Brother Ray

also by David Ritz

Biography

DIVIDED SOUL: THE LIFE OF MARVIN GAYE

FAITH IN TIME: THE LIFE OF JIMMY SCOTT

Autobiography

BROTHER RAY (cowritten with Ray Charles)

INSIDE MY LIFE (cowritten with Smokey Robinson)

THE RHYTHM AND THE BLUES (cowritten with Jerry Wexler)

RAGE TO SURVIVE (cowritten with Etta James)

BLUES ALL AROUND ME (cowritten with BB King)

GUIDE TO LIFE (cowritten with Sinbad)

FROM THESE ROOTS (cowritten with Aretha Franklin)

THE BROTHERS (cowritten with the Neville Brothers)

REACH (cowritten with Laila Ali)

GUILLAUME (cowritten with Robert Guillaume)

HOWLING AT THE MOON (cowritten with Walter Yetnikoff)

Novels

SEARCH FOR HAPPINESS

THE MAN WHO BROUGHT THE DODGERS BACK TO BROOKLYN

DREAMS

BLUE NOTES UNDER A GREEN FELT HAT

BARBELLS AND SAXOPHONES

FAMILY BLOOD

PASSION FLOWERS

TAKE IT OFF! TAKE IT ALL OFF!

Songs

SEXUAL HEALING

BROTHERS IN THE NIGHT

LOVE IS THE LIGHT

RELEASE YOUR LOVE

CAN YOU TELL ME WHO THE HEROES ARE?

Ray Charles and David Ritz

BROTHER
RAY

Ray Charles' Own Story

DA CAPO PRESS
A Member of the Perseus Books Group

For our mothers, Aretha Robinson and Pearl Ritz

Cataloging-in-Publication data for this book is available from the Library of Congress.

First Da Capo Press edition 1992
Second Da Capo Press edition 2003
Third Da Capo Press edition 2004
This Da Capo Press paperback edition of *Brother Ray* is an unabridged republica-tion of the edition published in New York in 1978, with the addition of an Epi-logue, discography, and some new photographs. It is reprinted by arrangement with the authors.
ISBN 0-306-81431-5

Published by Da Capo Press
A Member of the Perseus Books Group
http://www.dacapopress.com

Da Capo Press books are available at special discounts for bulk purchases in the U.S. by corporations, institutions, and other organizations. For more information, please contact the Special Markets Department at the Perseus Books Group, 11 Cambridge Center, Cambridge, MA 02142, or call (800) 255–1514 or (617) 252–5298, or e-mail j.mccrary@perseusbooks.com.

1 2 3 4 5 6 7 8 9—07 06 05 04

Contents

Acknowledgments

This project could never have existed without the wonderful example set for me by my passionate, music-loving father when I was a very young boy. And without the love of my family—my wife Roberta, my daughters Alison and Jessica, and my sisters Esther and Elizabeth—I surely would have suffered some wild breakdown before completing the book.

I am grateful to Joyce Johnson for her splendid editing and to Aaron Priest for his splendid agenting.

And for their assistance, I thank Joe Adams—who first let me in—Mrs. Joshua Kahn—who patiently transcribed every word of this book into Braille for Ray—Ron Boyd, Ivan Hoffman, Vera Tussing, Darryl Hardy, Gwen Cavitte, Beatrice Williams, Ruth Reams, Milt Garred, Quincy Jones, Nancy Jeris, Robert Foster, Jeff Brown, Norman Granz, Percy Mayfield, Paul Behn, Clarence Nelson, Lowell Fulson, Hank Crawford, Ahmet Ertegun, Mac Rebennack, Betty Carter, David Newman, Eddie Palmer, James Clay, Billy Brooks, Bill Tallmadge, Sid Feller, Charlie the Collector, Jack Lauderdale, Jorgen Grunnet Jepsen (for his *Jazz Records*), and Jerry Wexler, whose enthusiasm came at just the right time.

—D.R.

Introduction

by Ray Charles

Before I decided to work on this book I thought about it a long
time. I considered all the possible consequences and rewards.

Would I be hurting myself? That was my first question. Would
I be hurting anyone else? Did I really have anything to hide, anything which I couldn't tell, anything which I was ashamed of?

The answer to those questions is no. Looking back, I couldn't
see anything that needed to be censored. There was no reason
not to be straight. What's done is done. Ain't no taking it back. I
can't turn around, and I don't want to. That's not my nature. Besides, I've been there already. So I decided to tell you all I can remember, according to my truest memories.

I never planned to write a book about my life. Had no earthly
idea. So I've been sloppy about keeping things—even my own
phonograph records—and I've come to these pages cold. No
notes, no diaries.

It's all coming from my mind, from months and months of
talking, from letting my thoughts run loose and free. Sometimes
my memory's been sharp as a tack; other times my brain's given

out and I've just drawn blanks. I've tried to recall everything—the good along with the raunchy—but I know I haven't succeeded.

I've been hearing about myself for a long time. Some of the things people say are just opinion—good or bad. Some of the items are highly inaccurate or misleading. And there's also lavish praise—folk calling me a cornerstone of music or a legend in my own time.

That's strong language, and lately I've been trying to figure out how *I* really feel about it. How do I look upon myself? Well, in order to figure that out, I must look *into* myself.

That requires going back. Putting everything in the right perspective. Seeing where I come from and what I've actually been through. That takes some time and some thought.

I intend to go back and relive it. And I'm pleased to have you come along with me, pleased that you're interested enough to sit there and listen to me tell my story.

Brother Ray

Home

Before I begin, let me say right here and now that I'm a country boy. And, man, I mean the real *backwoods!* That's at the start of the start of the thing, and that's at the heart of the thing. All I ever saw—and I'm talking literally—was the country.

I didn't lose my sight till I was seven. It happened gradually. So I have years of pictures of country places, country people, country animals in my mind.

I was born in Albany, Georgia, on September 23, 1930. A few months later we moved to a little town in northern Florida, only thirty or forty miles from the Georgia border. On the map it reads Greenville, but we always pronounced it Greensville, with an *s*. That was home. Greensville's very much like Plains, Georgia, if you'll pardon my comparison. Same part of the country and same sort of tiny rural village.

You hear folks talking 'bout being poor. But listen here: When I say we were poor, I'm spelling it with a capital *P*. Even compared to other blacks in Greensville, we were on the bottom of the ladder looking up at everyone else. Nothing below us 'cept the ground.

Fact is, I was fairly old when I got my first pair of shoes. Indoor plumbing was something we never even dreamed of. And yet I was taken care of. Two women loved me. It sounds strange, but I actually had two mothers.

My father's name was Bailey Robinson, and to tell the truth, I wouldn't bet a lot of money he and my mother ever were married. My mother's name was Aretha. 'Retha was what everyone called her.

The old man wasn't part of my life. He was a tall dude—I remember that. But he was hardly ever around. He drove steel or spikes on the crossties on the railroad between Perry, Florida, and Adel, Georgia. Sometimes he came around to see Mama, but not very often. He was so big and she was so small that people often confused them for father and daughter.

I recall one morning—I still must have been a very small child—when he was leaving the house and I asked him if he was going to get on top of Mama and play with her. I knew they were always doing something like that when I was supposed to be sleeping. But I didn't know exactly what it was.

Those little shotgun shacks were tiny, and you were just about on top of each other anyway.

So Bailey came and went. I didn't really get to know the man. Maybe 'cause he worked on the railroad and was always gone; maybe 'cause he didn't care. Can't say.

But in the country we had two kinds of marriages—common law and the normal type. Relationships between men and women, though, are things that a little child can't easily understand, and to this day I'm not certain what the entanglements were all about.

I do know that Bailey's first wife—a woman named Mary Jane—was someone who loved and cared for me like a mother. Probably it was during his marriage to her that Bailey had a love affair with 'Retha—which is how I got here. Bailey had another wife after he split up with Mary Jane. Her name was Stella, but I didn't really know her.

Yeah, Mary Jane took to me like I was her own. She'd lost a son named Jabbo, and maybe I became a substitute. Who knows?

There's a lot about this part of my life—the earliest years—that remains mysterious, but you have to remember that I was too young to do any serious questioning. And besides, a little kid wasn't supposed to be asking any questions.

In spite of all this confusion about who was loving who, living with who or leaving who, I do know that two women—Mama and Mary Jane—bathed me in affection and cared for me as long as they were both alive. Fact is, I called 'Retha "Mama" and Mary Jane "Mother."

Mama was small—110 pounds or so—and she was also sickly. It wasn't that she couldn't work. In fact, she worked all her natural life. She quit school after the fifth grade and worked the tobacco and cotton fields, snapped beans, and hulled peas.

But now her main job was washing and ironing. Other women in our neighborhood gave her some of the extra work they got from white folks. It was like subcontracting. Hardly made any money at it, but whatever there was went toward clothing and feeding me.

Mama was a rare human being. She was no softy; really strict as hell. I mean discipline was her middle name. She showed me that discipline is a kind of love. And that's something I believe to this day. Mama taught me all kinds of things—big lessons, little lessons—which I've kept with me and use every day of my life.

She was a weak woman, but that was only physically. In all other ways, she was strong. Didn't drink, smoke, or swear. Lots of rules. Lots of practical, down-to-earth common sense. And at the top of the list were two: You do not beg and you do not steal.

We slept together—Mama and me—till I was eleven or twelve. Or else I slept on the floor. It was very cool down there, specially on hot summer nights.

We lived in all sorts of different places, moving from pillar to post. Often we found ourselves in the kind of shack which could have gone up in smoke at the drop of a match.

But somehow we made it.

Mary Jane and Mama were two very different women. Mary Jane had a couple of good jobs. Her first gig was for white people, supposedly one of the older families—the Osbys. And she also worked at the sawmill. Actually, Greensville was a sawmill town, and women worked there alongside men. Truth is, most men today would shy away from the sort of work Mary Jane did—lifting huge wet boards and throwing 'em into the steamer.

This might surprise you, but Mary Jane and Mama got along just fine. Mama was a lot stricter and Mary Jane much more lenient—but that didn't matter none. For instance, Mary Jane wouldn't let Mama whip me. And usually Mama didn't argue with her. Maybe that's because she knew that Mary Jane was always giving me stuff—little foods that I specially liked and small articles of clothing.

I also remember that when they were still together, Bailey and Mary Jane ran a café not far from my grandmother's house, the kind of place that sold candies and breads and beer. I must have been around three years old at this time.

Mary Jane called me her "monkey doodle." Yeah, that was her name for me, and she was an awfully protective woman. On the other hand, Mama had a little more vision about preparing me for the real world. She let me roam, let me make my own mistakes, let me discover the world for myself.

There were two sons born to 'Retha—my brother George and me. George was a year younger than me, and he was a phenomenal kid. By the time he was three, he could add, multiply, and divide. Neighbors came by just to watch him do his little mathematics; they were fascinated by him.

George also had a highly developed talent for inventing games and designing toys. Since there was no money for stuff like that, you had to make your own. And George did just that—putting together tiny cars and other devices with strings and wires. The kid was inventive and, in many special ways, brilliant. I could see that Mama was amazed by George, and so was everyone else living around us.

The two of us were little free spirits. We ran off into the woods, threw pebbles and rocks into the streams. We picked blackberries and we laughed when Mama yelled, "Get outta that berry patch 'fore a rattlesnake up and bites your head off."

I can see the landscape—the pecan, chinaberry, and pine trees, the pigs and cows and chickens. I remember hog killing time. I can see men shooting hogs in the ear and cutting their throats to let the blood drain away. Then a short while later we'd be chewing on that same animal for dinner.

Country folk don't miss nothing on the pig—ears, feets, insides, and outsides. We ate everything on the hog except the oink. Neck bones, chitlins, collard greens, rice smothered with onion gravy, cabbage with thick pieces of ham, sweet watermelon. . . . Man, we might be poor, but we ate good.

If we had chicken, it had to be on Sunday, our church day. Oh yes, Lord, Mama believed in going to church. Ours was the Shiloh Baptist Church, and I liked it best for the singing.

Church was simple: Preacher sang or recited, and the congregation sang right back at him. Hardly any accompaniment—we didn't have a piano in church until I became much older—and the services were basic and raw. That's how I got my first religion and my first music.

I was a curious kid, a little mischievous, but for the most part well behaved. I was raised to obey my mama. In the country, you did what adults told you to do. If you didn't, you got a licking. Never more complicated than that.

I was a happy kid. I loved the country with all its colors and mysteries. At night, when it got so dark that I couldn't see my hand in front of my face, I snuck out back with a box of matches and struck 'em all. My eyes glowed with wonder, and I felt like I was lighting up the whole world!

By day I gazed into the sun—maybe too much for my own good. And during storms I waited for the lightning. Most kids were frightened of lightning, but to me it was beautiful. I tried to jump into it—that's how stupid I was. The white streak running across the black sky thrilled me.

And so did the radiance and glow of the sun. Thinking back, I see that I could have been an arsonist; it was a miracle to witness the power of light and heat.

And then there was music. I heard it early, just as soon as I was seeing or talking or walking. It was always there—all shapes, all kinds, all rhythms. Music was the only thing I was really anxious to get out of bed for.

I was born with music inside me. That's the only explanation I know of, since none of my relatives could sing or play an instrument. Music was one of my parts. Like my ribs, my liver, my kidneys, my heart. Like my blood. It was a force already within me when I arrived on the scene. It was a necessity for me—like food or water. And from the moment I learned that there were piano keys to be mashed, I started mashing 'em, trying to make sounds out of feelings.

Sometimes I'm asked about my biggest musical influence as a kid. I always give one name: Mr. Wylie Pitman. I called him Mr. Pit.

Now you won't find Mr. Pit in any history of jazz, and the man's not in the Down Beat Hall of Fame. But, sweethearts, you can take my word for it: Mr. Pit could play some sure-enough boogie-woogie piano. And best of all, he lived down the road from us.

Red Wing Café. I can see the big ol' red sign smack in front of me right now. That was Mr. Pit's place. It was a little general store where he and his wife, Miss Georgia, sold items like soda water, beer, candies, cakes, cigarettes, and kerosene. Mr. Pit also rented out rooms.

Mama and me were always welcome there and, in fact, during one period when we were really down and out, we lived at the Red Wing Café for a while.

Mr. Pit's place was the center of the black community in Greensville, and when you walked into the café you saw two things—right off —which shaped me for the rest of my life.

Talkin' 'bout a piano and a jukebox.

Oh, that piano! It was an old, beat-up upright and the most wonderful contraption I had ever laid eyes on. Boogie-woogie was hot then, and it was the first style I was exposed to. Mr. Pit played with the best of them. He just wasn't interested in a musical career; if he had been,

I know he would have made it big. He just wanted to stay in Greensville and lead a simple life.

Well, one day when Mr. Pit started to playing, I waddled on up to the piano and just stared. It astonished and amazed me—his fingers flying, all those chords coming together, the sounds jumping at me and ringing in my ears.

You'd think an older cat would be put off by this young kid hangin' round. Not Mr. Pit. Maybe that's 'cause he and Miss Georgia didn't have children of their own. But for whatever reasons, the man treated me like a son; he lifted me on the stool and put me right there on his lap. Then he let me run my fingers up and down the keyboard. That was a good feeling, and forty-five years later, it *still* feels good.

I tried to figure out how he could make all those notes come together. I was a baby, but I was trying to invent some boogie-woogie licks of my own.

Some days I'd be out in the yard back of the house. If I heard Mr. Pit knocking out some of that good boogie-woogie, I'd drop what I was doing and run over to his place. The man *always* let me play.

"That's it, sonny! That's it!" he'd scream, encouraging me like I was his student or his son.

He saw I was willing to give up my playing time for the piano, so I guess he figured I loved music as much as he did. And all this was happening when I was only three.

I couldn't spend enough time with that gentleman. I was there for hours—sitting on his lap, watching him play or trying to play myself. He was a patient and loving man who never tired of me.

"Come over here, boy, and see what you can do with this pie-ano," he'd say, always helpful, always anxious to teach me something new. And when I look back now, I know he saw something in me, felt something in me, which brought out the teacher in him.

The jukebox was the other wonder. There was a long bench at Mr. Pit's place, and I had my special place, right at the end, smack against the loudspeaker. That's where I would sit for hours, enthralled by the different sounds.

I heard the radio round town, though there were only white stations on it. No way they'd be playing real blues—I mean hollering-through-the-hollow-log blues. But records were also around, and the first ones I listened to were on Mr. Pit's jukebox.

Boogie-woogie, baby! The jukebox was jumping with the stuff. There was Pete Johnson, Meade Lux Lewis, and Albert Ammons. And you better believe that there was also some filthy blues, some *country* blues, coming out of that same box—Tampa Red, Blind Boy Phillips, and Washboard Sam.

Sure, I listened to the blues and boogie-woogie, but I also heard the big bands of the time. And you gotta remember that this was the Deep South, and the airwaves were running wild with hillbilly tunes from morning till night.

The earliest part of my life was filled with music of many styles, and I liked it all. I was also curious 'bout it. I wondered . . . hmmm, how'd they do this, or how'd they do that?

There's a mechanical side of music which has always fascinated me: the way the thing is put together. Actually mechanics of all kinds interested me. 'Round Greensville my nickname soon became "Mechanic," 'cause even as a toddler I was poking my nose inside engines and motors to see what made 'em tick.

When I wasn't called Mechanic, they called me RC. My full name is Ray Charles Robinson, though how and why I dropped the Robinson is something I'll tell you later.

I remember seeing colors. Red. Well, that was hot and bright and brilliant. Brown and blue were cooler colors. White was pale. And green was soothing.

And though I went blind before I got to look at a big city or an airplane, I did see cars. Mr. Pit had an old brown Plymouth, and he let me ride in it with him, showing me how to shift gears, how to steer, and how to apply the brakes.

Can you picture this little country town? You must remember that it was simple—a simple time and a simple place. We were back in the woods, and the feeling of life and the spirit among the people was good. There was something very nice about these early years.

Of course Greensville was segregated to the teeth—blacks on one side, whites on the other. But I was a little kid, and what did I know? To me, it seemed like a connected community. Everyone had a link to everyone else. Folk really cared about one another.

There were chitlin switches and giant fish fries. Since Greensville was in a dry county—Madison—some of the men drove to Georgia and brought back what we called sealed liquor. And if they didn't do that, they filled themselves silly with moonshine.

Us kids slurped down Kool-Aid, went racing off into the woods and played games, exploring that world of ours back among the trees and the ponds. And naturally my brother George and I were always together; he was my first and my best pal.

On my fourth birthday Mama gave me a party. Someone had an old-fashioned ice-cream churn, the kind that's packed with salt and ice. We had to stir the thing by hand, and it took lots of manpower and womanpower. But when we were through, we were glad about the results. Never tasted anything before or since so good.

Didn't bother us any that we were poor. Didn't bother us 'cause we didn't know any better. Folks who don't have much—and ain't ever had much—can get along just fine. Just fine, that is, till they start seeing that there's more to be had.

The main thing I saw, though, was Mama. She and Mary Jane were the only ones to really take care of me, and naturally I still remember the way both those women looked.

I often shared Mary Jane's bed, too, though I never saw her or Mama naked. They were always careful to be right proper around me.

Mary Jane was a bit larger than Mama, and her attitude toward me was more like a grandma doting over a grandson. She indulged me. Still, it didn't bother Mama none if I went to Mary Jane's to spend the night.

They were both beautiful women, I know that for sure. Both brown-skinned with clear, lovely complexions. And though they worked hard doing rough, burdensome chores, they had gentle souls.

Thing I remember most 'bout Mama was her hair. Wasn't like the hair you see on so many women today—all teased and toughened up, sprayed and shellacked, so when you touch it you might get cut. No, sir.

Mama's hair was like a good cat's fur, if you can feature that. And it was long: it trailed all the way down to her buttocks. There was a fine sheen to it. And one of the prettiest pictures in my brain is that dark black hair, soft and velvety. I loved stroking it; I loved running my fingers through it. To this day, I've never felt a woman's hair as smooth as Mama's.

Life went on for our little family in the country. There was nothing spectacular about it. George played with his numbers and constructed his little toys. I fooled around any piano I could get my hands on. Mama looked after us both. And between going to church and playing on the dirt roads and back paths of Greensville, not much changed. Until one day.

It was afternoon when it happened. Can't recall it all, but I can remember the main thing. I can see it almost too vividly. It shines inside my head. It's hard to look at it again. Hard to recreate the scene. It hurts. It was my first real taste of tragedy and, even after more than forty years, the taste hasn't left my mouth.

George is a little older than four. I'm five. We're playing out back, just messing round. Mama's inside ironing. There's this huge tub—a number four tub I think it's called—filled with rinse water. Me and brother love to splash around in those things and play like we're swimming. It's one of our games.

George climbs inside the tub and I think nothing of it. Happens all the time. I'm close by, and I watch him kicking his legs, hooting and hollering. Seems like he's having a good time. But suddenly I realize something which sends a chill up and down my body: I realize he isn't playing; I realize he's in trouble. My heart starts pounding like it might explode. Waves of fear pass over me. I shiver. I'm watching my brother drown.

And I find that I can't do anything. Has someone ever thrown something at you—a bottle, say—and you can't duck? You see it coming, you know you're about to be clobbered, but for a few seconds you can't move. You're frozen.

Well, that's what happens to me when I first see that George is in trouble. He swings his little arms around and kicks his little legs. He screams, and finally—after those first moments—I run to the tub and desperately try to yank him out. I can't do it. I'm too small and weak myself.

"Mama!" I scream with all the strength I can find. "Mama! Mama!" I keep on screaming all the way to the house.

I run—run to the house like I'm on fire, yelling, hollering, crying for Mama who's at the ironing board. She drops everything and comes running, pulls George from the tub and tries to breathe life into him.

I'm shaking like a leaf as I watch her.

Now she's pumping him, now she's blowing air into him, now she's breathing inside his mouth, now she's slapping his back, and now I see her tears spill onto his face.

Now she stops.

I look at her. Seems like she's drowning in her own tears. I also weep uncontrollably. I'm scared. I want to help.

She rests her hand on my small head, and then she lifts George—who's limp and still—and quietly carries him inside. Following her, I understand what she already knows:

It's too late to do anything else. My brother is dead.

Don't ask me why, but now my mind goes blank. I know there was a funeral. I know there was mourning and weeping. I know there was a cemetery and a grave. I know I was there when it all happened, but for some reason I can't see it. I can't even remember crying.

Who knows what goes on in the mind of a five-year-old? Sometimes I think I might have been feeling guilty 'bout not being able to save my brother. But that's something I think about *now*, as an adult. As a kid, it just happened to me.

It was a powerful thing to have witnessed. And it came at a strange time in my life. Turned out to be one of the last things I would ever see.

Just a few months after my little brother drowned, my eyes started tearing. And they weren't real tears, but matter that was thicker than tears; it was mucus. Some mornings it'd be so thick I'd have to pry my eyes open. It didn't take Mama long to figure out what was happening.

Going Blind

Going blind. Sounds like a fate worse than death, doesn't it? Seems like something which would get a little kid down, make him afraid, and leave him half-crazy and sad. Well, I'm here to tell you that it didn't happen that way—at least not with me.

That's probably 'cause it took me two years to lose my sight completely. It slipped away gradually. And I suppose that's the reason I was never too frightened.

Images began to blur, and I saw less and less. When I woke up, my little eyes were shut tight as a door, crusted over and so sticky that my eyelids were matted together. Sometimes Mama took a damp cloth and gently mopped around my eyes. After five or ten minutes, I'd slowly start blinking and adjusting to the morning light.

But soon my horizons grew shorter and shorter. Faraway distances were fading. I was like a guy who stands on top of a mountain and one week sees fifteen miles off, the next week only ten miles, the third week only five. At first, I could still make out large forms, then only colors, then only night from day.

There were only two doctors in Greensville—a Dr. McCloud and a Dr. King. Dr. King was the more expensive of the two, and white folk went to him. Dr. McCloud—who was a white man—took care of everyone. He tried to help me as best he could, treating my eyes with ointments and drops, but there wasn't much he could do.

Finally he suggested that we go to a clinic in Madison, a town close by. So we went. Just Mama and me. We walked into the office of the doctor there and he looked into my eyes and examined me every which way.

"Is there any hope?" Mama asked.

"Well," the doctor answered, his face glum, his head hanging down, "I don't think so. I'm afraid the boy's going blind."

"I understand," Mama said. She was not afraid; she didn't weep or scream for the Lord's mercy. Mama was a strong woman—a smart woman—and she knew what she had to do.

Mama always wanted me to learn things. Even though she didn't have much education herself, she taught me all she knew—the numbers, the alphabet, the way to spell, how to add and subtract. So when I started going blind, she began looking into schools for me. Remember, I was the only blind person in Greensville; people just didn't know what to do with me.

Mama sought out advice. She asked Miss Lad who worked at the post office. She talked to the banker and to Mr. Reams who owned the general store. Soon everyone in town learned about my plight.

It was the white folks who told Mama about the State School for the Blind in St. Augustine. I think a few of them saw something good in me and cared about making sure that it was nurtured. Maybe they knew I had half a brain; maybe they heard I had some musical talent. I don't know, but Mama was able to get good advice, and I'm certain that many white people were encouraging her to send me to school.

It didn't take her long to decide. I was going to have to go to school and live in St. Augustine.

Now Mary Jane felt differently. She didn't want me to leave her. Ignorance and love sometimes mix in strange ways, and I think she simply had a fear about letting me go.

Mama knew what was best, though, and she insisted that I get some education in one form or another. She couldn't see me growing up without knowing how to read and write. She understood that one day I'd have to be on my own.

My own reaction to leaving was a big fat NO. Didn't want to leave Mama and didn't want to leave Mary Jane. That simple. Going blind was one thing; I was getting used to that. But leaving these women was something else. They were all I knew. They were my whole world.

No matter. Mama told me I was leaving, so I was leaving. End of discussion. I had a couple of months to get used to that idea, and during this last period at home I was treated the same as a normal child. Fact is, I was made to do the same chores I had done when I could see.

Mama was a country woman with a whole lot of common sense. She understood what most of our neighbors didn't—that I shouldn't grow dependent on anyone except myself. "One of these days I ain't gonna be here," she kept hammering inside my head. Meanwhile, she had me scrub floors, chop wood, wash clothes, and play outside like all the other kids. She made sure I could wash and dress myself. And her discipline didn't stop just 'cause I was blind. She wasn't about to let me get away with any foolishness.

So I still had the freedom to fend for myself on the outside. That made me happy. Even though I couldn't see much, I wasn't afraid of running around. I knew every inch of Greensville, and I didn't lose my confidence about finding my way; I went wherever I wanted to.

Some of the neighbors gave Mama a hard time. They got on her case when they saw me working out back or helping her in the house.

"He's blind," Mama told them, "but he ain't stupid. He's lost his sight, but he ain't lost his mind."

Mama was looking way down the line.

Blindness didn't break my spirit, but it might have added to my already shy personality. Many kids' games required sight, so I couldn't play with 'em. On the other hand, I had my own circle of friends, and I still raised some hell with the other kids.

I still went over to Mr. Pit's place and climbed up on the piano stool. By then, even at age six, I could fake a little black-bottom blues of my own.

I started teasing and messing with little girls the same time as the rest of the boys—maybe a little earlier. I played around like all kids, getting into more trouble than I should and less than I might. Luckily, Mama held the reins tight, and I was taught to mind my elders. Either that, or my butt would be burning for days.

I wouldn't want you to think I was a model kid.

Look here: Some friend would show up and convince me to follow him down the road, just before dinnertime.

"C'mon, RC, let's go, man."

I was dumb, I was stupid, and even though Mama had instructed me to clean the house, I'd leave anyway. Two hours later I'd come back and Mama'd be burning mad. She wouldn't whup me right away, though. She had the good sense to realize that you don't hit someone when you're full of rage and anger. No, she'd wait till she was calm— maybe an hour or two later—and then she'd come after me.

But the discipline didn't bother me. I came to expect it. No, I loved my home life, loved my mama, loved Mary Jane, loved the feeling of roaming round the woods with my friends. So when they put me on the train to St. Augustine, I was one unhappy boy.

The idea of leaving Mama and Mary Jane was almost more than I could bear. What did I know 'bout St. Augustine and some strange-sounding school for the blind?

"Mama," I cried, "don't make me go, Mama. I wanna stay with you." But she remained firm.

"You gotta go, son. How else you gonna learn to read and write? I can only take you so far."

I understood that I couldn't go to school in Greensville and learn like normal kids. But at the same time, the thought of getting on a big train and going far, far away—leaving everything and everyone I knew behind—man, that was enough to get me down and keep me down.

Remember, I'd never really been outside the country, and here I was going off on my own.

Mama and I had always been very, very tight. I told you how we'd even sleep together in the same bed. It didn't seem possible my life could go on without her. I was just a seven-year-old kid. It didn't seem possible that I had to leave. None of it seemed possible. But let me tell you: It sure enough happened.

First Year
at School

Like it or not, when the train pulled out of Greensville early one morning toward the end of September 1937, I was on it.

It was the old Seaboard line, and there was a special car just for the blind kids going to school in St. Augustine. Other little boys—in the same shape as me—were on the train, but I was in no mood to socialize. I stuck to myself and moped.

The trip wasn't that long—160 miles or so—but to me that was much too far away from home. Man, I was homesick the minute I climbed aboard. This little country boy ain't ever been on a train before, ain't ever been with strangers before, ain't ever left home. And on top of that, my vision was near gone. By this time, I could only make out obvious colors—day from night—and very large shapes.

Once I got to school, I still stayed to myself. I hardly talked to anyone. Everyone else seemed to know each other; there was all this laughing and carrying on, reuniting and celebrating about the beginning of school. But to me they were all strangers, and I didn't care about them. With all these people around me, I was still alone. And I hurt. Deep down inside, I hurt bad.

My eyes also hurt. Every time I looked at light, I had trouble. So it wasn't much fun trying to get these things straight in my brain—the new surroundings, the new kids, the changes going on inside my eyes.

I was suffering plenty. The first couple of weeks I did nothing but cry. Missing Mama. Missing Mary Jane. Missing the whole little town of Greensville and everyone in it. Yeah, I was feeling mighty sorry for myself; all this newness had me afraid.

The other kids were no help. They saw me cry and right away they got on my case:

"Little sissy boy, crying for his mama."

"My, my. Baby don't do nothin' but cry."

You know kids. They got no tact; they can be awfully cruel. So I continued to pout and moan, feeling all sullen and gloomy. But then —don't ask me why—I finally came round and started getting into the swing of things. Strange, I must say, but that's me: Finally, I do adapt.

Listen here, I say to myself, 'tain't much you can do about this here situation. So you better just continue to continue.

That's one way of looking at my life. I was able to adjust. Sure, it was a struggle, but I somehow muddled through the emotional mess. Downhearted and lonely, scared, nervous, and unsure of myself, I finally realized I had no choice.

No use boohooing for Mama. She wasn't coming. I was all alone. So very slowly I forced myself into the routine of day-to-day life at school, and I tried to make the best of the thing.

To tell you the truth, school wasn't all bad. It was run by the state, and us kids didn't have to bring anything but our clothes. In some cases, when we were too poor even for that, we'd get hand-me-downs. I was given some secondhand clothes. Of course the other kids—blind or not —learned that I was wearing these hand-me-downs, and that didn't help my status none.

Now in those days—and it's the same today—the school housed the deaf and the blind, boys and girls, black and white, from around ages six through eighteen. And talk about segregation!

First, everything was broken down between white and black. I don't have to tell you about that. There was a white side and there was a black side. If you were black, you were made to understand—right quick— that there was no crossing over the line, unless you were asked to. If you had to go to the hospital, for example, you were allowed to travel over to white territory. Even our teachers had to be black.

Then within each color group there was another division—between the blind and the deaf. And then within the blind and deaf groups, the girls were separated from the boys.

There must have been around thirty or thirty-five black kids who were blind, and a good many of those, unlike me, could see something. This was my little family, the kids I'd be living with for the next eight years of my life.

Thinking about all this makes me laugh now—at least in one respect. I didn't realize it then, and I suppose that's because I wasn't all that aware of the race thing. Going blind made me even less conscious of it. But imagine the nonsense of segregating *blind* kids. I mean, they can't even see!

I can't say it made me angry. It didn't. I was too far into my own problems and, besides, I just didn't think in those terms. Actually, the whole race business didn't hit me till years later. As a musician, I went on the road and discovered that I couldn't pee where I wanted to; that's when the chickens came home to roost.

Anyway, it's awfully strange thinking about separating small children —black from white—when most of 'em can't even make out the difference between the two colors.

School routine was tight. Up at 5:30, breakfast, chapel, classes, recess, more classes, dinner, workshop, play, supper, and a study hour at night. (We called lunch, dinner.) The place was strict, and they didn't put up with any monkey business. That didn't bother me too much. I was a Southern boy who had been raised by a woman who didn't exactly let me run wild. I knew that obeying was part of life, though I wasn't always crazy about the idea.

All the blind kids lived in a single building—the boys' dormitory in one part of the building, the girls' dormitory in another. The supervisors of each section—Mr. Knowles for the boys, Miss Katy for the girls —lived between the dorms, making sure there was no trespassing between the boys and the girls.

I made some friends. There was Clarence Nelson from Pensacola and my bunkmate, Joe Walker (who's now a disc jockey). Once things started rolling, I quickly got the hang of the place and was able to get around very easily. I spent lots of time seeing how the big boys did things.

The big boys. That was a popular phrase. The big boys did this, the big boys did that. Among the kids, they had the power, and soon I could see things would be much hipper when I got to be a big boy myself.

First off, I had to learn Braille. It was easy; in fact, it only took ten days or so, and within a couple of months I was able to read storybooks like *Living on John's Farm* or *The White Rabbit.* We called those primers. Didn't seem like much of a chore.

A couple of years later—maybe at nine or ten—I also discovered that I was good at workshop. I actually learned some crafts—how to carve, how to weave cane for chair bottoms, how to put together brooms and mops, pot holders and leather goods. I dug it. And soon I could turn out the merchandise like a pro. I was a specially hot weaver, and I could really cook with that cane.

In the afternoons, after classes, I played in the yard with the boys. I loved to run, and I was plenty fast. I was not a great all-around athlete, but I was okay. We had our own silly games, and there was one which I really liked. Here's how it worked:

We'd take a magazine, roll it up and fold it a couple of times so it became hard, and then tie it with cord string. That would be our ball. Then we'd take a broomstick and use it as a bat. The hitter would put the paper ball in his left hand and drop it as he swung at it with the broomstick.

You'd be surprised how many guys missed the ball—even those

who could see. There were three or four players on each team. Wherever the ball stopped, that's where the other team would hit it back. And by hitting the ball back and forth, we marched on each other's territory.

It was a dumb game, but I loved it. (We also played football, just like regular football, except we didn't pass.)

I'd say I was about a B student. Math and music were my best subjects, and now I realize that's because they're very related. Didn't know that then, but I could sure feel it.

After I got used to the place, I'd wander over to the rooms where the big boys or the big girls were practicing the piano. I'd love to just hang around and listen.

I was always on the prowl for new sounds. I tried to copy anything I heard just for the fun of it. I didn't really begin formal lessons till I was eight, the following year.

But just when I began to settle into the groove of school, something happened which threw me off balance.

At Christmas, everyone got to go home. Everyone, that is, except me. Mama didn't have enough money to send for me. (The state only paid for transportation to and from the school at the beginning and end of each nine months. Holiday transportation was paid by the parents, if they wanted the kids to come home.) And, baby, when everyone had gone home for the holidays and I was left alone, I was *really* alone. That was something I wasn't ever gonna forget. That's when I knew how poor poor can be.

Course it wasn't Mama's fault. If she had the bread, she would have sent it. She wanted to see me as badly as I wanted to see her. The money just wasn't there. And, man, I was miserable. My heart ached for Mama, Mary Jane, and all the folk back home. It had been nearly four months since I left Greensville.

So there I was. Christmas at the State School for the Blind in St. Augustine. Alone. I cried my little eyes out during those weeks.

I suppose I've always done my share of crying, especially when there's no other way to contain my feelings. I know that men ain't supposed to cry, but I think that's wrong. Crying's always been a way for me to get things out which are buried deep, deep down. When I sing, I often cry. Crying is feeling, and feeling is being human. Oh yes, I cry.

These were tough times for me, but I cannot remember praying to God for help. That's not my style. When I was going blind, I didn't turn to God. It didn't seem to me then—and it doesn't seem to me now—that those items were His concern. Early on, I figured I better begin to learn how to count on myself, instead of counting on the supernatural forces.

I never felt worse in my life than I did those couple of weeks. Didn't seem fair. My friends had split. *They* got to be with *their* families. Why not me? Now I was really feeling sorry for myself. In Greensville, being poor didn't mean all that much to me. We were all in the same boat. But now I was the only one left in school.

Only months earlier I had been scornful about the other kids in the school and didn't want to talk to them, didn't even want to get to know them. But, boy, when I heard them romping down the halls and screaming and hollering, when I knew they were coming back from vacation, I was as happy as a mud duck in the rain. Never had been so glad to see people in my life!

The second part of the year was rough for a completely different reason: My right eye started aching in the worst way. It throbbed with pain from morning to night. Then someone at the school told me that the eye had to be removed.

Removed! Oh man, that's all I needed to hear. Take out my eye! No way. I was scared—real scared—at the very thought. Going blind didn't seem half as bad as actually losing an eye. And what did I know about operations and stuff like that?

They took me to the hospital and removed my eye. Had no choice. Couldn't live with the pain.

I was laid up in bed for a few days, and then I slowly returned to the normal routine. (Years later, as a man, I've asked a few doctors what they thought my ailment was. They've speculated that it was glaucoma, but I'll never know for sure.)

So the second part of the year wasn't much easier than the first. After all this time, I just wanted to go home and see Mama and Mary Jane. It had been nine long months.

Summertime in Greensville

When I stepped off the train in Greensville it wasn't long 'fore I was wrapped up in Mama's arms. It felt good all over. I didn't realize how homesick I had been till I actually set foot back in my own stomping grounds.

Life in a little country town is like a soap opera; nothing really changes much. You can be gone for a long spell, return, and find the same things as before. Oh, maybe someone's left town or someone's died, but for the most part, things are as they've always been. And always will be.

My old friends were all there: Talkin' 'bout people like Johnny Williams—we called him Johnny Cake—and his sister Lou Dell, Beatrice (who later married Johnny), Mary Lee, and Wilbur Miller. These were the kids who always messed around with me, even before I went blind.

When I had left Greensville I could still see something. But now all my vision was gone, and yet I wasn't all that different. I was still the same little RC. I could get around by myself. I'd take walks round town, usually barefooted. I'd try to stay on the grass during those hikes 'cause the sand roads would be hotter than burning hell. I learned to use the transportation I was born with.

Mama didn't mind letting me wander off on my own. She knew, blind or not, that I was able to watch where I was going. If I was sent to the commissary to buy some meats, I'd walk downtown—a couple of miles from where we lived. And of course I knew not to go wandering over to the white side of town without a specific purpose.

Naturally I went to the Red Wing Café whenever I pleased. That was my hot spot in town. I was always asking Mr. Pit to show me something new on his piano, and he never refused.

Sometimes I heard a piano being played in someone's house. But I'd never ask if I could play. I was raised to wait until someone asked *me* to play. And even then, I'd have to turn to Mama or Mary Jane—whoever was with me—and say, "Is it okay if I play for the people?" Judging by most folks' reactions, I must have been sounding pretty good, 'cause they kept on asking me.

Confidence was building in me, and that applied to girls as well as music. I must tell you that the opposite sex has always intrigued me. Like my feeling for mechanics or for music, I've always been curious to see what makes women tick, from the inside, down underneath.

And on the romantic side, I liked those sorts of little love friendships where you get stuck on someone and start smooching. Actually it was fairly early in my life—couldn't have been older than ten—when Mama caught me under the house with a little girl. Listen to what happened:

You know, the way houses were built down South, you could creep under the foundation and play around so no one could see you. Or so I thought. One bright afternoon I had this gal down there and managed to climb on top her, the way I thought older folks did it. Well, she didn't seem to mind—no, didn't mind at all—but Mama, who spotted us, sure as hell did. She came after us with a Georgia peach tree switch, swinging away and whipping the daylights out of us both. Me, I straightened up so fast I didn't have time to think, and I almost knocked my brains out against the bottom of the house. Mama kept swishing and I kept banging my head, trying to duck those hard licks. The little girl was able to escape, and Mama chased her all the way home.

As I got older, I sometimes wondered why Mama hadn't found another man for herself. I knew that there were several who had come around to court her. But none of them stayed for very long. She was a fragile lady, and maybe she didn't want to burden a man.

She also had this blind boy to look after, and maybe she wasn't too anxious to take care of anyone else but me. I never asked her, but I couldn't help but wonder.

During those summers when I was home from school, I was always around Mama and Mary Jane. Almost every weekend I spent one or two nights with Mary Jane, and she was constantly buying me baloney, weenies, and candies, the kind of food Mama couldn't afford. She also gave me clothes; there was nothing the woman wouldn't do for me.

Mary Jane's job was rough. Working at the sawmill was no picnic. She flung round those soaking-wet boards like they be made of straw. But that was country life—women side by side with men, doing manual labor and not thinking twice about it. You can imagine how strong these women were. They had to be; the times demanded it.

In those days no man just took his pussy—not unless he had his gun. No, sir. You got what you were given. And there was no way you could throw your weight around. Gals were used to real labor. And if they didn't want to give you a piece, Jack, you just weren't gonna get any.

Fact is, I'd say the average gal of 125 pounds back then could whip the average cat of 160 pounds today who sits around an office, talking on a telephone, and getting fat.

Chores at home weren't exactly lightweight either. I know, 'cause I did most of 'em. You be lifting huge tubs filled with water. You be lugging round heavy pots. You be carrying frying pans, three-legged iron kettles, and skillets big enough to kill a grown man. You be washing clothes. You be scrubbing. You be snapping beans and you be cleaning fish.

'Nother thing: Back in the country we had our own way of dealing with cuts and bruises. It might not have been the most scientific method, but we'd take clay—the kind you find around water wells— and put it on the wound. That be your Band-Aid. Or you could also use cobwebs.

We also had what we called a slop jar. That's a bucket made of granite with a tin top. That's where you'd pee at night—right into this slop jar.

Now, let's say you got a boil on your behind. Well, you'd take a brick, put it on the stove, and let it get red hot. Then you'd place it on the bottom of the slop jar. Next, you'd sit on the slop jar and pee on the brick. The steam from the pee would rise up, hit that boil, and bust it. Or we'd cover the boil with the skin from an eggshell. That would also draw it.

Aside from these home remedies, we also used Sloan's liniment or heat liniment. We'd apply turpentine to wounds to make them heal. I know a lot of you city folks will be surprised by this sort of medicine, but I'm here to tell you that such cures ain't half bad.

Mama had a dual problem in dealing with me. She wanted to treat me like an average boy, and she often did. On the other hand, the folk living round us were convinced that she was some sort of witch inflicting pain upon me. You can appreciate how much pressure was on her.

Mama had no coaching from anybody. No professional or educated advice. This was a little ol' country town and like I said, I was the only blind person there. What's more, in those days the attitude was that the blind were helpless. No one expected them to do anything but be led around.

So you can imagine how strong Mama had to be—and how intelligent—to fight against this outlook and allow me to go out on my own. And she did all this even with the other folks looking down on her.

Not only did she make me help around the house, she made certain that I did the job right:

One day, for instance, she told me to scrub and mop the floor. I thought I might as well get off easy, so I skipped the scrubbing part. I just sloshed some water around the floor and mopped up.

Mama came back and blew a fuse; I mean, she was smoking with anger. Made me do the whole thing over again, from scratch. That hurt. But I do believe I learned something 'bout doing a job right.

Mama was big on those sort of lessons. She knocked them into my brain with a sledgehammer. She had no choice. I wasn't an easy kid. I was as stubborn and mischievous as any other boy. So she treated me like a naughty puppy and rubbed my nose in my own mistakes.

The woman never let me get away with anything just 'cause I was blind. I was treated like I was normal. I acted like I was normal. And I wound up doing exactly the same things normal people do.

Take my bicycle. Somehow—I can't remember the exact circumstances—I was given one. Couldn't have been much older than ten or eleven. Riding was something I learned to do quickly. I loved the feeling of motion, and being blind wasn't gonna stop me from enjoying the bike.

I knew practically every road and dirt pathway in town, so getting round was no problem. (If you go to Greensville today and ask about me, I bet the thing they remember most is the way I raced around town on my bike, as though I had 20/20.)

Somewhere in the back of my mind I knew I wasn't going to hurt myself. Sure, I rode pretty fast, but my hearing was good and my instincts were sharp. Never got into any wrecks. Can't even remember a close call.

Now most mamas would die rather than let a blind child scoot around on a bike. And at first I know Mama was scared for me. She had to be. But she let me do it. She let me find out for myself. She let me stray, little by little, further and further away from her. And once she saw I was capable of maneuvering this bike, she became less afraid.

In her own way, she was preparing me for tougher times—times which weren't very far off.

On another day Mama asked me to chop wood in the backyard, and a neighbor got on her for that:

" 'Retha, now look here, woman. What you doing allowing that po' child to go cutting that wood? Don't you know a splinter's gonna up and strike him in the eye!"

But Mama paid no mind. She understood that the same thing can happen—and often does—to the sighted. Those wood chips fly so fast that no mortal has time to move out of the way.

Same thing went for cooking. I've heard it said how dangerous it is for a blind person to be frying something in a skillet. The grease might pop up and burn 'em.

Well, as a kid I learned to cook, and it was Mama who showed me how. When she was at the stove frying some sausage or bacon, many is the time she got hit in the arm with a wad of burning fat. She could see, but she couldn't get out of the way in time. No one could.

I went to the Shiloh Baptist church in Greensville every Sunday of my childhood. (I never was what you'd call *extra* religious. I'm still not.) I went 'cause Mama made me, even though she was never that hard on my case. We had what was called BYPU—Baptist Young People's Union—and we'd sing and mess around and learn our little Bible stories.

To me, church was like listening to music at Mr. Pit's café or fooling around at fish fries. Only difference was that I couldn't leave when I wanted to. It was just part of life, part of growing up in the country. I accepted it because it was there.

I never expressed my opinion about church because I wasn't asked for it. I was a kid, and in the woods little children were taught to be seen and not heard. Yeah, that was a very popular expression in Greensville. That was Mama's philosophy. And lemme tell you—she wasn't shy about enforcing it.

Don't ever forget: Not only was the South old-fashioned, but blacks in the South were also extremely old-fashioned. Older folk just didn't let kids butt in with their little opinions. When you were punished, chances were, it'd sting.

Nowadays a kid might be sent to his room, but when he gets there he finds a TV, a stereo, a radio, and three dozen toys. In my day, living where I did, I was taught to say "yes, sir" and "yes, ma'am." I was taught respect.

On the other hand, adults in Greensville also showed respect for kids. You rarely heard a grown-up curse in front of a child, for example. Kids were taught to mind their manners all right, but as far as I could tell, the older folk set a decent example.

That's probably the reason why I was able to do all right at school: I was the product of a strict Southern home, and, even though I was a shade wild and restless, I understood the meaning of rules.

Back to School

Second year at school was a whole different story. I was relaxed, and I was even happy to be there. By then I had my own friends. I knew everybody and everybody knew me. They gave me a nickname—Foots —though I don't remember exactly where that came from.

That second year even the Christmas vacation worked out. The whole staff got together, chipped in, and raised enough bread to buy me a round-trip ticket home. I figured they must really like me.

Main feature was my music instruction. For the first time, I got formal lessons, learning little exercises and classical pieces. I took to it right away.

One time, though, I was almost kicked out of school for something I did during one of these lessons:

My music teacher—Miss Mallard—asked me to play my exercise. For whatever reasons, on this particular day I couldn't get the piece together in my brain. So I flubbed it. You know, there are days when your fingers won't do what they should.

Well, Miss Mallard got mad. Real mad. I tried a little bit more, but I still couldn't cut it. Finally she got so upset she cracked me 'cross my knuckles with a ruler.

Man, that sent me reeling! I hauled off and whacked her in the chest. Didn't know what had come over me. Guess I was just reacting to someone messing with my most valuable parts; I knew I needed my hands to play. And I was real sensitive about anyone fooling with 'em.

Anyway, I hit her. And that's something you did not do, specially in the South. Teachers would not take that kind of crap. And she didn't. She told the principal. (We called him Prof.) And he told the president of the school, Dr. Settles, who was about to kick my young ass out and send me home to Mama. I was scared to my bones. If Mama found out, she'd murder me.

When Miss Mallard discovered what Mr. Settles was gonna do, she intervened on my behalf. She told him to cool it. She figured I was only going to be whipped, and she thought that expelling me was too severe a punishment. Lucky for me.

I know Mama would have taken the side of the principal—no questions asked. That's how it went back then. Parents didn't question teachers.

You could see how important the piano was to me, even at age eight. When I was a kid, I never thought about being famous or rich, but I did think about being great. I wanted to be a great musician, and, early on, I understood who the great musicians were. I could hear them.

From the earliest days—listening to Mr. Pit back home—I was interested in winning the respect of genuine musicians. High standards had been set for me. I knew what real blues singing and boogie-woogie were all about. I had learned about jazz piano. The older I got, the more keen the competition became. Musically, I was raised during a time of absolutely no compromise: Either you could play your instrument or you couldn't.

I wasn't allowed to play boogie-woogie or blues in school. It was mainly simple things by Chopin or little waltzes by Strauss. The gutbucket music might have been our own, but it was not tolerated during lessons.

I bet you that deep down every one of the three music teachers I had during my school days—Miss Ryan, Miss Mallard, and Mrs. Lawrence—loved the blues. But it just wasn't thought to be proper. Makes me think of a time years later:

As an adult, I once attended a fancy NAACP dinner. I saw prime rib on the menu and I asked the woman in charge why we were eating white folks' food. I wondered why we weren't putting away some collard greens and pigs' feet, the goodies I knew everyone *really* wanted.

"Honey," she said to me, "if we had down-home food here, no one would leave home."

Although there was nothing really down-home about the music I learned at school, all music fascinated me. I was happy to play melodies I hadn't heard before. We learned silly tunes like "Won't You Come Out and Play with Me?" and when I was eleven or twelve, I joined the choir where I was the youngest kid in the group.

Every chance I had, I imitated the hits of the day. We had one radio at school, and naturally it was controlled by the big boys—kids like James Kendrick, who was a real power, Otis Mathews, and James Young. They decided what everyone else would listen to. And if you tried to turn the knob, you'd get your hand slapped.

I was hearing what everyone else in America was listening to—the big bands. I learned the Glenn Miller numbers and all the big tunes by Tommy Dorsey, Glen Gray, and Benny Goodman. I liked them fine, and I was interested in studying the arrangements and hearing how the diffferent sections—the horns, the reeds, the rhythm—were doing different things.

Now you didn't find no muddy Mississippi blues on the radio. That music was available only on what we called race records. But those low-down sounds were things I already knew. They were as much a part of me as my nose, my teeth, or the hair on my head.

These other sounds were new, and I was pleased to pick 'em up and learn 'em. One cat in particular knocked me out. They always talked 'bout Goodman being such a great clarinetist, but to me he wasn't in the same category as my man—Artie Shaw.

When I heard Artie Shaw do "Stardust" or, sometime later, "Concerto for Clarinet," I flipped. I loved his sweet sound and I loved his pure tone. It was Artie Shaw who inspired me to take up the clarinet —something I did when I was about ten—and Artie's Gramercy Five was one of the first small combos which made me sit up and take notice.

There were three pianos in that school—one in the practice room for the girls, another in the boys' practice room, and a third—the best one—in the chapel. (The chapel, by the way, also had rows of desks in the back and was used as a classroom.)

There were also a few cats at school who could always play for real. The best of 'em was Joe Lee Lawrence. He was one of the big boys. And I'm here to tell you that he could play the piano. Joe Lee was blind, and so was his brother Ernest, a teacher of mine and also a piano player. (Mrs. Lawrence, my music teacher, was Ernest's wife.)

Course Joe Lee couldn't play exactly like Art Tatum—who could? —but he was able to approach that amazingly fast style, and, man, I was impressed. Anyone who could sound a little like Tatum had my vote. For my generation, Art Tatum was the main cat on piano. He was our hero, and I still haven't heard anyone who could do so much with two hands.

Must say that even later, when I got fairly good at the piano, I knew that I couldn't even carry Art Tatum's shit bucket. The man was alone and no one could touch him. I loved how he played standards, and I also knew that he could play very filthy blues if he wanted to. He could do anything.

Over the years, my respect for Art Tatum has grown. There are other pianists I like. I admire Oscar Peterson tremendously. In fact, I love Oscar to his drawers. But Oscar will be the first to tell you that he ain't Tatum.

Yeah, Tatum was God. And if God walked in the room, you stood up and paid your respects.

Whenever Joe Lee—our local Art Tatum—showed up in the dorm, all the kids started yelling:

"Wow! It's Joe Lee! We gonna be hearing somethin' *hot!*"

He came through the door and right away he'd be thumping and singing like a bass fiddle—"boom boom boom boom." Sure 'nough, he'd start working out tunes and have us all jumping, dancing, and carrying on like lunatics.

Not long after that I found myself doing the same thing, playing "Honky Tonk Train" or "Beat Me Daddy" while the kids got up and slid around. All this, you understand, was done after hours, on the sly, in the practice rooms when the teachers were nowhere to be found.

By this time I was pretty sociable at school, even though I was shy with folk I didn't know.

I was one of the few blind kids who could communicate with the deaf. I did it just 'cause I wanted to talk to them. I learned the sign language so the deaf kids could "speak" to me in the palms of my hands. They made signs or letters against my skin. And of course they read my lips. It was fun.

Not that I was a goody-goody. Far from it. I was among the nervier kids, I'd say, and there was also a vicious side to me. If I was provoked, I'd almost always respond.

Let's say a cat did something mean to me—squeal to the teacher that I was messing with a girl in the hallways or throwing spitballs. Once I found out who ratted—and I always made it my business to find out —I retaliated. Oh yes I did.

I'd tie a piece of wire between two benches. Then I'd settle back and wait till the kid started walking down the sidewalk. I'd take great pleasure in hearing him fall on his face.

Yeah, it might take awhile, but I'd always pay back these kinds of debts. And I always did it in a way where I wouldn't get hurt. Toe-to-toe combat never appealed to me. If you're after revenge, there be better ways of getting it than hitting someone upside the head. Now and then I was forced into a fight, and I recall one time when I clobbered someone in the face with a piece of coal.

I got into other kinds of trouble. If I was being punished, for example, they'd turn my plate down at the dinner table, so when the food was served I wouldn't get any. Sometimes that made me mad, so I'd tilt the table and everyone's food and drinks would go spilling on the floor.

Course that would just make them punish me even more. Now I'd have to wash the dishes with the girls, say, for three or four days. And that would be tough, 'cause everyone would be laughing at me like I was the biggest fool on the face of the earth. Not that I didn't want to be with the girls. On the contrary. Anyone who knows me, knows how I love women.

I learned the facts of life at school. Somewhere around eleven years old. I think the first time I ever beat off was with a group of boys. We had this game: We'd lay around and jack off together, trying to see who would come first.

You can imagine that I had a problem with masturbating. All the blind kids did. Maybe I did it every week or every two weeks, but I had to be careful. I didn't want to get caught, and of course I couldn't see if anyone was looking at me. The supervisor could walk in and bust me before I had a chance to pull up my pants.

So I had to wait till nighttime when everyone was asleep. I had to wake myself in the middle of the night. But lots of times I was too tired and just slept on through. A school for the blind ain't the easiest place to jack off.

Never did have any bad feelings about sex. Never felt it was a sin of any kind. It gave me a buzz, and it felt awfully nice. Man, that was enough for me.

I was always trying to get girls to sneak into the practice rooms so I could finger 'em a little. That was a favorite pastime of mine. Course another big hazard of being blind was getting caught with a girl. So you just had to take your chances, trying to be as cautious as you could. You couldn't get a girl in the practice room every day. No, that was a rare treat, something you were able to do maybe once a month.

I had several girlfriends during this period. The one I remember best was Geneva. She sat next to me in class and had a sharp little mind. I liked that.

I teased a lot of the other girls. I found saddle spurs, for instance, and placed them on their seats, covering them with a piece of paper. When they sat down, the girls jumped ten feet in the air, screaming bloody murder.

But I didn't do that with Geneva. I dug her. There was something soft and sweet about her. I thought we were cool. She had a mellow voice and a graceful manner. Sure, it was puppy love, but when you're into it—even at that age—it's some serious stuff. Least it was for me.

Lots of adults laugh when they see little kids having their first love affairs—but not me. I can dig it. I recall many of mine, and at the time they were vital to my body and soul. Onstage these days I sometimes do a spoken introduction to the tune, "Crying Time." And the story I tell is partially based on just the kind of thing I had with Geneva:

> When you're small, grown-ups don't realize how important it is to you when a friend moves away. Specially if it's a girl. They say, it ain't nothing. But to you it's a whole lot.
>
> I remember when my girlfriend was gonna move away. She was eleven, and I was what you might call a hard twelve.
>
> Yeah, I remember the day she was moving away. I finally got up my courage and went next door. Tapped on the door and said, "Miss Janie Lee"—that was her mother—"would you please let your daughter come out and play? I promise I won't do nothing to her."
>
> So she came out. She didn't know what to say. And I didn't know either. But eventually I perked up and said, "Oh, it's crying time again, you gonna leave me . . ."

I never got to make love to Geneva, though God knows I always wanted to. The school was strict about those things. The girls were examined each year at the beginning and at the end of the school year. The officials were always suspicious and had to keep an eye out for everyone—me included. That was why I tried to cool it most of the time.

I liked the romantic angle as well as the physical. Not that I didn't love exploring little girls' pussies; it's just that I also enjoyed all the small talk that came first.

Sounds strange, but I've always been shy when it comes to females. I have to talk to my baby first, then cuddle up, then do some coaxing, then maybe make a move or two. Can't just grab.

Blind cats can be real aggressive with women. When they're introduced, sometimes they'll be putting their hands all over the girl's face. Or they'll be feeling up her titties. They'll use their lack of sight as an excuse. They call it the Braille method.

I don't like that. I think that's pretty jive. And I don't do it. I have another method:

When I meet a girl, I just shake her hand and then place my other hand slightly above her wrist. By doing that I learn all the necessary data. If she's built, you can bet that I know it from the first touch. I immediately understand her contour—and that's most important to me. I can come close to telling the size of her arms, her thighs, her breasts—almost everything, all from that first touch.

I must have been around eleven or twelve when I started venturing off campus a bit and exploring St. Augustine. I got to know the town real well, and took long walks by myself, just the way I'd done back in Greensville.

Now it's important that you understand that there were three things I never wanted to own when I was a kid: a dog, a cane, and a guitar. In my brain, they each meant blindness and helplessness. (Seems like every blind blues singer I'd heard about was playing the guitar.)

It wasn't that I wanted to fool myself. Hell, I knew I was blind as a bat. But I didn't want to go limping around like I was half-dead. I didn't want to have to depend upon anyone or anything other than myself. So I learned certain tricks going around St. Augustine. And I still use 'em today.

If I was in a part of town for the first time and needed to find my way somewhere, I'd have someone take me. I'd pay attention to the path we took—remembering a building here, a step down there, listening to the changing sounds and memorizing as much of the trip as I could. I'd never count steps; that'd be too complicated. I'd keep the method simple.

On the return trip I'd have another chance to see where I was going. And before long I'd be able to do it myself. That's about all the help I'd ever need. From then on, I was on my own.

It was like learning a musical score which has been written in Braille. You memorize five bars first . . . then another five . . . then maybe ten, until you have the entire thing straight in your head. That's what I did with Greensville, St. Augustine, Tallahassee, and later Jacksonville, Tampa, Orlando, Seattle, New Orleans, Dallas.

I don't want to sound like I'm bragging, but when I walked around those towns, my pace wasn't halting or even cautious. Man, I moved. I set my own rhythm, and I do believe it was usually a little faster than most other people's, blind or not.

One of the first things I did off campus was play the piano. Sometimes my music teacher found me jobs at tea parties for the ladies of St. Augustine. Those were my first playing experiences on the outside, and I loved them. Yes indeed. The idea of getting out, playing a new piano, and pleasing all these people—that was a big deal to me. I dug the idea of being an entertainer and I could always figure out what the ladies wanted to hear.

Now these women were black. Deep down, I knew they'd dig some filthy blues. But these were proper parties, like the NAACP dinner I mentioned to you before. You were expected to play with a certain dignity, even though you can bet your sweet ass that every one of those mamas was *dying* to hear something nasty.

Still, I played the part. I played the proper tunes—"String of Pearls" or "Jersey Bounce." I knew those pop hits like the back of my hand.

I liked them, and I took pride in the fact that I played them well. I was paid very little, if anything. Mostly the ladies gave me candies or fruits. (I loved getting tangerines; that was my favorite.) Occasionally they gathered up some coins which could come to two or three dollars. To me, that was a tremendous sum of money.

This was a time in my life when my musical horizons were expanding. Course I already knew church music. I had been singing it all my life. On records I heard gospel singers like Wings Over Jordan and the Golden Gate Quartet. In school I sang in the choir—they even gave me a little uniform—and some of us kids put together our own informal singing group, doing the same kind of rhythmic gospel music. (I was the youngest boy in the group. When it came to music, seemed like I was always with people much, much older than me—whether singers or instrumentalists.)

You also have to understand that the South was full of country-and-western sounds—hillbilly music, we called it—and I can't recall a single Saturday night in those years when I didn't listen to the *Grand Ole Opry* on the radio. I loved Grandpa Jones and those other characters. I could hear what they were doing and appreciate the feeling behind it. Jimmie Rodgers, Roy Acuff, Hank Snow, Hank Williams, and later Eddie Arnold—these were singers I listened to all the time. I wasn't fanatical about their music, but I certainly dug it and paid it some mind.

At the same time I didn't lose interest in the big white bands—Dorsey and Miller and Goodman and Krupa and Shaw. And naturally I knew the black bands—Jay McShann and Jimmie Lunceford, Lucky Millinder, Buddy Johnson, Basie, Ellington, and later Billy Eckstine, whose version of "Blowing the Blues Away" is something I still play.

Al Hibbler singing with Duke, Ella singing with Chick Webb or the Ink Spots—this was music which hit me hard. I also knew all the white singers of the time: Bing Crosby, Dick Haymes, Vaughn Monroe, Tony Martin. Of the whites, only one—Jo Stafford—impressed me much. She had a silky quality to her voice which I liked; there was something haunting about her style.

I listened to the *Hit Parade* on the radio in those years and heard the early sides of Frank Sinatra, though I don't think he really started wailing till later in his career; he's one of those people who has improved and mellowed with age.

I knew jazz. I loved jazz, and I could play jazz.

Art Tatum, as I've said, was Big Papa to all us piano players, but I also had great respect for Earl "Fatha" Hines and Teddy Wilson. Nothing escaped me, and I was always trying to imitate the new sounds, just to see whether I could do it. Usually I could.

But there was one guy who sung and played the piano in a way which changed my life. He influenced me above all others. This dude did it all for me, and I couldn't hear him enough. In fact, I followed him for nearly a decade. Musically, I walked in his footsteps until I found a stride of my own. I stole many of his licks. And I got his vocal style down to a T. He was my idol: Talkin' 'bout Nat Cole.

Folks forget that Nat Cole started out as a piano player, a *jazz* piano player. Sure, he played pretty tunes and pop melodies, but if he wanted to, he could turn out the blackest blues you'd care to hear. When bop came along later in the forties, he could do that too.

Yeah, Nat Cole could play the piano, pure and simple. And I knew it. I also loved the way he sang, the way he phrased, the way his voice was deep and romantic and sexy. He caressed a ballad, got under it, and stroked it for all it was worth.

No one accompanied himself quite like Nat Cole—that was another thing. You might think playing the accompaniment is easy, but I'm here to tell you it ain't. No, sir; those little fills he ad-libbed behind himself were gems—always tasty, always clean, always inventive as hell.

I was also aware of Nat Cole's popularity in the forties, the fact that everyone loved him, and that he was making big money playing this kind of music.

So that was my first program—to become a junior Nat Cole. Many of those early tunes—"All for You" or "Straighten Up and Fly Right" —soon became part of my repertoire. His style wasn't my style—that would come years later—but it was one that put together so much of what I loved: jazz improvisation, pretty melodies, hot rhythms, and an occasional taste of the blues.

There were other piano players and singers of that school who were powerful influences on me: Charles Brown, for example, in the early part of my career, especially when I was struggling down in Florida. I made many a dollar doing an imitation of his "Drifting Blues." That was a hell of a number.

But I don't think anyone quite affected me like Nat Cole. I quickly learned that by being able to duplicate his popular hits, I could enjoy some recognition of my own. So between that and the jazz I was learning from Joe Lee Lawrence at school, my music was starting to shape up. Even though I wasn't a teenager yet, my confidence as a musician was slowly building.

Summers
in Tallahassee

I loved going home for the summers. Mama was there and so was Mary Jane. And when I look back now, it surprises me how quickly I was able to adjust to living in two different places.

School was one thing. It was September through May. I liked it fine. I was doing okay and, aside from light mischief, I stayed out of trouble.

But home was something else. It was a place where these two women loved me and cared for me. It was a town where I knew practically everyone, where people—at least in the mind of an eleven-year-old—seemed to genuinely care 'bout each other.

Sure, the South was full of superstitions and dozens of different forms of segregation. But none of that meant very much to me then. Man, I just liked Greensville; it was where I belonged.

The only taste I had of the South's wicked history came from my grandma—my father's mother. She told me stories about the days of slavery. Her name was Margaret Robinson, and she was a big, light-skinned woman. She probably had a white mother or father. I'd guess she had been a slave herself. We called her Muh.

Muh, who lived till she was ninety, liked to tell me stories. Stories 'bout how it was "way back then." She told me what white folk did to black folk. And I must admit to me it was like a wild adventure, like a comic book or a radio program.

Wow! I'd think to myself. Imagine that! Oh man, that's amazing!

Can't remember the stories exactly, but they were about things which happened on the plantations—rapes and raids against the blacks. They had as much reality for me as a novel about pirates or the tales of Robin Hood.

In addition to Mr. Pit and Miss Georgia, another couple was particularly fond of me—Henry Johnson and his wife, Miss Alice. When I first knew them, they owned a café, with a jukebox, far away in another section of town. That was another place where I spent lots of time, listening to whatever music was being played in those years—Louis Jordan, Big Joe Turner, Erskine Hawkins, Tiny Bradshaw, Muddy Waters, Lucky Millinder, Earl Hines, and Nat Cole.

As a matter of fact, many times while I was at Mr. Johnson's, people came up to give me nickels to buy ice cream and candy. But instead of buying ice cream and candy, I always put the money in the jukebox. And if I didn't have any money, I'd wait for other people to put their nickels in. If there was a way to get to listen to music, I'd find it.

Mr. Johnson had a car, and like Mr. Pit, he sometimes let me drive. He'd sit next to me, telling me when I was swerving too much in one direction. By then I was pretty good at it. After a while, Mr. Johnson and Miss Alice moved to Tallahassee—forty miles west of Greensville—and I often went to visit them during the summer.

They opened a club there—and Mr. Johnson also belonged to a fraternal lodge. I'm not sure about the exact nature of the organization; it might have consisted of church elders and folk like that. Anyway, I do know that Henry convinced them to raise money just to buy me a clarinet.

That was really a thrill—a brand-spanking-new clarinet! I carried it around like it was part of me, a third arm or leg. On top of that, Miss Alice, who saw that I rarely wore shoes, was always giving me clothes and special foods which she knew were my favorites.

I liked to move around. Fact, I've always liked to move around and suspect I always will. I had energy to burn, and whenever I could, I ran over to Tallahassee to visit the Johnsons.

Met some other nice folk during that period, or maybe a little later. I think I was around fifteen when I ran into a man called Mr. Bison. I called him Kiddy Boo. He had a wife named Dolly and a daughter named Lucille. They ran a grocery store down the street from where the Johnsons lived and I hung out there a lot.

We were good friends—Lucille and I—though nothing more than that. Kiddy Boo and Dolly were also very sweet to me, and it was at their store that I first learned how to use a cash register.

Might seem like a little thing to you, but it made me feel awfully good to be able to ring up sales and give change to people. To this day, I can still tell you where the various keys on the register are placed.

Lucille had the run of the store and she'd often let me have moon pies or maybe some Nu Grape or True-Aid orange soda. She and her mama and papa treated me like·one of their own, and they were another reason I spent so much time in Tallahassee.

Then there were motorcycles. I learned to ride one in Tallahassee when I was about fourteen or fifteen. I had a friend who owned one. During the day he worked at a drugstore where he made deliveries using the store's motorbike. That meant I could borrow his.

I got to know the town pretty well, and soon I felt confident about riding round. Tallahassee was full of hills, and I loved racing up and down 'em, sometimes trailing my friend or riding next to him, so I could hear the sound of the exhaust and make sure to follow closely, and yet not too closely.

I know it sounds strange—a blind teenager buzzin' round on a motorcycle—but I liked that; that was me. I had always been nervy, and I always had a lot of faith in my ability not to break my neck.

Well, one day some people saw me riding around the city and didn't believe that I was blind. So they reported me. Since I was going to a state school for the blind—and therefore receiving a form of state aid —they insisted that I be examined by some board. I was examined and, of course, they learned I really couldn't see. So I hopped right back on the motorcycle.

I always say that I'll try almost anything once. I'll try it, all right, providing that deep down inside I don't believe I'm gonna get hurt. If I can control the machine—whether it's a car, a truck, a motorcycle, or a plane—then I can be pretty sure I'll survive it. I suppose that one proof of the rightness of my attitude is that, as a kid, I was never seriously hurt and there were only a few close calls.

One day at school a classmate and I both fell and I somehow cut my forehead on a broken pipe. The scar's still there today.

And another time, also in St. Augustine, a friend and I were crossing a street when I thought I heard a noise. My friend had partial sight, so I asked him whether he saw anything.

"Nothing," he said.

I believed him and followed him across. Next thing I knew I was picking myself up a block away, where I had been thrown by a car. We were just shaken, not really hurt. But it did teach me a lesson: to follow my own instincts, blind or not.

During those summers my instincts almost always led me to Tallahassee. Mr. Johnson and Miss Alice were there, Kiddy Boo and Dolly and Lucille were there, and there was also a band. In fact, that's where I met a cat they called Cannonball Adderley.

He played in the Florida A. & M. band, and in those days we mostly called him Julian. I sat in with the group, playing piano, and come to think of it, this must have been the first big band of its kind that I played with.

They'd be doing the current stuff going round, very hip charts of "Tippin' In" and "After Hours," the big Erskine Hawkins hits. I especially loved "After Hours," with that nice bluesy piano feel.

There was also a guitar player around Tallahassee named Lawyer

Smith. He had a small combo and once in a while he'd call me to play a gig for a dollar or two.

When I got back to Greensville, of course I thought I was a pretty big little man, playing these gigs just like a grown-up. But it didn't take Mama long to put me in my place. I'm sure she was proud that I was learning to become a musician, but that didn't stop her from teaching me the lessons of life.

Once she caught me with a cigarette. She made me smoke the entire pack, one after another, till I nearly choked to death.

"If you wanna smoke," Mama said, "then smoke."

I got to swimming in the head so bad I thought I was gonna pass out. That taught me good. Years passed before I could look at another cigarette.

'Nother time I tried to chew some tobacco. It was called "Brown Mule," I recall, and it belonged to Uncle Johnny B. Wise, who was really not an uncle but a distant cousin. It made me sick as a dog.

There was another lesson Mama taught me which I'll never forget:

That year we happened to be living in a shack with a fireplace, which is where folk in the country like to roast sweet potatoes. On this particular night, two fat potatoes were cooking when Mama gets up and leaves me alone in the room.

I want a potato, but at first I hesitate. In those days, kids asked for things before they took them. But Mama isn't there to give permission, and the aroma of the sweet potatoes is really getting to me. I can practically taste them, and in a split second I reach into the fire and grab one.

At that very moment, I hear Mama coming back into the room. What can I do? I decide to hide the potato and, like a fool, stuff it in my pocket. At first, it's cool, 'cause the skin isn't all that warm. But the insides of the potato—the meaty part—is hot as a raging fire, and it doesn't take long for the heat to reach the skin.

Well, you can imagine the scene: I'm hurting now, I'm movin' and slippin' and slidin', I'm bouncin' back from one leg to another, I'm steamin'.

Now Mama just sits there. Doesn't say a word. Just waits. Finally I know I need to take this hot potato out of my pocket. Either that or take my pants off. So I meekly dig out the potato and put it down.

"Let that be a lesson to you, boy," Mama says. "Anytime you want something, you ask for it. If you steal, son, you sure to get burned."

Making Out

That was my life until I was fifteen—nine or ten months in school, then the summertimes in Greensville or Tallahassee.

As I got older, I found more places in St. Augustine—off campus—where I could do a little damage. But I never did much. In those days, I was partying if I drank a bottle of beer in a bar; I mean that was a big thing.

Yeah, the state school for the blind was a no-nonsense operation. And the amount of sin and sex was kept to a bare minimum. I never even heard the name of any drug while I was there, much less tried any.

There was a lady who had a tavern in St. Augustine, and we went there 'cause she let us sit in the back room and served us beer. She had a piano which I played for the crowd, free of charge. And there was also a jukebox.

So between the music and the smooching we'd be doing with the girls, everyone had a fine time. I had already discovered my weakness for women, and that tavern was one of the few places where I was able to do a little light loving.

There were cats who were braver than me when it came to getting some pussy at school. (In those days we sometimes called pussy "poon tang," or, as we said in the country, the stuff "down there.")

I told you before how the girls slept in their dorm, separated from the boys. Well, there was one girl who actually drew her boyfriend a map, and together they formulated an elaborate scheme. It was a special Braille diagram which showed him how to sneak into the girls' section and find his way to her bed.

This diagram was really somethin' else—all detailed and precise—and even included a contingency option for dealing with the night watchman if he happened to show up. It was a very hip strategy and an especially creative plan. You gotta remember that both these kids were blind. But then again, sex is a bitch of a motivator; it don't need no eyes.

One time the mention of lovemaking in a musical context almost got my ass thrown out of school. You see, we had these little assemblies, shows where the kids did acts, recited poems, or played songs. When it was my turn and everyone expected me to play some innocent classical piece—maybe "Moonlight Sonata"—I sang a popular tune of the day instead: Lil Green's "Romance in the Dark."

The words were raunchy for those times. The first lines went something like, "In the dark, I get such a thrill, when she presses her fingertips upon my lips. And she begs me to please keep still . . . in the dark."

Then there was another line: "In the dark we will find what the others left behind. Oh Lord, just you and I, in the dark!"

I tried to sing it good, with lots of feeling. Actually, I might have given it too much feeling, 'cause it didn't sit well with the teachers. They weren't ready for this, didn't appreciate it, and found the words a little upsetting.

It might have been too obvious that I understood what the sex part was about. Anyway, the kids dug it. They yelled and stomped and hollered for more. The result of all this was a small musical scandal. I was instructed never to perform such tunes again. Shut my mouth, I was told. And I did.

A couple of years later—maybe I was twelve or thirteen—I got my first little piece of pussy. As best as I can remember, it happened during the summer in Tallahassee. I was playing at a club, probably with Lawyer Smith's combo, singing like Charles Brown or Nat Cole. Those styles, you know, had a certain romantic lure about them.

Anyway, some gal dug my act. She had been hanging around, and it was after midnight when she came up to the bandstand. Now I didn't know much, but I'd been listening to the older cats talking for a long time. You know how musicians talk; they just love to bullshit about fucking. And I always paid a whole lot of attention to that chatter.

It was late and I was sleepy, but suddenly I came to life when she said, "You wanna play?"

Yes, ma'am, I wanna play. Sure 'nough, darling! Oh my, do I! Indeed I do wanna play! Hello, honey!

I knew my time had come. And, Jack, I didn't hesitate. She took me to a gas station where she whisked me into one of the rest rooms. She had been juicing and was awfully anxious to be loved.

Inside the bathroom there wasn't the kind of toilet bowl you see today, but more or less a platform with a seat. Don't know how old she was. Maybe nineteen, maybe twenty. But I do recall how she pulled up her dress, leaned against the wall, and rested one foot on that platform. We made love just like that: She was arched against the wall, and we were both standing up, pumping the prime.

She made me feel nice and comfortable. I loved it. It was smooth and easy, sweet and hot. Everything it had been cranked up to be. Finally I was able to understand what everyone had been bullshittin' 'bout for so long.

Growing up was particularly strange if you were a musician. Seemed like you got to things faster than most kids. And it seemed like I was always around older kids. That's 'cause they were the ones who were in the bands.

I was an advanced player. I was able to do more than most kids my age. And being around the big boys had an impact on me. I saw what they were doing—whether it was with music or with girls—and I wanted to do it too.

School might have been a little slow for me. It never provided the challenge, say, of music. There wasn't much reading material around school other than what we got in class. There was no library.

I read *Huckleberry Finn* and *Tom Sawyer*—those books were about country life and I could relate to them—and I also dug *Robinson Crusoe*. The only other books I remember were the Bible and Funk & Wagnalls dictionary.

There was study hour every evening. That's when we were supposed to be preparing our lessons. But I was usually able to do the homework for one class while sitting in another. The lessons were easy; I think they were too easy, and, as a result, I got bored. So during those study hours, I either fucked off or nodded out.

I needed challenges. And I'm sure that's why at school mechanics interested me; a mechanical problem—say, breaking down an engine —could take days to figure. It was something I could get into, a way for me to lose myself.

Same thing with music. I was intrigued by harmonics and arranging. Those things represented great challenges. The idea of writing for an entire band fascinated me. I wanted to learn how to compose parts for all the instruments, and I wanted to know how to make them blend.

By the time I was fourteen, I could do it. I called off the various notes to someone who wrote them down, part by part. I use the same method today when I want to write an arrangement. I do it in my head.

I learned some other stuff at school. Dominoes and cards, for example. I even invented my own method of Brailleing the cards, and I'm still using it. We played crazy games like dirty hearts, whiz, tonk, coon can, or pity pat. I wasn't a shark, but I could hold my own.

I also learned to type. That's how I wrote letters home. We had old Underwoods, and I banged away, always setting the machine for the heaviest touch. (When I played piano, I also played so I could be heard; I'm no soft touch.)

The main thing was still my piano playing. That kept my interest like nothing else. Whether I was banging out "Cow Cow Boogie" in the rehearsal room with all the kids dancing round me, or whether I was fooling with the blues on Mr. Pit's piano back home, I played wherever I could.

There were white people in Greensville who let me use their piano: the Reams, for example, the folks who owned the general store. And there were also black folk, aside from Mr. Pit and Miss Georgia, who had musical instruments. Maybelle Grey and her mother, Middie King, who lived right around Mama, told me I could play their piano anytime. Everyone knew that among the music I toyed with—swing, boogie, blues, hillbilly, jazz—something was bound to please 'em.

So between my life at home during the summers and my time in school during the winters, nothing was going too wrong. I was growing up. I was pretty popular among my classmates and among my teachers. I was a decent student, and I was learning and playing as much music as I possibly could. I was happy.

Maybe you'll have a hard time believing it, but even blind kids can adjust and lead normal childhoods.

It was in the middle of May of 1945 that my world suddenly changed. I was in school when they brought me the news. I had nothing to prepare me for the shock. There had been no warnings. No early signs.

They just came and told me: Mama was dead.

They might have said that she was very sick, they might have said that she was calling for me, they might have said that she was in critical condition and needed me by her side.

But they didn't say that.

All they said was Mama was dead. She had died the night before.

I was supposed to go home. She was going to be buried in the ground. Mama was dead.

Nothing had ever hit me like that. Not George drowning. Not going blind. Nothing. No, this was something new.

Mama had raised me, and now she was gone. I couldn't deal with that. And for a while, I went a little crazy.

Suffering

"I'm not always gonna be with you."

Those were Mama's words, and I can't tell you how many times she must have said them to me. Still, they didn't start meaning anything until she was gone.

"There are two sides to life."

That's something else Mama would say. There's happiness and pain. Joy and sorrow. When things seem like they're going good, watch out: Trouble and heartache may be just around the bend.

Sure, Mama warned me. Sure, she told me over and again that one day she wouldn't be here. Sure, she let me know that I'd have to make it alone. So when I went blind, she said, "Don't worry, child, there are two ways to do everything." And she'd show me the other way— whether it was walking or cooking or drawing water out of a well.

I heard her words. I listened to her voice. I knew she was sick and frail. But I was still a boy—even at fifteen—and I couldn't imagine a world without Mama. I couldn't feature it. I couldn't deal with it.

What did I know about death? How could I understand it?

I've heard about premonitions in dreams of other people's death. That didn't happen with me. I had a lot of dreams as a kid, but not about death. Sometimes when the covers were pulled too tight, I dreamt that I was falling or that someone was chasing me. But I never dreamt that Mama was dead. In fact, when I was home dreaming in my own bed, it was always Mama I turned to—lying right there next to me—and it was Mama who comforted me, mopping my brow and telling me that everything was gonna be all right.

I can't remember who gave me the news at school—one of the teachers, maybe Ernest Lawrence. I heard the words, and suddenly a series of shocks attacked my brain.

All my memories of those first days are silhouettes, shadows hanging over me. I wandered around in a trance. There was no way out. My mind couldn't handle the fact that there was no possibility of seeing or hearing Mama again. I couldn't go to anyone for help. I didn't pray and I didn't break down. A big lump formed in the middle of my throat and just stayed there. Like a rock.

They told me I was going home, and I went. Even after I arrived in Greensville, the lump didn't budge. I couldn't eat; food seemed to expand in my throat; I couldn't sleep; I couldn't communicate with anyone.

I knew why the lump was there—it was my brain fucking with me —but I couldn't do anything about it. I kept all my feelings bottled up inside. And I was getting sick, seriously sick.

Folks started worrying about me. No one knew what to do. I was a zombie. I had real trouble, and all I could keep thinking was why, why couldn't I talk to her again, why couldn't I see her, why couldn't I kiss her again?

It was rotten; it was unfair. I hadn't been with Mama since Christmas, and here it was May. I didn't have even a chance to tell her good-bye. I was too young for this to be happening. I was fifteen, and she was just thirty-two. (It's hard to be sure of Mama's exact age— thirty-one or thirty-two is close. The only records country folk kept were notes we'd jot down in the Bible.)

There were other people—Mr. Pit and Miss Georgia, Mr. Johnson and Miss Alice—who treated me with kindness and tried their best to comfort me. But they weren't Mama. My father wasn't around, and even had he been, there's nothing he could have done.

Mary Jane stood by me in those next months, but it was not the same thing. Mama and me were close; after George died, there were just the two of us. Now no more.

Dr. McCloud—the same doctor who cared for me when I went blind —told me that Mama died in her sleep. Something she ate—potato poon, a mix of grated sweet potatoes—gave her gas, forced her stomach to blow up, and choked her heart. At least that's what he said.

In the country, everyone died of a heart attack. You never heard about no other diseases besides heart attacks, rheumatism, and arthritis. There were no hospitals, no specialists. Who knows what happened or what the real name of her sickness was? But it didn't matter: Anything would have seemed senseless.

When a boy has just one parent—a mama—he'll cling to her like she's life itself. And he'll never even start thinking about what life would be like without her. The thought's too terrible. I still couldn't get a lot of things together in my mind: Why couldn't I talk to Mama again? Why couldn't she talk to me? Why couldn't I hear her voice? I was unable to deal with the facts of death; I was unable to accept the reality of death.

I'm not sure why I didn't go off my rocker. I was pretty close to the edge and maybe, at least for a few days, I might have been a little over it. I kept thinking that I should have been there that night 'fore she died. Maybe I could have helped. At least I could have talked to her one last time, heard her voice, kissed her face. It all seemed bizarre: alive in the evening, dead in the morning.

I sat alone, silent, not moving a muscle or saying a word. Not crying, not eating, not praying. My mind just drifted somewhere out there in space.

Mama rested in the funeral home for a week. She'd died on Monday and wasn't buried till the following Sunday. I was motionless that whole week, too stunned or saddened to do as much as say hello to anyone.

SUFFERING

Many people were alarmed about me. They were convinced I was becoming dangerous to myself. My despondency was growing too heavy for everyone. It was a disease which wouldn't leave.

Then a woman came to me. She was known in Greensville as Ma Beck. She had twenty-two children—three had died; nine boys and ten girls were still living. She was a remarkable and wonderful person.

This was the lady you'd go to if you were sick—I mean sure-enough sick—'cause the people of Greensville were convinced that if there was a heaven, Ma Beck would be going there. She was a staunch Christian, everybody's friend. If you needed to ask God for help, it was thought that she had more influence with Him than anyone else.

Ma Beck was the salt of the earth, and when it came to matters of the heart and of the soul, she knew her business. She let me have it:

"Boy, don't you remember what your mama told you? Well, you better. You better remember what your mama said. Your mama wouldn't want you acting this way. No, she wouldn't. You know the things she tried to teach you. You've been acting like a crazy boy, and if she was here, she wouldn't put up with it. So stop acting like a crazy boy. Stop feeling sorry for yourself. Your mama spent her whole life preparing you for this here day. You know what she taught you. You know what she told you. You gotta carry on. That's all there is to it. That's what she'd want. And that's what you gotta do. You gotta carry on, RC."

That did it. Suddenly I fell into her arms. Now tears were streaming out my eyes; now my body was shaking with sobs. She held me, not saying another word, just letting me weep for hours. I howled like a tiny infant, crying for all the pain that had been stored up, crying for the loss and the grief and the sweet memories that Mama had given me.

Ma Beck broke me.

I went to the funeral. I wanted to see Mama again. And I did. I touched her face that one last time. I still remember what it felt like. I still remember the chills running over me.

How strange it was. Until then I had been terrified of dead people. Even the sound of an ambulance frightened me. But now, being next to my mama didn't bother me. The day of her funeral I had no fear.

It was important to me that I touch her; it was my only good-bye. I loved her very much. I still wanted to speak to her, and I still wanted her to speak to me, to hear her voice, to have her miraculously come back to life. But slowly reality worked its miserable way to the insides of my brain, and I understood that Mama was cold now and about to be buried in the ground.

The church was crowded with black folk and white folk. Everyone was weeping together. Thinking back, I know there was something decent about Greensville. In spite of the hang-ups and hypocrisies of the times, on some occasions you could feel a sympathy and a love between the races. Mama's funeral was such a time. Seemed like all of Greensville broke down and wept for that woman.

So together we walked to the graveyard—I could hear everyone moaning and praying—and we paid our last respects. Mama was gone, and now I had to figure out what I was going to do with the rest of my life. Standing there by the grave, in spite of the folk surrounding me, I had never felt so alone.

By forcing me to break up, Ma Beck might have kept me from breaking down. Once the tears started to flow, once I had that initial flood pass over me, I started to remember Mama's old-fashioned wisdom:

"You will not beg and you will not steal. You gotta believe that you can do what you can do. If you don't, you gonna sink, boy; you gonna sink to the very bottom."

I knew that I had to have faith in myself; I had to start buying my own line. And as those months passed after Mama's death, I realized that point had come. I wandered around Greensville and spent my time wondering and wondering.

Those summer months after Mama's death were a turning point for me. There was no one else to tell me anything. I had to make up my own mind, my own way, in my own time. Never really had to do that before, and in many ways I found the situation frightening. But that week of silence and suffering also made me harder, and that hardness has stayed with me the rest of my life.

I didn't go round asking a lot of advice. I was going to make up my own mind. I was firm in my convictions, maybe even a little foolish and headstrong.

No, I didn't ask no preacher and I didn't ask no doctor. I knew what they'd say: Go back to school, boy. And I wasn't sure that was what I wanted. I knew I had to make this decision alone. I sought no one's help.

I didn't turn to God either. I didn't believe He had much to do with Mama's death or any of this personal stuff. I didn't have an ax to grind with Him, but I didn't have much to say to Him either.

What strength I was able to find came from people like Mama herself, or Ma Beck, or Mary Jane—country folk who understood what it meant to be tough. Women from that neck of the woods saw deeply into life; they weren't afraid and they weren't pampered. They could stand up to anything—natural disasters or personal misfortunes —and I knew that they were the ones who would keep me from cracking.

There weren't lots of people crowding around to comfort me. I didn't act like that was what I wanted. I sure as hell didn't enjoy having other people feel sorry for me. Fact is, I hated it. I'd rather be off in a corner by myself than have bunches of friends and neighbors patting me on the head and telling me how, yes indeed, it was all gonna be all right.

So I kept my head up, took long walks round town, and chewed the fat with my old friends—Johnny Cake, Beatrice, or Lou Dell. But my brain was working all this time, trying to put the pieces together in the right shape.

There were really only two things I could do: go back to school or quit. Going back would have been the easiest path to follow. I had been boarding there for eight years now and knew the place as well as I knew Greensville. Everyone there liked me okay and life on campus was pretty easy. It was a state school, so even if I didn't have a cent of my own—which I didn't—at least I knew I wouldn't starve.

Money had a lot to do with my decision. I didn't have any, and I knew I was gonna have to learn how to get some. School was all right, my grades were decent, but I really wasn't enthusiastic about the place or about my studies. I had gone because Mama told me to.

Now for the first time I had a choice—one enormous choice—and it wasn't long after Mama died that I knew where I was headed. At fifteen, I thought I was ready for the world, and I decided that I'd better learn sooner than later what scuffling was all about.

I spent part of that summer in Tallahassee. And it was there that I decided to get my courage together and quit school. I wouldn't go back to St. Augustine. Instead, I made up my mind to move to the biggest city in Florida—Jacksonville—and see what was cooking.

It was actually Mary Jane who helped me make up my mind. She knew some people in Jacksonville—the Thompsons—who told her they'd take me in. That gave me an excuse and, more important, a place to stay.

Not that Mary Jane wanted me to leave. She didn't. She offered to let me stay with her, and I could have lived with her forever. I loved the woman, and I knew that she loved me as good as any woman ever loved any child. But I couldn't accept. I couldn't see myself being a burden like that. And besides, I was already curious about what the rest of the state looked like—even the rest of the world. I suppose that's why I couldn't stay in Greensville for long after Mama's death.

I was fifteen and I wanted to move on. I had shaken off this tragedy as best I could. I had spent a couple months in Tallahassee with my old friends and now I was certain which path to take.

I came home to Greensville, packed my two pair of pants, two shirts, my underwear, my sox, my tennis shoes and put 'em all in my little steamer trunk. I took the clarinet that Mr. Johnson's lodge gave me and put it under my arm. With Mary Jane walking beside me, I headed for the train station.

I didn't tell anyone that I was going off to make my fortune. Didn't think that would make much sense, since one day I might be coming home, wagging my tail behind me. I just split. Mary Jane bought me my ticket and gave me the name of her friends in Jacksonville. Besides that, I had maybe a dollar or two in my pocket.

I was on my way to the big city—126 miles off. I was alone. I was beginning a new life. I settled back and listened to the rhythm of the wheels turning over the tracks. I liked the motion. I liked the forward thrust. I was thrilled about what was going to happen to me. Now there was movement to my life.

Deep inside I was also scared out of my wits. But that was all right. Sometimes it's fear which makes you move. And keeps you moving. No matter, nothing could ever go back to what it was.

Mama was dead and under the ground. I finally got that through my brain. I was alive and on this train. And inside my head I heard music. Driving music. Spirited music. Man, I always heard music. And I knew I could play most any kind anybody wanted. Playing music made me feel good, and that's why people liked it. I could make them feel good too.

So what the hell: I was carrying on. I was healthy and young and nervy as the next kid. I knew I was going to have to make my own way. But so what? What choices did I have? I wasn't about to get a tin cup, a cane and find myself a street corner. No way I could do that.

I could sense something ticking inside me—a rhythm, a beat, a pulse —something very strong and very steady. Even with all the wild fears and terrible pain brought on by Mama's death, I could feel a new sensation: I was starting to generate a little faith . . . in myself.

Scuffling
in Jacksonville

There were lots of sounds around Jacksonville in 1945 and 1946, and I heard 'em all. It was the first big city I ever lived in. I was pretty close to the center of things, staying with Fred and Lena Mae Thompson at 752 West Church Street, right near downtown.

Lena Mae's sister, Louise—we called her Big Sister—was Mary Jane's close friend, and that was how I was introduced to the family. They were kind, considerate people who took me into their home like I was one of their own.

Something inside me wanted to call Fred "Mr. Thompson" and Lena Mae "Miss Lena Mae." I was still used to saying "yes, ma'am" and "yes, sir." But they wouldn't hear of it. They knew I was a country boy who minded his manners, but they also wanted me to start thinking of myself as a little man.

Whatever the Thompsons had, they shared with me. I even slept in my own small room off the kitchen. It was an upstairs apartment, nice and comfortable, and there were two radios in the house—Lena Mae had one and Big Sister had another.

They also made sure I had something to eat, and they even would have bought me clothes if I had let them. I tried my best to stay independent. Whenever I made some money, I stopped by the grocery store, got some goodies, and left them on the kitchen table. That was the only way they accepted anything from me.

They were the type folk who wouldn't take payment of any kind. Thinking back, I can see how they helped to make my change of life —from the country to the city, from school to the real world—easier than it might have been.

They treated me like a son, and I had to come home at a certain hour each night—either that or tell them where I was. They were firm with me, making sure I didn't go hog wild with my new freedom.

In spite of some rebelliousness in me, I still had respect for my elders. You learned that in the country. It was something Mama had drummed into my brain. Besides, as a kid I found that most older people were good to me. Maybe that's 'cause I played piano and sang for them, or maybe 'cause I was blind and they thought, Good God, the child can do all that and he can't even see! Don't know, but to this day I have a good feeling about older people—people like the Thompsons—and I try to treat 'em right.

Funny, but there were also times in my life when I felt like older folk were being too good to me.

For example, just before I left Greensville for Jacksonville, a group of white people wanted to buy me a Seeing Eye dog. I said no without blinking an eye. It was nice of them, I appreciated the kind thought, but there was no way I was gonna have some animal lead me around.

As I've said, that was one of the three big NOs—no dog, no cane, no guitar. I'd rather stumble a little and maybe bang my knee once or twice—just the way sighted people do—than be dependent on a four-legged canine. Besides, it wasn't something I needed. Contrary to what most folk would say, it wasn't essential.

I was lucky in Jacksonville 'cause we lived close to the musicians' union. Fred took me there once or twice and, in my usual manner, I memorized the route. I paid attention to little things like drainage pipes, sewers, or cracks in the sidewalk. And after a trip or two with Fred, I could get there and back by myself. In fact, I got to know the city quickly and had no trouble racing round on my own.

Big changes were coming down. I realized I wasn't a little boy anymore. And I could no longer act like one. I didn't have a mama, I never did have a papa, and in my mind I had to start acting something like a man. Tough job for a kid, specially for one who had always worn short pants. Fact is, it wasn't till Mama passed that I started wearing long britches every day.

Now I could go out at night and maybe stay gone till midnight or later. I was full grown at fifteen, about the size I am now—160 pounds or so.

I began to understand how things worked: If I got into trouble, that was *my* doing. Or if I did something halfway worthwhile, *I* could take the credit. Responsibility came awfully early to me.

Not that I shone like an angel. Far from it. But I was never too wild, particularly during this period down in Florida when I still hadn't even heard the name of any drug. Besides, music was my main passion.

I'm sure I was born with some natural musical talent, but I also know that I've always felt the need to perfect my skills. I still feel the need today. I'll always feel the need because perfection isn't attainable.

Music's the only way I've ever thought about making a living. Back in Jacksonville, I never even entertained other ideas. I suppose I could have been a mechanic, or a carpenter, or a weaver. I also think I would have been a fairly decent electrician; that's a favorite hobby of mine today. Maybe even a lawyer, since I love to argue.

But I never featured these things in those early days when I first hit the streets. It was music which drove me; it was my greatest pleasure and my greatest release; it was how I expressed myself.

Probably it was this same thing—my need to shout out the blues or moan some pretty little love ballad—which helped me adjust to most situations. Here I was in Jacksonville trying to fit into something new:

new people, new surroundings, new chances, new dangers. And I responded by seeking out any piano I could find.

The first one was in the union hall, and I played it whenever I could. I went in and heard what the other cats were up to. I was specially interested in the piano players. But after a while, when those guys saw me coming, they stopped playing; they knew I'd be copying their licks and they didn't want to give 'em away.

"Here comes that kid," they'd say.

And I could understand how they felt. They were right. Once I heard what they'd be putting down, I started running with it. Like a thief in the night.

But I also let the cats know that I was ready, willing, and able to boogie-woogie for my dinner. I wasn't proud; I might say to some guy, "Say, man, I'll play, and if you don't like it, don't pay me."

I went ahead and took some jobs like that. I told the leader that he didn't have to guarantee me a dime. And even though they weren't forced to, they always paid me something.

Local Union 632 in Jacksonville was the first one I joined. From then on I suppose you'd say that I was a professional, even though I didn't view myself or my playing any differently.

Little by little other musicians around town started hearing 'bout me. That's because I was making myself known by playing and jamming whenever I could. I didn't want to be a flash in the pan; I never wanted to be known as a "teenage star." I wanted to be able to play for real—the blues, jazz, boogie-woogie, swing—whatever was called for. I played to eat, and I had to be sure I could play anything.

Besides, I wanted to be able to play good—not for my age, but for *any* age. I remember a black kid who played piano back then. His name was something like Little Sugar Charles. He was young, and he could do a few things. But the big deal was his age, not his playing.

Years later, I was doing a concert in Detroit when the promoter asked me if a ten-year-old kid named Stevie Wonder could come up and perform onstage. I said yes, and I immediately understood that the child was phenomenal—and his age had nothing to do with it.

In Jacksonville—especially in those days—the musical community was small and word got around fast. There was also a certain kind of fellowship among the guys who played. I don't mean it wasn't competitive; man, it was a wild-assed horse race. Cats could play their instruments, and I mean from top to bottom.

But we all knew that we were in the same boat, struggling to stay afloat. I hung around the hall where the brothers were always weary of me. But just by being available, I started making connections and soon began getting calls for gigs now and then.

First big band I played with was Henry Washington's. He was a drummer and had a regular sixteen- or seventeen-piece outfit which followed the style of Basie and Billy Eckstine's big band.

I wasn't the regular pianist, but once in a while Henry let me sit in. I wasn't even supposed to be in the club—the Two Spot—'cause they served liquor and I was way underage. But somehow I prevailed. I did my Nat Cole and Charles Brown things. And people seemed to dig me.

There was another character in the city—Tiny York—who had a combo that I worked with sometimes. Tiny didn't play an instrument. He was just the leader, and he did a Louis Jordan routine. (In those days Louis Jordan was very, very big.) Actually, Tiny York turned out to be the cat who helped me leave Jacksonville a year or so later—but we'll get to that in a little while.

My social life wasn't anything to scream and holler about. But it wasn't terrible either. Lots of times I stayed home in the evenings with the Thompsons and listened to the radio. I liked that.

The *Grand Ole Opry* was still a favorite with me, and I also got a kick out of those mystery and FBI shows. I picked up on *Inner Sanctum* or *Suspense* or *The Shadow*. And of course everyone could relate to Jack Armstrong, the all-American boy.

Must make special mention of *Amos 'n' Andy*. I loved those two cats; they made me howl till I cried.

Fred and Lena Mae had friends who owned pianos, and Fred took me over to these people's houses where I could play. But I didn't get a chance to practice. When I went into a home I always felt obligated

—out of simple courtesy—to play something to please my hosts. They didn't want me to be learning and fumbling around; they wanted to hear something I already knew.

Round this time I met a cat named Fats Webb. He played trumpet, and the strange thing is that Fats wound up playing in my band— twelve or thirteen years later.

Fats had a relative who had two pretty daughters—and a piano to boot. So you can imagine that I was anxious to spend a lot of time in their home. I liked one of the daughters real well. We called her Lovie Herman, and she and I got very tight, though—much to my displeasure —we never did get into bed. Even back then my thing with girls was a little funny. I liked them fine, and Lord knows I was always looking around to see if any chicks were coming my way. But I didn't have the same confidence about my women that I had about my music. By the time I was fifteen, I had been feeling my way around a piano for over ten years, doing serious playing and serious singing. I might even have been a little cocky. I knew a song couldn't talk back the way a woman might.

During my day, there were two types of sounds. Least that's how we country folk viewed it.

You had race records. Those were the black-bottom goodies, the low-moaning blues which you listened to if you wanted to get all the way down. Colored artists only. And I'm talkin' 'bout Big Boy Crudup, Tampa Red, Muddy Waters, Blind Boy Phillips, Washboard Sam, Elmore James, Sonny Boy Williamson, and the boogie-woogie piano players—Meade Lux Lewis, Pete Johnson, and Albert Ammons—who I loved with all my heart.

On the other hand, there was music from the radio. Most of it was swing, black or white. Here I'm referring to Shaw, Goodman, Dorsey, Basie, and Ellington.

I also understood that certain black cats—Fats Waller, Cab Callo- way, Louis Armstrong—were popular among whites. But they did more to entertain me than to really influence my playing. Still, I knew that

Louis was a bitch of a trumpet player and a great song stylist. And I also knew that you weren't going to back Fats into a corner; the man could play.

By the time I hit the streets of Jacksonville, I'd been schooled on all these different sounds way 'fore I ever heard the word school; it was part of my natural upbringing.

And at school, of course, I'd been exposed to Bach, Beethoven, Mozart, Sibelius, Chopin, and all the other big names. I thought that Beethoven had lots of feeling, though Bach—in spite of the fact that the cat was a genius—made me a little nervous.

Once I got started playing in the big city, I could jump back and forth from different styles—doing piano boogie here or playing big-band swing there—depending upon what the boss wanted. I didn't really think about my own style yet, didn't even dawn on me that I needed one.

Hell, I was so happy to be able to duplicate things I was hearing around me, I didn't see any problems. And besides, I did my imitations with real feeling. I was doubly proud when I found out I could imitate other singers. Sometimes I came so close that you might confuse me with the original. I'd never had a voice lesson in my life. At school I had instruction for the piano and the clarinet. But my singing went its own merry way—free as the breeze.

'Nother fact to keep in mind during this period: I played a lot of music which originally had been done by blacks and then reinterpreted by whites. Good example was Freddie Slack's "Cow Cow Boogie," or another big song, "Pistol Packin' Mama." They were white hits, but were based on black sounds and black rhythms going round years before.

These tunes got dark all over again—in a hurry—when I got my hands on them. I reclaimed them and brought 'em back to where they started out. It wasn't that I was angry at those white cats for taking from blacks. I've always said, just 'cause Bell invented the phone doesn't mean Ray Charles can't use it. No, I gave those ofay boys some credit for having good ears. And besides, in a short while I'd be in Tampa playing with a white hillbilly band myself.

Essentially my life in Jacksonville was spent trying to get the word out that I was a musician. The gigs were few. And I took whatever I could hustle up, playing whatever they asked.

I got around by myself. I'd walk to the job or take a cab—they only cost ten or fifteen cents then.

I was suddenly in a world of adults; everyone around seemed at least five to ten years older than me. And I was impressed with the idea of being able to play in a nightclub till midnight, or maybe even later. That was a big deal to a kid.

I mentioned Tiny York to you before. Well, one day he asked me to do some out-of-town gigs with him—in central Florida. I went. But then while we were in Orlando, the job fell through and we didn't get our bread. I wasn't angry at Tiny and I didn't feel cheated. It was just part of being a musician. In fact, I don't think I've been ripped off any more than most people in show business.

People ask me if being blind has been a handicap that way. They want to know if clubowners or other cats are inclined to steal from me 'cause I can't see. I don't think so.

I basically trust people, and for the most part the trust has been justified. Oh, I've had bread taken from me—and we'll get to that later. But I've been very careful. I always asked to be paid in singles, and I patiently waited till the money was counted out. I understood how to care for money, how to make sure it was all there. And I never presumed anyone was going to steal.

Mama used to say that everyone's entitled to a clean slate. I believed that. Later on, I learned to watch closely to see if the slate got dirty.

In Orlando, I was really cleaned out. I had little money and few prospects for work. But I still wasn't all that anxious to go back to Jacksonville. I had been antsy there for some time. The Thompsons had been wonderful to me, but I was still seeking more independence. As good as these folk were, I wanted to be on my own.

Orlando was a chance to cut loose even more. I was still in Florida, still in my home state, still not all that far from Greensville, where I could go back and visit each year. But this was a new adventure. I wanted to see what living *completely* alone was like. And besides, I was sixteen and just didn't know no better.

Hungry
in Orlando

This was the bottom.

These were my hardest days, and sometimes in Orlando I actually wondered whether I was going to starve to death. For a while I thought I was dealing with malnutrition. I worried plenty. I went to live with a lady who rented out rooms. And when I had the money, I paid her $3 or $4 a week.

Work was tough to come by. Bands were stranded everywhere I looked. Musicians were coming out of the woodwork. Yeah, times were dismal. A couple of days might pass without me having a meal. And now there was no one around—no Mama, no Mary Jane, no Lena Mae —to put something in my stomach. It was me—all by myself—getting a feel for what being busted was all about.

This was when I had to dig down and see what was really going on inside me. Mama had said many a time, "Just keep yourself clean, and use what you got."

Well, I had a shirt, a pair of pants, some shoes, underwear, and sox.

The rest was all in my fingers, my chest, my lungs—and mostly in my mind. So I wandered around Orlando—alone with myself—looking for any kind of work I could find. I didn't know many people, and like I said, the competition among musicians was ferocious.

I made my way round town using the same methods I learned in Tallahassee and Jacksonville. If I wanted to cross a busy street, for example, I'd wait till I heard some women who were also crossing. Then I'd snuggle into the middle of their group and cross when they did.

I spent my days and nights hanging out in the clubs, searching for jam sessions and asking everyone I met if they'd heard of a job where I could play.

Oh man, this was some slow-moving shit.

Eating almost became a luxury. When I could get a little bread together, I'd buy a can of sardines and maybe some soda crackers. That and a glass of water became my dinner. Or maybe a couple of cats and me would chip in and cop a six-cent bag of beans. We'd get hold of some fatback, throw the beans in a pot, add a little salt, a little pepper, and to us that'd be a banquet.

I'm not sure what kept me going. There wasn't a lot of hope for a brighter future. I suppose I just didn't have any choice. The idea of selling pencils wasn't too appealing.

Here and there small jobs started to trickle in. Just enough to keep me from literally starving to death. You also got to remember I was a kid—just sixteen—and I had lots of stamina, at least enough to get me through those lean times.

Somewhere along the line I met a tenor player named Joe Anderson. He had a big band which worked the Sunshine Club. Joe gave me a few gigs, and that was really my only small break in Orlando.

Anderson was something like a black Woody Herman. He wasn't the greatest instrumentalist, but he had charisma as a leader. And he always recognized and appreciated musicianship.

Joe's band was like Henry Washington's back in Jacksonville. It was a good outfit, even though it might not have been known outside the area. Lots of guys were getting out of the army around then, and Florida was flooded with excellent players.

Matter of fact, you'd be surprised how many of them were first-quality musicians—I mean real motherfuckers—you never heard of. Cats who just hung around home and lacked the drive to go after fortune and fame. These two bands, for instance, would compare favorably with most of the famous ones you'd be hearing on the radio or on records.

Many of Joe's arrangements were stock. That means they had been written by someone outside his band and then published and sold like books; anyone could buy 'em. But once Joe found out I could write, he started asking me to do original arrangements for the band, and suddenly I was thrown into a whole new arena.

This was a big step in my musical life, the first time someone had ever used me as an arranger. And I was so thrilled that something I wrote was going to be played by a big band that I forgot to ask to be paid for it! Shows you how young I was.

I used my old method for arranging, calling off the notes for the individual instruments—part by part—to someone in the band who wrote out what I was saying. I could hear the whole thing in my head. I knew how I wanted it to sound, and it was just a matter of getting it down on paper. And I did it without using a piano or a score; I did it like I was dictating a letter.

My writing gig gave me a lift. I figured that my worth as a musician had increased—at least in the long run. In addition to singing and playing the piano, now I could legitimately call myself a writer. And the more I could do musically, the better my chances of survival.

I still had my clarinet, and I loved to play it. But by this time the sax was really king. Louis Jordan and Illinois Jacquet were big men back then, and, as a result, alto and tenor saxes had become all the rage.

While I was still at school, I had taught myself alto, and I wasn't too bad at it. Actually you can learn any sax pretty easily if you already know clarinet. Later in my life, I'd play alto much more and even do some recording with it.

Combos were coming on strong in this period—'46 and '47—and I joined with a couple of them in Orlando:

First one belonged to Sammy Glover. He played trumpet and his main man was Roy Eldridge—just the way Roy was Dizzy Gillespie's idol. We played mostly in a jazz bag. I did some writing for Sammy, and it was just about this time that I composed a tune called "Confession Blues."

A guy named A. C. Price also had a combo. He was like Tiny York; he just led and didn't play an instrument. He gave me some work now and then, and I was awfully grateful for any little crumb thrown my way.

Most of the clubs we played were black, but once in a while we'd get gigs in white places. And then you'd have to know the right songs to play. "Ace in the Hole," for example, was one of the tunes that white folk would always request. I had been careful to learn it 'cause I wanted the tips. Besides, it helped build my repertoire. The more tunes I knew, the better off I was.

The joints we played—black or white—always had drinking and dancing. And once in a while, a fight broke out. Well, that could get a little nasty. And in my case, I couldn't see where the punches were being thrown or where the bottles were being hurled. So I tried to find the location of a window as soon as I started working a new place. If a fire or a hot brawl started up, I wanted to know how to escape. In those days, I was known to jump out of windows.

Orlando was a down period for all kinds of reasons: And the lack of bread—the kind you munch and the green kind—was just one of 'em. Another heavy experience really dragged me down into the dumps. And even telling you about it now—some thirty years later—doesn't make me very happy:

Lucky Millinder is a big name in the music business in 1946. And one day he and his big band happen to blow into Orlando for a gig. Some cat suggests that I go over and audition for him. Baby, I'm ready. I've been listening to Lucky for years, and I like his sound. His band's got a real snap. I also like Sister Rosetta Tharpe who's singing with him back then. "That's All," I remember, is a smash hit.

I decide to give it a shot. I figure this is going to be my big break. It's my first attempt to go with a national outfit, and I'm pretty confident. I don't think the chances of tagging on with Lucky Millinder are all that remote. After all, everyone's been telling me how good I am.

Someone arranges a meeting. I go over to the club. And there he is, just sitting in a chair and waiting for me to play. So I do. I sing a couple of songs, I play a couple of tunes. I give it all I got. And, when I'm through, I just sit there, waiting for the verdict.

Lucky is straight with me; he doesn't mince words:

"Ain't good enough, kid."

"W-w-w-what?" I stammer.

"You heard me. You don't got what it takes."

Those are the man's words—"You don't got what it takes"—and, brother, that hits me between the eyes like a bolt of lightning!

No one—I mean nobody at no time—had ever said that to me before. And for a self-assured little motherfucker like me, that was a very heavy blow. I just wasn't prepared for out-and-out cold rejection.

Lucky wasn't mean, just matter-of-fact. And that almost made it worse. It bothered me so bad that I went back to my room and cried my eyes out for days.

I met Lucky again years later, after I had done some things on my own, and talked about what had happened. He explained his feelings to me in a way which made sense, particularly considering the times.

He thought I had potential, but he didn't think I was already there. And in the forties, potential wasn't enough. Lots of people had promise, but there were so many cats who could play good, no one needed to wait around while *you* developed. If you couldn't cut it, you'd be sent home to your mama. And that's what Lucky did to me. I got to give him some skin for having high standards, even though he cut me to the bone.

When I hit the streets in the forties, playing was competitive. Lord, have mercy! All kinds of dudes be throwing knives at your head. You had to know your stuff. And, darling, you had to know it good.

You'd fall in a jam session. There'd be a cat on tenor, someone on alto, a cat on trumpet, a trombone player, guitar, bass, and drums.

They'd be waiting for you. They'd be ready. And you'd try your luck on piano.

Now some wise-ass would call for "How High the Moon." Or someone else would yell out, "How 'bout a little 'Cherokee.' " Or maybe a cat would start playing "Lady Be Good." And these tunes be moving fast—with chord changes you just didn't hear every day.

Coleman Hawkins's version of "Body and Soul," for example, was a huge favorite among jazz musicians, and invariably some dude would say, "Okay, give me some 'Body and Soul' in D-flat."

Now there's a change in the middle of that tune to D natural which would truly tell whether or not you could play. I've heard guys wail away till they came to that change. And if they were skating, you'd be able to tell when they reached the tricky part. Then they suddenly get real soft and quiet.

Other times cats would call a song and then do it chromatically. That means you'd play it in all the keys, one by one. If you'd be fumbling around, getting your finger caught in your ear or up your ass instead of hitting the right notes, you'd be laughed out of the place. You'd be sent on your merry way, little boy.

But if you could handle those tunes, the cats might respect you a little—and that's what I was aiming for.

It was merciless back then. Cold-blooded. You either cut the mustard or had mustard smeared all over your sorry face.

Lucky came from this kind of background, so it was natural for him to cut me down. It became part of my education. We called it developing chops.

Thinking back, I can't recall anyone, outside of Mr. Pit, who encouraged me much. But then again, I wasn't the type who sought encouragement. Real musicians weren't pampered. They figured out what they had to do, and then they went out and did it. Sure, it was cruel and hard-nosed, but, baby, you did learn to play.

I was pretty crazy at sixteen, and if you need any proof, just listen to what I did when I was finally able to rub a couple of dimes together:

I didn't run out and buy a mess of food. No, nothing practical like

81

that. Instead I got me a record player—right there in Orlando, in the midst of the worst economic depression of my life. I figured that was all the nourishment I needed.

I wanted to hear all the Jazz at the Philharmonic records. Those early sessions had everyone on them: Illinois Jacquet, Benny Carter, Charlie Parker, Lester Young, Nat Cole, Roy Eldridge. I remember a particularly wild blowing session on "Lady Be Good."

Many musical schools—from swing to modern—were coming together and coming apart then, and I loved 'em all. I could hear what everyone was doing, and I played those records over and over again.

It's strange when I think back to those sides. Norman Granz, who produced the concerts, is now a friend of mine and someone who's booked me in Europe for years. And Benny Carter would one day write arrangements for my own big band. I'd get to meet and play with many of those cats on that record within fifteen years.

Sitting around Orlando and listening to these guys blow in the forties, though, I was just a kid admiring the great jazz artists of my time. Way down in Florida, those records were the only way we knew what the heaviest dudes were up to.

I learned from everyone, not necessarily piano players or singers. Charlie Christian, for example, was a bitch of a guitarist. Listening to his records I educated myself about phrasing and ad-libbing. Same went for the great drummers. They taught me the importance of keeping time. And as far as I'm concerned, there's no greater lesson.

I bought a lot of the 78s. Strange, but I didn't break a one, even though they were made of shellac. I was like the folks back in Greensville who lived in shacks which could have gone up in flames at the drop of a match. That just made them more careful.

I also had a healthy supply of Nat Cole's hits—maybe "Gee Baby, Ain't I Good to You?" or "I Just Can't See for Looking." I had me a Lionel Hampton side of "Flying Home." And I know at some point I owned Lester Young's "Lester Leaps In" and "DB Blues." I especially admired Lester's playing—his cool, laid-back phrasing and his salty sound.

Among the vocalists of the time I continued to follow Ella Fitzgerald. For me, she's always been in a category by herself, a musician so good that even nonmusicians appreciate her.

I liked Sarah Vaughan, too, and had great admiration for her range. I like to compare Ella to Cannonball Adderley—they're both so lyrical —and Sarah to John Coltrane—they're both calculating, masterful technicians.

Sarah was singing with Eckstine back then and, as I said, Mr. B's band turned me around several times. He had Gene Ammons, Dexter Gordon, Charlie Parker, Dizzy Gillespie, and Fats Navarro; it was a complete gas.

I could certainly relate to the way Al Hibbler and Duke did "Don't Get Around Much Anymore" or "Do Nothin' Till You Hear from Me."

And of course Billie Holiday always destroyed me. There was something Lady Day had that no one else could claim. People have told me that she and I share the same sort of sadness in our voice. I know what they're talkin' 'bout. I don't know where that comes from—in her or in me—but it's there.

Billie could sing her ass off any given night of the week. And I remember back during the forties how her version of "Hush Now, Don't Explain" stopped me dead in my tracks. I couldn't listen to it enough; it made a lasting impression inside my brain. The woman was a natural, always her own, strange self.

Orlando was no high point in my love life. Aside from my extravagance on the record player, I led a Spartan existence and barely had enough greens to feed Ray, never mind any females. Things were tough enough—being turned down by Lucky Millinder and having a bitch of a time finding work.

I had been hearing cats talkin' 'bout going down on chicks, giving them head or whatever the hip term happened to be in 1946. I hadn't done it yet, and to me it seemed disgusting. What did I know? I was still fresh out of the country.

Well, the more talk I listened to, the more curious I became. I also heard how some chicks actually gave blow jobs, but I wasn't about to have it done to me until I was ready to reciprocate the favor.

I was curious, sure, but I was also cautious. Didn't want to make a wrong move, or a false move, or a stupid move. And that was my attitude when I met a girl singer with a big band that happened to get stranded in Orlando. She was older than me, and in those days, that was almost always the case. Can't remember her exact age—maybe twenty-two—can't remember her band—but it was a biggie, from New York or Chicago. Can't even remember the woman's name.

Well, we started into the normal routine and then, out of the blue, she began kissing and sucking my breasts. That felt wonderful. Man, I was ecstatic. And she didn't stop there. She kept coming on down, and when she was through with me, she lay back, indicating that it was my turn. Now I could dig it. And I did.

The lady was a sweet teacher, and for that reason, I'm glad her band was stranded, even though it seemed like half the population of Orlando consisted of hungry musicians ready to take any gig.

It got to be too much.

So I figured what the hell, it was time to hit the road again, Jack. And the next time I went out of town on a gig—I think it was with Joe Anderson's band—I decided to make it a one-way street and not return to Orlando.

I looked around and saw that I was in Tampa. Seemed all right to me. Another day, another city.

A year in Jacksonville. A year in Orlando. Time for a change. I was all of seventeen years old and figured I'd make out okay.

What I didn't figure on, though, was falling in love.

Floppin' Round
Tampa

I started out in a flophouse. That was some beginning. And I stayed there for as long as my bread held out. But when my money started getting funny, I had to find someplace to live. Didn't even have a dollar for a room.

Luckily I met a guitarist—Gosady McGee—who became a friend of mine. Gosady introduced me to two women, sisters who lived together in a little stucco house at 813 Short Emory Avenue.

Freddie, the older sister, was a teacher. And she was also Gosady's girlfriend. Her younger sister Lydia was a scatterbrain like me—young, silly, and crazy. I dug them both, and Lydia and I became very good buddies. When the Simmons girls saw my plight, they invited me to live with them. Of course I was delighted. And what made it even better was the piano sitting in their living room.

Imagine! A piano living under the same roof with me! Ain't ever happened to me before; this was a first. Freddie played some, but she also insisted that I use it whenever I wanted. You can't feature how happy that made me; that meant I could bang whenever I felt like it.

So after a flaky start, I hit upon some good luck—meeting up with Freddie and Lydia—and during those early months they made my life in Tampa sweet and mellow.

I also found a good gig in a hurry. Cat named Charlie Brantley had a seven-piece combo and he hired me to play piano.

Now when I say Charlie was into Louis Jordan, I mean with both hands and both feet. He almost *became* Louis. Like Jordan, he played alto, and he did all those numbers—"Ain't Nobody Here but Us Chickens" and "Saturday Night Fish Fry"—like he had eaten the original recordings for breakfast.

Charlie had a singer—Clarence Jolly—so I really didn't have much of a chance to get into my vocals. Clarence's main man was Billy Eckstine; he loved doing "I'm Falling for You" and "Jelly Jelly." He could sound like Mr. B and also do a slick version of Jordan; yeah, Clarence had both bases covered.

Business was pretty good for Charlie. We found ourselves making gigs in towns like Gainesville, Ocala, Cocoa, and Sarasota.

I started making new friends and meeting more musicians. Sam Jones, the jazz bassist, was living in Tampa then. And a piano player named Jimmy Tanner showed me all kinds of things on the keyboard I'd never seen before.

At some point, Charlie Brantley got sick and was forced to curtail his activities. So I found another gig with a drummer, Manzy Harris, who formed a trio with me and Otto McQueen on bass. I played piano and did my Nat Cole and Charles Brown vocals, then maybe a couple of blues of mine written in that same style.

The color thing was not a big item for me then—and that's probably 'cause I couldn't see. Playing white clubs just meant I had to do tunes like "Laura," "I Surrender, Dear" or "Poor Butterfly."

Some white dude might come up to me, half drunk, and say, "Hey, kid, I'll give you five dollars if you play 'Ace in the Hole.'"

Well, shit, five dollars was big money, so you can bet your ass that I'd have all those tunes covered.

In other white clubs, you might play just for the kitty. After you were through, the folk would give you whatever they wanted to. So you sure as hell were going to do the kind of sounds *they* liked.

Besides, it was easy for me. I'm not sure I made all those black and white distinctions you're always hearing about. Years later, when someone asked me the difference between, say, a black band like Chick Webb's and a white one like Tommy Dorsey's, I said, "Oh, about a hundred dollars a week."

I knew back then that Nat Cole was bigger than ever. Whites could relate to him because he dealt with material they understood, and he did so with great feeling. Funny thing, but during all these years I was imitating Nat Cole, I never thought twice about it, never felt bad about copying the cat's licks.

To me it was practically a science. I worked at it, I enjoyed it, I was proud of it, and I loved doing it. He was a guy everyone admired, and it just made sense to me, musical and commercial sense, to study his technique.

It was something like when a young lawyer—just out of school—respects an older lawyer. He tries to get inside his mind, he studies to see how he writes up all his cases, and he's going to sound a whole lot like the older man—at least till he figures out how to get his own shit together.

Today I hear some singers who I think sound like me. Joe Cocker, for instance. Man, I know that cat must sleep with my records. But I don't mind. I'm flattered; I understand. After all, I did the same thing.

As a teenager, and even in my twenties, my voice was light. But during this period in Florida, I learned some of the tricks of working with a PA system. I could make my voice heavier; I could give it more resonance by turning on a little more bottom and tweaking up the treble end at the same time. That kept me sounding clear, but also deep.

My voice never changed drastically. As I got older, it developed more resonance of its own. But I experienced no dramatic fluctuations, and

I really never lost my old voice or gained a new one. The kid sound and the adult sound just blended together.

Even today my voice is hard to categorize. You can't call it a tenor 'cause it ain't high enough; you can't call it a baritone 'cause it ain't low enough. If there's such a thing as a true lead singer, that's me.

I can sing real well and still be heard as low as an A-flat in the bass clef. My natural top would be a high C in the treble clef. But then again, I can make a lot of other notes—higher and lower—by going through my own crazy contortions.

Strangest job I had in Florida—and one of the nicest—was with an all-white country-and-western band. All-white, that is, except me. They called themselves the Florida Playboys.

Can you feature that? The Deep South, 1948, a black dude playing piano in a hillbilly band? Well, it happened. And I'm glad to say that it happened to me.

I met this guy at the Arthur Smith Music Store in Tampa. That's a place where I hung out and fooled around with the instruments. I can't remember the cat's name, but he was one of the Playboys. He knew me. He knew I could play piano, and one day he told me that his band needed a piano player. Was I interested?

Course I was. It was money, wasn't it? So he took me over to meet the rest of the band. I sat in with them, and they immediately heard that I could play their style of music. They offered me the job and I grabbed it. I was a Playboy.

Pay was around $15 or $20 a night, much higher than what I was used to. And it was a tight band. There was a regular guitar, steel guitar, a couple of fiddles, a string bass, drums, and me on piano. We played all the country hits of the day—"Kentucky Waltz" and "Anytime." And every once in a while I'd get to sing. I remember doing "Waiting All for You." But my main work was on piano, even though I also learned how to yodel.

You might think that by working in such a group I'd encounter all kinds of nasty crap—tomatoes being thrown at me, folks making fun of the blind nigger trying to play white music. But I'm here to tell you that it just ain't so. No one said a thing. I was accepted and applauded along with everyone else.

I'm sure part of the reason was 'cause I could play the music right. I didn't give 'em anything to laugh at. They were being entertained, and I wasn't about to play any wrong notes. I could do country music with as much feeling as any other Southerner. And why not? I had been hearing it since I was a baby.

But I also have another notion about why I was left alone: A lot of the black/white thing in the South was caused by white men worrying 'bout black cats fucking with their women. Since I couldn't see—and since they saw I couldn't see—I wasn't much of a threat. In their minds, there was no way I could be checking over their little ladies. My gaze couldn't offend them. So they thought I was cool.

I was happy to let 'em think whatever they wanted. I was making a living playing music. Far as I was concerned, hillbilly music was fine; I enjoyed it. And after the gig, the guys went their way and I went mine. But that was no different from when I played with black bands. I found my way to and from the clubs by myself; I was a loner.

I knew about the segregation in those years. But it still didn't weigh on my mind. Ever since I was a little kid, I'd understood that white folk could go wherever the hell they pleased, but that we were restricted to our own place. And that place had been determined by whites. Sure, I could comprehend the system, and I knew it was rotten. But I was just too busy trying to stay alive to let it drive me crazy.

Not only did I avoid black/white conflicts, I also didn't get entangled in any black/black fights. Where I came from a man could get cut for calling another dude "black." That expression wasn't exactly the rage in the forties. Lighter cats seemed to be getting better jobs, and the black-is-beautiful thing was still twenty years away.

So you'd be very careful about how you'd shade your description of a brother. If not, someone soon be describing you as red—bloodred. I watched all these goings-on from the sidelines and I never got involved. I valued my health too much.

About the time I was playing hot hillbilly piano, I recorded my first tunes, though at the time I just considered it fooling around.

I bought a primitive wire recorder—it was really a toy to me—and some guys came by Freddie and Lydia's place just to practice. I can't even remember who the cats were. In those days we were always practicing, playing, jamming, and inventing new items

I had written a song—hell, I can't even say that; I didn't consider it a composition, just a blues I made up. Called it "Found My Baby There." It was a nasty little number, and that day we worked it out— along with a couple of other songs—with the recorder going. The sound quality was so bad it sounded like we were all locked away in a closet.

Funny thing about that song: After the first chorus, I took a solo on the piano and accompanied myself vocally. I hummed the actual notes I played on piano and worked a unison duet with myself. I had never heard anyone do this before, and, to tell the truth, I'm not sure what gave me the idea. Might have been listening to T-Bone Walker, the blues singer. He was able to get a sound out of his electric guitar— bending and extending the notes—which always fractured me.

You can't do that on piano; you can only suggest it with a grace note here or there. But by singing on top of my playing, I was able to create —at least in my own head—a guitar-like, bluesy effect.

Years later the song popped up on several albums. This was after I had a name. Someone must have found it down in Tampa collecting dust. I never got any money from it. And I never even bothered to find out who had gotten hold of it. Early on in the music business I learned to enter certain fights, swinging with all I got, and to avoid others, knowing that I wouldn't accomplish anything even if I won.

Tampa really became my stomping grounds. I was feeling full-grown, making a small amount of change, and working halfway decent clubs. Even bought myself a pair of dark glasses—my first.

They were just regular sunglasses. My friends had been telling me that my eyes didn't look good. Lots of times they were tearing and caked with matter. So for the sake of appearance, I got some dark glasses, and I've been wearing them ever since.

My wardrobe wasn't much. It consisted mainly of my work clothes —black suit, white shirt, black tie, black shoes, and black sox. You might have taken me for an undertaker.

But drab clothes aside, I was chipper most of the time, and during the day I wandered around Tampa by myself. There was a cabstand near the Simmons's house. And I often went over there to bullshit with the boys, listening to their tales of fast-moving women.

Talkin' 'bout women, I met a few of my own. A girl named Marian became close friends with me. She and I courted each other for a while, though we never got into bed. And it was over Marian's house one Sunday night that I met the girl who would become my first sure-enough sweetheart: Louise.

Something happened when Louise and I met—the chemistry began popping—and it started a long chapter in my life. We had our own little love story, with all the ups and downs, the heartaches and the awful pain which go along with such romantic adventures.

Now Marian was a popular girl. She had a nice house. Her people had some bread. And lots of kids used to congregate over there. For me, the central attraction was the piano in the living room.

I was probably playing "Drifting Blues" on that piano when I met Louise. I remember I liked the sound of her voice immediately. It was sweet and soothing. She was about my age—seventeen—weighed maybe 110, was five feet three inches, and had quite an enticing figure. Might say fabulous. We got tight right away. Something clicked. I could see Louise understood that I didn't want anyone to mother me or lead me around.

She liked good loving as much as I did. That was always the best part. So we became serious and hung out together nearly every day. We fell in love. I wanted her to live with me. I wanted her to cook food for me. I wanted her to make love to me. I wanted her to be my woman. And I could see no reason in the world why we shouldn't set up house together.

Her folks found a reason or two. They didn't see much future for a blind musician. Musicians never had nothing anyway, but a sightless one just made matters worse, far as they were concerned. They were hard on her case from first to last.

Course the more they bitched, the closer we snuggled together. She came to my gigs at night. And during the day we strolled around Tampa, holding hands, talking about how much we loved each other. I mean, we were far gone.

But her family kept its evil eye aimed our way. And soon we decided to do something crazy. We were tired of being watched. Tired of being bitched at. I had saved money from when I was with the Playboys. So we made up our minds: We decided to run off to Miami. That would show them. Once we got there and contacted them, they'd be so glad to hear Louise was safe and sound, they'd approve of us and finally leave us alone. At least that's what we were thinking.

So we went to Miami. We found some folks who had a big house and we rented a room with cooking privileges. Course we never bothered saying that we weren't married.

We were in our own little world down there, stoned silly and smashed on love. No liquor, no dope—Louise didn't even smoke cigarettes—just an ample dosage of high-quality screwing.

Couple of days after we arrived, I found work in a club called O'Dells. And for three or four weeks we had a nice time, just being together in Miami.

But soon it became clear that her family wasn't leaving us alone. Our plan hadn't worked, and it wasn't going to work. They kept on bitching —mostly at her. That pissed me off; I figured that I wasn't forcing her to do anything. She was as starry-eyed in love as I was. And I couldn't understand why her folks couldn't accept that fact. That was nothing new, though. Parents always do wild things, especially when it comes down to their daughters and sex.

We decided to go back to Tampa. But we also decided that there was going to be a difference when we returned. This time we were going to live together. So when we got home, we rented a place in a lady's house across the bridge in West Tampa. We paid her $3 a week for the room, and we kept our love light burning. Man, it just shined, shined, shined all over us.

Louise was my first heavy girlfriend, and my memories of those days and nights with her are all sweet, or maybe bittersweet; you'll soon see that the story doesn't have a happy ending.

At this same time—besides flipping over Louise—I found myself going through another change. I was almost eighteen. Mama had been dead three years now. And for three years I had been out there alone. Somehow I'd survived, kept myself out of trouble and free of debt. I'd learned to believe in myself. I'd seen I was able to find work if I looked hard enough.

When Louise and I returned from Miami, I found a good gig at a white club in Tampa. I was making decent money. But that was not enough. I was still itching and scratching to see more of the world. And I was determined to become great at what I did.

Most of the cats I was playing with were years older than me. And I knew I had as much energy—maybe even a little more—than the next guy. I could sing, I could play piano, I could play clarinet and alto, I could not only write songs, but arrangements for combos or big bands.

I saw all these other bands always passing through Florida. And the cats in those bands always seemed to come from faraway places— Chicago or Detroit, Cleveland or New York, Los Angeles or St. Louis. Everyone was from somewhere except Florida.

I got to thinking about all this. And it suddenly dawned on me that I had never been more than three or four hundred miles from Greensville. By this time I knew Florida as well as anyone needed to. I had been through the state—east, west, north, south, the big cities and the little towns wedged in between.

Now it hit me that I have to get away. I have to go exploring. I've been able to save some bread—a couple of hundred dollars. And it slowly starts burning a little hole in my pocket. Yes, Lord, I think that's enough scratch to buy a bus ticket to practically anywhere.

One day my partner Gosady McGee comes over to our place. I ask him to find me a map of the United States.

"Gosady," say I, "take that map, brother, and locate Tampa. Put your finger on it and keep it there. Now I want you to find the big city furthest away from here. Go as far as you possibly can without leaving America."

I wait while Gosady does his figuring. A minute later he simply says, "Seattle."

"That in the state of Washington?" I ask.

"Yes it is."

"Well, brother, count me as good as gone. 'Cause that's where I'm going. And I be leaving soon."

Moving
Cross-Country

Didn't want to leave Louise, but I had to. Had to move on.

Moving on was my main item, and nothing could stop me once my mind was made up. I've always been pigheaded that way. Got to go and do what I want to do, what I think is right for me. Besides, I promised Louise that I'd send for her as soon as I could. That's an old line, but it proved to be true sooner than either of us would have guessed.

I had done as good in Florida as I was going to do—at least that was my reasoning. I could have gone to New York or Chicago, but I didn't think I was ready. Besides, I was afraid of those big-sounding cities. Seattle had a nice ring to it—medium-sized and manageable. A place where I wouldn't get swallowed up.

I didn't know anything about Seattle, I didn't know anyone living up there, and I hadn't heard a thing about the town. It just seemed like a reasonable place to go. All mystery and adventure. I also liked the fact that it was way on the other coast—real far away. That term

—West Coast—was appealing to me. I came from the woods, and the idea of heading west was enticing as hell.

I didn't take anything but my clothes which fit into one small suitcase. That's all I had. So I went down to the bus station, kissed Louise good-bye, and headed out, like many a man before me, toward what I expected would be greener pastures.

Five days and five nights, they tell me. And that doesn't sound bad. Until I actually do it. The bus ride's a bitch, let me tell you. A nightmare of a trip. Total boredom, man, for hour after hour after hour. Nothing for me to do 'cept try to sleep or munch on a candy bar.

Course there's no air conditioning. And they make me sit in the back. That means I'm right on top of the motor which is blowing out hot, disgusting fumes. So I'm squirming and sweating, fidgeting and fooling round. When the bus finally comes to a rest stop, I'm restricted to the colored side—at least as far as Chicago—where there's nothing to eat but pathetic sandwiches and other tasteless shit.

Jesus, I'm an unhappy traveler; I think the days will never pass. To make matters worse, in Chicago I have to be put up in a hotel by the Travelers Aid. I didn't know about overnight stops in hotels, so I haven't brought any bread for that purpose. Sure, I have money, but that's the little bit I've saved to keep myself going in Seattle. I'm not about to spend it on a hotel. Anyway, the Travelers Aid gives me a couple of dollars and finds me a place. What bread I have, I clutch to my heart.

It's 5:00 A.M. when the bus finally rolls into Seattle. I'm a mess. Tired, groggy, lost. I ask someone where a hotel is and get directions to a place near the station. I find my way there.

I check in right away, go upstairs, and sleep for almost twenty-four straight hours. I'm out of it. When I wake up, I'm still zonked, and I can barely remember where or who I am. Just know I'm hungry. So hungry that it hurts. Reach over and pick up the phone by my bed. Talk to the lady downstairs:

"Do you know where I can find somewhere to scarf?"

"Eat," she says, "at this time of the night? No. Nothing's open."

"There has to be someplace open."

"Well, there's a nightclub not far from here. That's the only joint I can think of."

"What's it called?"

"The Rocking Chair."

All right. Put myself together, get dressed, go downstairs, catch a cab, and find myself outside the Rocking Chair. Now I'm staring another problem in the face: the big, burly bouncer guarding the door.

"What's happening here?" I ask.

"Talent night."

"Let me in."

"You too young, boy."

"Too young! What you talkin' 'bout! I can sing! I can play!"

"Sorry, you too young."

"Listen, man, you just got to let me in. I mean, I'm really a musician. You oughta hear me."

"You kidding?"

"Would I jive you?"

"Well . . ."

And with that, I'm in like a flash. I wait around and listen to the other acts—some singers, a few musicians, tap dancers, stuff like that. Then it's my turn.

I go to the bandstand, sit myself down, and do my version of Charles Brown's "Traveling Blues," then "Drifting Blues." I must tell you, I really sing my ass off. I mean I'm singing the *blues!*

I know that song as well as my own mother, and when I'm through, I can tell that the folks dig it: The place rings with applause.

Just a few minutes later, a man approaches me with the best news I've heard in a year:

"You play okay, boy. Think you could get a trio together?"

"Yes, sir! Of course! Just name the time and place!"

"Have your group over to the Elks Club on Friday night and you got yourself some work."

Man, now my head is really reeling! Only one day after I land in this strange city and I got myself a gig. It's 4:00 or 5:00 A.M. Wednesday morning when all this happens, and I'm already halfway to heaven.

It was cool when I got to Seattle. That first gig was cool and the weather was cool. Had to be around March of 1948. The town was still wide open. And the entertainment business was in something of a boom. Competition was fierce.

Many cats had just left the armed forces bands—and don't think those outfits couldn't play. In one respect it was just like Tampa: There were lots of musicians roaming the streets who'd blow your ass off the stand if you gave 'em half the chance.

But I wasn't about to get blown off the stand. I'd been on my own for three years. Florida toughened me up. Mama had been gone for a long time. And not much later—when I was sixteen or seventeen—my father died without me ever knowing him. I never even learned the details of his death, only that he passed in Adel, Georgia, while he was still a young man.

Anyway, now I was starting to think of myself as a man. I had moved to a new part of the world. And as far as I was concerned, I was my own boss.

Seattle was different than any place I had seen. It rained continually, it was cold and frosty much of the time, and, most amazing of all, it snowed. I even wrote a blues to celebrate—or to bemoan—the weather: "The Snow Is Falling."

I adapted to these changes quickly. The Elks Club gig worked out fine. I found a couple of guys at the union, and we formed a Nat Cole–sounding trio. A little while later, my pal from Tampa, Gosady McGee, came to town. And with him on guitar, a cat called Milt Garred on bass, and me on piano and vocals, we had a permanent group.

We called ourselves the McSon Trio. The name came from the "Mc" in McGee and the "son" in Robinson.

By the way, it was right about now that I dropped the Robinson altogether. Sugar Ray caused that. He already had a name for himself, and I figured two Ray Robinsons might be one too many. So for clarity's sake, I started going by just my first and middle names: Ray Charles.

We were at the Elks Club for a while, and after that we started playing the Rocking Chair—the place I originally stumbled into my first night in town. The club opened at midnight and we worked from 1:00 to 5:00 A.M. We were a pretty hot attraction there. I even wrote a happy blues about the place:

> *If you're feeling lowdown, don't have a soul to care,*
> *If you're feeling lowdown, don't have a soul to care,*
> *Just grab your hat and start for the Rocking Chair.*
>
> *There's Dubonnet Judy, Gin Fizz Flo,*
> *Cocktail Shorty and old Julip Joe.*
>
> *I'm telling you, it's the gonnest place in town;*
> *If you don't have your rubbers, take a taxi down.*
>
> *If you're a regular guy, you're bound to get a souvenir,*
> *If you're a regular guy, you're bound to get a souvenir,*
> *And when you write back home, you can say you're spooning at the*
>   *Rocking Chair.*

I had my Nat Cole/Charles Brown routines down clean by now. Yes, by 1948 and 1949, I had my program together and was ready to kick some ass. I'd been working on my repertoire for three years—three long years of on-the-job practice—and you'd be surprised how many people actually confused me for Nat or Charles! I could see that in a city like Seattle—a place which was more sophisticated and open than what I was used to—my act was going to pay off.

When I think back on this part of my life—blowing into new cities and trying to make it—I can see that music was my means of survival. It was medicine for my brain.

Music allowed me to eat. But it also allowed me to express myself. I played because I had to play. I rid myself of bad dreams and rotten memories that way. I got everything out of me. I'm sure that if I hadn't found a job I would have just sat up in some room and sung my heart out.

I continued writing arrangements for big bands in Seattle. I remember two I did back then: one was the standard, "Ghost of a Chance," and the other was Dizzy Gillespie's thing, "Emanon," which was pretty advanced for that time.

And even though I was listening to lots of Charlie Parker, I was also very much into Woody Herman. That was my group. He had a very loose, very swinging big band—particularly the Herd with Bill Harris on trombone. I especially loved "Four Brothers."

I also paid some attention to Stan Kenton. I thought of his band as a white version of Lionel Hampton's. Very screamy. Very brassy. It didn't swing nearly as much as Hamp's band, but it had that same sort of blaring brass.

Cat called Bumps Blackwell had a well-known combo around Seattle. Bumps played vibes and worked a great deal in white clubs. From time to time, he used me on piano.

And there was also my good friend Gerald Brashear. He was a tenor saxophonist who gigged with Cecil Young's group.

There were a lot of faces around Seattle, and I tried to make mine familiar so I could keep working.

The McSon Trio played all over—Fort Lawton, Kirkland, Tacoma, and places in Seattle like the Washington Social Club or the 908 Club. The race thing was cool in Seattle; most of these joints were integrated.

After a couple of months, someone asked us to play on the radio—KRSC—and we told the cat sure; we'd do it, as long as we could advertise ourselves. He agreed and we played for free. We gave Gosady's phone number over the air in the hopes of finding some gigs.

The radio bit led to a little TV show which also ran for five or six weeks, just featuring the trio. Someone told me that this was the first program of its kind with blacks. As far as I can tell, it must have been one of the first live programs up there of any kind. After all, this was 1948.

So our star slowly started rising in Seattle. Nothing real spectacular, but some straight-ahead, steady progress.

There was no individual star, by the way. We were really a leaderless trio. We all got the same bread—as much as $25 each a night—and no one even suggested otherwise. All I wanted was to please the audience and to keep eating.

The one thing which bothered me about some jazz players I met around that time was their strange attitude: They'd say to a crowd, "This is my music. If you like it, cool. If not, fuck it!"

I thought that was wrong. People give you their bread and are entitled to some kind of musical return on their dollar. I don't mean you got to give them *exactly* what they want. But you do have to keep them in mind.

Upstairs at the Rocking Chair there was a room where people gambled. And one dude in particular liked to hang out there. This was Jack Lauderdale. He dug our music, and I think he particularly liked the way I sang. One night he approached me and told me that he had a record label. He called it Downbeat. (Later it would be changed to Swingtime because the magazine *Down Beat* threatened to sue.)

A record! Man, that was the ultimate! I had been listening to records my whole life—back when I was four or five on Mr. Pit's jukebox—and here I was, actually about to make one.

Yes, we'll cut a record, Mr. Lauderdale. Good God Almighty! Just show us the way, Papa. Nothing I want to do more.

We found a little recording studio in Seattle. First tune I did was the one I wrote back in Florida, "Confession Blues." The other side was a song written by my friend from school, Joe Lee Lawrence. It was called "I Love You, I Love You," and I did it in my very best Nat Cole voice.

This happened in 1948. A recording ban was going on at the time and later I'd have to pay a $600 fine. Burned the shit out of me. Even if I had known, though, I probably would have gone on and recorded anyway. I just knew that I wanted to record and nothing—short of grabbing me, sticking me in some closet, and locking me up—was going to get in my way.

Few months later I went down to Los Angeles. That's where Jack

Lauderdale lived and where his label had its office. I made some records without the regular trio. Oscar Moore played guitar on that date and so did his brother, Johnny Moore. I believe Johnny Miller played bass. These were some big-time cats, the same guys who played with Nat Cole and Charles Brown. So you know how ecstatic I was.

During the L.A. session we cut a tune of mine called, "Baby, Let Me Hold Your Hand." I sang it in the Charles Brown style, and it turned out to be my first national hit. It made the charts—the black charts—and within two or three years it sold a hundred thousand copies or so. For those days, that meant something.

Recording back then was fun. We used transcriptions—huge discs —and we'd be recording right on lacquer. Everything was done in one or two takes; you had no more than a couple of hours to get in and out.

I was in hog heaven, just grooving on the fact that I was making a record of my own. Never thought twice 'bout publishing rights; never thought twice 'bout royalties.

The records from this period have been issued and reissued so many times it's pathetic. And I got very little money from them—just scale —but blame that on me; I was young, naive, and just up from the country.

It was in Seattle that I met Quincy Jones, and we've been partners ever since. He was only a couple of years younger than me, and at that point he didn't really have his program together. He was just a teenager.

Quincy was playing trumpet, but he really wanted to write jazz. So he asked me how to do it. I showed him my methods of arranging for big bands, and he soaked it all up. Q was hungry for all that information, eager to learn anything he could. He was a sweet, likable dude. We ribbed one another a lot—we still do—but that's 'cause there was love between us.

In those years, musicians had a close-knit community in spite of the competitive jam sessions—or maybe because of them. We were always borrowing from each other in all kinds of ways. There were fewer means of entertaining ourselves than you find today—no one had a TV then—and we spent huge amounts of time together: playing, bullshitting, smoking dope, trading off ideas, and teaching each other private tricks of the trade.

I had a good time floating round Seattle. It was easy traveling there, and I learned the bus system pretty well. In fact, I had this trick: I always listened for the bus to drive over a certain dip in the road. That told me that the next stop was going to be mine, so I pulled the cord. You should have seen how that knocked out the other passengers. They'd start whispering to each other, "How does that blind boy know that's his stop?"

By the time I was eighteen, I might have been a little cocky. You couldn't tell me nothing. I was running around with older cats. Started drinking a little, started smoking a little, and I discovered grass and smack. The drug thing really started in Seattle, and we'll get to that in a minute. But first I have to tell you what happened between me and Louise:

Couldn't have been more than a month after arriving in Seattle that I sent Louise a ticket. And you better believe that she came a-running. We were both hot to trot.

First we lived in someone's house, and then we found a place of our own, a little house we rented on Twentieth Street. Even bought a small dining room set. I suppose it was something like playing house. Like back in Greensville when some girl and me would take loose boards and build ourselves a hut to hide in.

We were rebels, still running away from her family. We made our own small world—far from Tampa in the wilds of Seattle—and we clung to each other for dear life.

She stayed home and cooked and cleaned and kept house. I went out and played my music. We were two silly kids, crazy and madly in love. And we spent a large amount of time fucking our heads off. While it lasted, it was beautiful.

But there were problems. We were both scared to death, even though I might not have admitted it. Louise was homesick. She had to be; this was her first time away from her family, aside from our fling to Miami. And I was always worried about money. When we set up our own house, I saw that I had no one to turn to for help.

When I had lived in ladies' homes, there was usually someone else's telephone to use. And there was always someone else there to make sure there was enough fuel to keep me warm. But not this time. Now *I* had to see about getting a phone; *I* had to go out and buy the fuel. For the first time, *I* was the provider, providing for someone else besides myself.

I was also pretty rigid. I was a workingman and thought highly of my worldly ways. I probably knew more about the real world than Louise, but I also knew a whole lot less than I thought I did.

We had our spats, and, brother, they were loud. But no matter how bad each brawl was, we'd usually wind up in bed. Funny how that quieted us down and made us forget what we'd been yelling about.

Sometimes we didn't have enough money for the rent. If I was between jobs, we might be lacking for food. And that would really make us edgy—living from day to day. That kind of hand-to-mouth situation, though, can also make you strong. You can only push a man so far when he's already down. Hard times can do a lot to build your character. And when you can honestly say that all you have—*literally* all you have— is the love for each other, well, that's a heavy statement.

I was playing it straight with Louise, at least as straight as you can expect of an eighteen-year-old kid who was being exposed to so much. Ever since I began singing and playing in public, I'd never had to ask for pussy. It was out there for the taking. All I needed to do was lightly suggest.

You know how it works: You don't ask, but you do ask. It's a little game where everyone knows their part. I learned mine well, and at an early age. By the time I was eighteen, I could play the game like a pro.

Other musicians will tell you the same thing. It's one of the fringe benefits which go along with the business.

I also believe that you can still love the person you're with and get an extra piece on the side every now and then.

During the time Louise and I were together, I might have strayed two or three times. But for the most part, I wasn't wild; the little girl really had me tamed. And the times I did slip around, I made sure it didn't get back to Louise. She was my woman, and I was her man. I loved her completely, even though getting some on the outside and being cool on the inside, for me at least, was and is a fact of life.

I think of one rooster and lots of hens. One bull and a whole mess of cows. There's a routine which I'd later recite onstage that would always get a laugh:

"Bible says that thou shalt not commit adultery. Moses got that law from God. It's a good law and I can dig it. Because back in those Bible days, if a man could have six wives, three hundred concubines, and still commit adultery, I'd kill him myself."

Yeah, slipping goes way far back. It's real natural business—and that goes for women as well. Ain't nothing I can fight. Ain't nothing I'm going to fight.

As Louise and I got closer, the love grew. And so did the tension. She wanted to get pregnant, and it was something I wanted too. It happened, but we lost the baby when Louise had a miscarriage. That broke our hearts.

Marriage wasn't something we thought about; it just didn't seem necessary. But we sure did want a child.

Meanwhile, Louise's family kept up their campaign against me, and they did everything they could to convince Louise to come back home. Louise's mama got me on the phone and stayed right on my case. I tried to be respectful, and most of the time I succeeded.

Every time Louise and I had a spat, Louise ran to the phone and called her mama for advice. Well, that didn't bother me none, except for one time. And that time turned out to be a tragedy:

I can't remember what caused this fight, but it was a heavyweight event. We had been shouting at each other for hours, and Louise was now all a mess—whimpering and crying.

"You don't love me," she said.

"Course I do."

"You don't understand me."

"Yes, I do."

"You don't care about me."

"Now you know I do."

And so it went. When I kept arguing my side, she finally gave up on me and pulled the usual number: She called Mama down in Tampa. Louise told Mama that she was miserable and that I was creating the misery. Mama asked to talk to me, and I figured I was going to get chewed out again. But this time there was a twist.

"RC, that you?" Mama asked.

"Yes, ma'am."

"Well, listen here, I want you to send my daughter home immediately."

"You want *what?*" I gasped.

"You heard me, RC, and I'm not interested in repeating myself. Just send that child home to me."

"Ain't gonna do it."

"I'm not asking you, boy, I'm *telling* you."

"Well, if you want her back so bad," I said, "you can send for her."

"Fine with me, RC."

"You send her the ticket, and I'll put your daughter on the bus. But *I* am not sending her home. I want her here with me."

That was that, and I didn't think much more about it. Thirty minutes later the fight between me and Louise was forgotten: We were back in bed, screwing our way to paradise.

But a few days later something happened which we didn't expect: The ticket arrived. We were both shocked. We couldn't even remember what the old fight had been about. Still, I had given her mother my word. I had told her that I'd send Louise home if she sent a ticket.

Now I was in a jam: I couldn't go back on my word. And besides, we were afraid that her mother would race up to Seattle and cause all kinds of trouble. No, the thing didn't make any sense; it tore us both up bad, and we cried like little babies for days, holding each other tight.

But we knew it was over. Our love affair was ending. And we were both hurt and confused. There was no counselor to guide us, no one to help us with these matters of the heart. All Louise had was her mother, who wasn't much of an objective third party. I had no one.

Nowadays couples like us may have more of a chance if they have the good sense to seek professional advice. But back then I didn't know what I was doing—trying to act like a big man, but really still a little boy.

We knew that we were nuts for each other, we knew that we fought like cats and dogs, and we knew that we had a hot physical relationship.

As much as we wept about Louise's leaving, she still left. And I let her. I was afraid about what her mother might do if I kept her.

Life was hell for the next weeks—me living alone in Seattle, Louise back in Tampa. I was sullen, sultry, and down deep in a state of salty gloom. I had a bad case of some serious blues. I have to rank it as a low point in my life.

I hung around for five dismal weeks and then split for Los Angeles. Jack wanted the McSon Trio to record some sides down there, and it was a great excuse for getting out of Seattle. But while all this was going on—while I was moving down to California—I was unaware of what was happening back in Tampa.

Louise was pregnant with my child. When she found out, she tried to let me know, but I had already left town and she had no idea where to find me.

I doubt I would have gone back to Tampa anyway. I'm not sure I could have taken her mama's hostility; I'm not sure I could have taken all the ducking and dodging and running away. I would have sent for Louise, sure, but I never had the chance. The thing wasn't meant to be.

My daughter Evelyn was born in 1950. Today she's a lovely woman, living in Tampa and studying to be a nurse. Louise got married and also lives in Tampa. We've kept in touch through the years, and I've always supported Evelyn.

And even though Louise and I have gone our different ways—to separate marriages with families of our own—I still have the feeling that spark between us is something which will never completely die. Our feelings for each other are unusually powerful.

I sometimes think the reason we fought so much those final months was because Louise was pregnant. That might have changed her temperament and caused her to get pissed at me all the time. And, like I said, I was acting like a jackass myself.

But if you spend too much time looking back and refiguring the past, you'll go insane. Our love was real, but it was also raw. And besides, I was ready to move out in different directions. Once again, my life was about to change.

Fooling
with Drugs

Before I launch into a description about how I started up with drugs in Seattle, I got to warn you: I don't push anything on anyone. I never have and I never will. And that includes drugs. On the other hand, no one ever pushed drugs on me.

I used various shit regularly for sixteen or seventeen years, and I certainly wouldn't encourage a single soul to start fucking with dope. But it may surprise some folk to learn that I have no horror stories to tell. Sorry, but I just don't. Lots of what's portrayed at the movies or on TV is pure fantasy to me. Maybe other cats have gone through it; I haven't.

So I can't deal in clichés. The subject is too important. I can only tell you what happened to me—plain and simple. No one did it to me. I did it to myself. It wasn't society that did it to me, it wasn't a pusher, it wasn't being blind or being black or being poor. It was all my doing. And besides—as crazy as it sounds—I have no regrets. It was another lesson in life. It was something I did, something I survived, something which became part of me.

I was a lot of different things in Seattle. I was still half-assed country, but I also thought I was hot stuff. And in some ways, I was. I had won the respect of most of the musicians in town. After all, I had a gig at the Rocking Chair. And in those days, that was real prestige. At jam sessions I could hold my own, I could play in a lot of different styles. But even though I was held in some esteem by other musicians, I was still a lot younger than most of them. Remember: I was just eighteen, and still as curious as ever. Curious about everything.

I told you about how wide-open Seattle was in those days—the booze was flowing, the women were plentiful, and there was an abundance of drugs around.

When I first arrived, I didn't even know what grass was. But after playing several gigs around town, I started smelling it. I questioned the other musicians about what they were smoking. During the breaks, I asked if I could follow them outside.

"No."

"Come on, man."

"None of your business, RC."

"Come on, man."

"Too much trouble, RC."

"You don't have to carry me out there," I said. "I'm not crippled. I'm not lame. I just want to see what you cats are doing."

And I kept pushing, kept pestering, kept poking them till they let me go with them and till they laid a joint on me. That's how I started smoking weed. It seemed all right to me. I liked the taste, and I liked the mellow effect it had on my body and on my mind.

Playing behind grass wasn't bad. I could really feel the groove of the music. And I thought it added to lovemaking. I thought it acted like an aphrodisiac. So like everyone else, I smoked it.

The next thing I did—maybe two or three months later—was to shoot heroin. But here I must interrupt myself again to give you another opinion:

It's bullshit that grass leads to heroin. I know too many people who have lived long, productive lives smoking grass every day—and never done anything else. No heroin, no coke—nothing.

I've always liked those counterarguments which show you that milk leads to heroin, since all addicts at one time drank milk.

No, marijuana is its own thing. It might be bad for you—I really haven't read all the reports—but I know goddamn well that there's no real link between weed and heroin.

Now in my case it happened because *I* wanted it to happen. That's all there was to it. Didn't take me long to figure out that before a gig, the cats might be doing something besides smoking reefer. Or if we were at someone's house, I'd hear them doing something in the kitchen. Before long, I discovered that they were cooking up horse, and I wanted to try some for myself.

I have to say it again: There wasn't no pusher hanging round the back alley who enticed me into it. No white cat or no black cat got me hooked or encouraged me to turn on.

Hell, the stuff cost money. And no one was giving it away. I had to look for it myself. I had to seek it out. And I wanted the shit bad enough so I found a way to get it.

I went back to bugging the other musicians:

"What are y'all fucking with now?" I'd ask some cats getting ready to shoot up.

"Nothing, kid."

"Come on, man, let me try that stuff."

"No way, RC, you're still a baby."

"Fuck that noise. If y'all are doing it, I can do it."

"Listen here, RC, it's bad for you."

"Don't give me that shit, man. If it's bad for me, it's bad for you. So why the hell are *you* doing it? Can't be all *that* bad."

Anyway, I kept pushing: I've always been able to argue, and I've always been persistent, specially if I want something bad enough. "Okay, goddammit," one of the cats finally said, "let's give the kid some shit just to keep him quiet. Better than having him drive us crazy."

And that was how I got my first hit.

There was no big profound philosophical or psychological reason. It was curiosity more than anything. The way I was around mechanical devices, the way I was around musical instruments, electronic playthings—well, that's how I was around drugs.

Once I started, I saw no reason to stop. In those days, it didn't even cost that much. You could buy a reefer for 50 cents, and if you had $5, you could buy twenty joints.

A $4 or $5 bag of heroin was plenty strong in 1948, and in the beginning, I might cop a bag once a week, or maybe once every two weeks. I didn't have to get high every day. And usually I didn't have enough money to do that anyway.

All my bread wasn't going for dope. Far from it. I had Louise to support. And I also had my music habit to feed. Around then I bought myself my first piano for $150 or $200. It was a little electric job. To me it was like a toy, and I loved it.

There were so many different changes I was going through in Seattle that even now I have to stop and think a while before I can sort 'em all out. I was being exposed to more things than I had ever seen before. And it was all coming at me at once. In a city full of good musicians —blues musicians, dance band musicians, bop musicians—I had gained my own little respectability. At the same time, money was still scarce, and Louise and I, lacking fuel for the heat, spent many a cold night together shivering like little puppies.

This is the background to my flirtations with dope. I don't tell you these things to excuse myself—I figure I don't need any excuses—but only so you'll understand what was running through my brain back then.

I suppose you could say that I was entering manhood.

On top of that, I didn't want to miss out on anything. And even though I was blind, I was still as observant as anyone else—maybe a little more so. I always knew what was happening.

As I told you before, I was a nervy kid. Well, that applied to all things—drugs included. The secrecy surrounding drugs made them even more intriguing. Many of the cats—many of the great cats—who could really play were on drugs. I wanted to find out why. And I wanted to see if the dope helped. I wanted to see what it did to you.

I heard stories later about cats strung out on shit, chewing up the sheets and acting half-crazy. I just never saw that side of it. Maybe it was there; but if it was, it passed me by.

If I had seen the bad effects of heroin—the vulgar side everyone talks about—I wouldn't have done it. I wasn't stupid, and I wasn't interested in messing myself up. I just wanted to get high, along with everyone else, enjoy life, and play my music. Remember: I love me, and I haven't ever wanted to destroy myself.

In some ways, Seattle was a very proud time in my life, in spite of the torture I was going through with Louise. I had figured out how to stay independent. I'd made a lot of progress since those days, only a year or so before, when I'd been scuffling down in Orlando. I'd managed to keep myself together without begging. Oh, I knew there were people in all those cities—Tampa, Jacksonville, even Seattle—who would have given me things, even money, if I asked. But I didn't want folks to feel sorry for me. I remember the way country folk talked down South:

"Look at this child. Poor thing. It's a shame 'fore God. Boy, ain't you got no mama? My oh my. And he's blind on top it all. Lord, have mercy!"

Well, I didn't like that talk. I didn't think I was helpless. And I didn't get no kick out of anyone's sympathy. I wanted to be in control of my own life. I wanted to see where I was going, and I had to make sure that I got there on my own.

Even up in Seattle I hadn't learned the difference between begging and asking. In my mind, they amounted to the same thing. And I just couldn't beg. God bless the child who's got his own.

Yes, Lord, it was wild up there. I saw more in a year than I had seen for five years before that. All kinds of strange shit. I saw cats bringing in huge cereal bowls filled with weed. I saw oceans of coke and heroin. I saw folk drinking whiskey like it was water.

Not that all of this was done in the open: Dope was something musicians did among themselves—privately—and they had to like you to include you in. Like I said, no one was stuffing it down your throat or up your nose.

Musicians did other crazy things—like pulling a train on a girl. That was where a lot of guys fucked a woman, one after the other. I never liked that and I never did it. But I saw the other cats doing it. It was just part of what was happening.

I left the guys alone to do whatever they wanted. If a cat liked to pull a train on a woman, that was cool. A cat liked coke, cool. Or horse, cool. Or whiskey or cigarettes or anything else. I had my own stuff going, and I never interfered. That was how I got along.

But this life didn't continue for long.

I had done what I needed to do in Seattle after a year or two. I had seen that I could come to a strange city, without a friend or a contact in the world, and still make it. I went in blind and I came out blind. And I was none the worse for it. I survived.

Once Louise split for Tampa, the town held very little for me. I was ready to move. I've *always* been ready to move. It suits my style.

Down to L.A.

It was 1950 when I moved to L.A.

As I told you, I had been there once before—to record for Jack Lauderdale without my trio. And it was that first L.A. session—sometime in '49—that produced "Baby, Let Me Hold Your Hand."

Now that was a strange tune. I sang it in my most authentic Charles Brown voice, but I added something of my own. At the beginning of the song, I played celeste instead of piano.

I got the idea from one of the most popular tunes of the day, "Dream," which also had a celeste part. "Baby, Let Me Hold Your Hand" was more or less a blues, though, so the celeste sounded weird in there. Anyway, it seemed to work; the record sold and became my first little success.

There was so much different music around this time—up in Seattle and down in L.A. Everyone was listening to Bird and Diz—that was

Charlie Parker and Dizzy Gillespie. They were the two main men among the younger musicians like me.

We also followed cats like Howard McGhee and Max Roach—all the guys inventing the jazz which sounded new and modern.

I knew how to play the music they called bebop, and I loved it. I respected these cats because they could play their asses off. I kept up with the changes so I could hold my own if I fell into a jam session.

But at the same time, I wanted to remain independent. I had to continue to make money. And in order to carry my own weight, I wanted to make sure I could do the popular music of the day. That still meant Nat Cole and Johnny Moore's Three Blazers featuring Charles Brown. Those cats were hotter than ever now, and so I kept on imitating them. It was working, and I saw no reason to stop. When it came to earning a living, I was a cautious man.

Naturally a great deal of other music was floating round. There was a mighty strong blues wind blowing up and down the West Coast. T-Bone Walker could be felt everywhere, and so could Big Joe Turner. Don't forget Louis Jordan either; he remained a popular figure with everyone—musicians *and* the public. My musical influences were still mixed. I loved much of what I heard and I tried to absorb it all.

The main thing—beyond pure bebop and pure blues—was my singing. I could sing before I even knew where a note on the piano was. I had been around my voice before any other instrument, and more and more I began to realize that my singing was more *me* than anything else.

Finally, though, I stayed loose in order to stay together. And in order to get work. That was the main thing. If a cat had a blues gig, or a jazz gig, or just a piano gig in a white club, I wanted him to think, Hey, I'll call Brother Ray. He can do this shit.

When I got to L.A. I was lucky enough to meet a woman—and that solved my housing problems. Her name was Loretta, and she was Jack Lauderdale's secretary. I was always hanging around Jack's office; that's where me and Loretta started flirting with each other.

I was living at the Dunbar Hotel on Central Avenue when Loretta invited me to stay with her; there was no hesitancy on my part. Loretta lived in a court where she had this cute cottage, and I was cozy as I could be.

After losing Louise, things were turning around a bit; Loretta helped my spirits to stop sinking and to start arising once again.

Things weren't so sweet for our trio, though. Milt and Gosady had come down to L.A. with me, and we recorded a bunch of tunes—things like "Honey, Honey" and "She's on the Ball"—for Jack Lauderdale's Swingtime label. But there weren't many gigs for the trio. And Milt and Gosady went back to Seattle.

It wasn't anything bitter or angry. The trio thing just wasn't happening, and Milt and Gosady ran out of bread. Meanwhile, I had a place to stay—with Loretta—and had managed to survive the move.

Jack was primarily interested in me. I think he was really fascinated by my voice, and the trio was something which just came along with the package. Maybe that's why we broke up so quickly. Maybe Jack wasn't all that concerned with pushing the trio. But he did want to push me. And in fact we became friends and ran together for a while. Jack's girlfriend's name was Betty, and often we double-dated and hit the L.A. nightspots.

I met many well-known people in this period of my life, but no one really impressed me much. No one, that is, until one evening in a Los Angeles nightclub when I found myself face to face with Art Tatum.

I was dazed, like I had been hit by thunder. This was my god before me. And I couldn't utter a word. Couldn't tell him how much I loved him, couldn't let him know that I had listened to all his records. I just stood there like an idiot, with my mouth open and my heart beating so fast that I was sure everyone around me could hear it thumping.

This had never happened to me before, and it hasn't happened since. I've met all kinds of people—little, big, famous, and notorious—and none of those encounters have had much impact on me. But Tatum was different. He wasn't merely the president of a country, a foreign minister, or a world-renowned movie actor. He was Art Tatum.

And Art Tatum was the ultimate, the last word with what could be done with a piano. Funny, because even though I loved his playing, I never got into his style myself. I was too divided musically to devote myself to the piano the way Tatum did. I also wanted to sing, compose, arrange, play sax. My own piano work was much closer to Nat Cole's; I concentrated on tasty fills and subtle ways to accompany my vocals.

Yet Art Tatum was the light which I followed. When I was twenty, he was still an example of what I might have accomplished if I had studied only the piano. He showed me what could really be done with eighty-eight keys, the way Charlie Parker showed saxophonists the way to play their horns.

Listening to Tatum, I was constantly reminded of how little I could play. He kept me humble.

I was starting to have a pretty good time around L.A., and much of that was due to Jack's friendship and his business interest in me. He got me gigs and even let me drive his car, sitting next to me and telling me which way to go. I really dug driving.

But the most important thing he did was put me on the road with Lowell Fulson. That was a move which changed everything. Lowell was also recording for Jack around this time, and he had a very big hit: "Every Day I Have the Blues." Sometimes Jack put together dances featuring his recording artists at places up and down the California coast. I remember that Lloyd Glenn, who was a very popular piano player back then, was on some of those shows with us.

So it was sometime in 1950—maybe March or April—when I first headed out on the road with someone who was a big star. Didn't know it at the time, but this was the same goddamn road that I'd be working for the next twenty-eight years, the road where most of my life—my musical life and my love life—was going to be spent.

The Road

Lowell had a little blues band.

I remember Earl Brown, his alto player, and I remember Eddie Piper, his drummer. At different times there were different horn players—Stanley Turrentine played tenor, Billy Brooks and Fleming Askew played trumpet—and the group was more or less modeled after the T-Bone Walker sound.

Lowell was a cat—like Pee Wee Crayton—very much in the T-Bone groove. He played the electric guitar and he sung the blues. And that was it. He had a good, down-home sound, and in the early fifties that style was very hot, specially round California.

I was put on the bill by Jack and an agent, Ben Waller. They put together the package, and naturally it was Lowell's show. I was a guest artist, and my "Baby, Let Me Hold Your Hand" was being played around the country in many black communities. I was just a little jive-ass celebrity. But Lowell's "Every Day I Have the Blues" was a *smash* hit; back then it was the biggest thing going. He also had a hot tune called "Blue Shadows."

Lowell opened and closed the show, playing maybe 75 percent or 80 percent of it. At some point, usually just before intermission, I came out and did my songs. And when Lowell was on, I also played piano with the band.

When I began, I was getting $35 a night; fifteen or sixteen months later when I quit, I must have been getting around $50. For me, that wasn't half-bad. I didn't have many expenses. Rooms were only $4 or $5. It cost me a couple of dollars a day to eat. To get my suit cleaned and pressed was 75 cents to 85 cents. So I still had $10 or $15 a day left over and was able to save some bread.

Most of the little towns we played, of course, didn't have any heroin around, so I had to wait till we got to the bigger cities—Atlanta or Dallas. And when and if the opportunity presented itself, I had saved some money for my little treat. But don't get me wrong. I didn't go around hitting on people. If I was going to buy from someone, I had to know that person very, very well. I had to be absolutely certain it was cool.

Through default I soon became the musical director of the band, even though in those days there was no such title. I was just the cat who wrote the charts and took charge of rehearsals. I whipped the band in shape, which pleased Lowell, since his thing was mainly singing the blues and playing his blues guitar.

I tried to add a little variety to the music. It wasn't that I didn't love the blues—I'll always love the blues—but as much as you might love cabbage, you don't want to eat it every day and at every meal. So I wrote a few other things, especially once we picked up our horn players. I never charged Lowell for any of these arrangements; in fact, I never charged anyone for arrangements back in those days, even when we were recording. Just didn't know no better.

To me the big thrill was just hearing the horns playing back something *I* had written.

I wasn't giving away my writing 'cause I was generous—far from it

—but because I was too busy being happy. Here I was—traveling, playing before people, recording, singing as a solo act, all at a very young age. I still hadn't been out of the woods *that* long.

I also wanted to be part of something good. If I could contribute to the band, I did it. The reward was in the music, in the sounds I created, in the pleasure it brought to me, to Lowell, to the other cats in the band, and to the people who paid to hear us.

Lowell had a station wagon and a Roadmaster Buick, and we drove for days and days and days on end. We hit every little town imaginable, and all the big ones too. First time out we ran through New Mexico and Texas and all round the Southwest. On another trip we went further into the South.

It was rough, and sometimes you thought you were going crazy. But there was so much good music back then, you'd always be meeting some new musicians and having a ball.

In Texas, I got to play piano behind cats like T-Bone Walker and Big Joe Turner. Sometimes they were on the same bill with Lowell, and our band would back 'em up. I especially loved playing behind Big Joe. I had grown up with his records, and here I was on the stage with him. That man has so much weeping in his voice. If it was just you and him in a room, he could sing the blues at you till you'd break down and cry. I don't care how cold-blooded you might be; he'd get to you.

Joe Turner reminds me of Lady Day when she was a young woman. He has a tear in his voice. And I ain't ever heard anyone sing the blues so raw and so pure. I also loved the way he sang "Chains of Love"; that was a heartbreaker.

I got to meet other big names of the day. Around this time I even ran into Charles Brown. And I also had a chance to see my friends. Quincy Jones, for example, was traveling with Lionel Hampton's band, playing trumpet. And whenever I was able to catch up with Q, we'd straightaway go off and find a place to jam.

I also knew many of the gospel men and women. Some were friends of mine, others just acquaintances. Among them were the best singers

I had ever heard in my life. And the very cream of the crop—for me at least—were cats like Ira Tucker of the Dixie Hummingbirds, Archie Brownlee of the Five Blind Boys of Mississippi, and Claude Jeter of the Swan Silvertones. These guys have voices which could shake down your house and smash all the furniture in it. Jesus, could they wail! They sung for real, and I loved their music as much as any music in the world.

Let's say, for instance, that I'm in Atlanta or Dallas or New Orleans. It's Sunday morning, and I sleep late after my Saturday night gig. I wake up to the sounds of a gospel group which happens to be in the same hotel with me. I can hear them practicing way down the hallway.

Well, I pick myself up and go follow the music. Maybe it's the Caravans. Maybe it's the Pilgrim Travelers.

I rap at the door.

"Yeah?"

"It's Brother Ray."

"Come in, man. Shit! Come on in, Ray, and help us sing."

So I walk in.

"What part you want, Ray?"

"Oh, I'll take what's left."

Yeah, that was always my thing: I was sharp enough not to get in their way. And because I could sing, the cats respected me. Just the way I liked to jam with jazz players, I also loved jamming with the gospel boys.

So while I was listening to all the new jazz, while I was playing dirty old blues with Lowell, I was also hearing all the churchy sounds.

Music was all over the place. When we got to New York, we hit the Apollo. And there were as many people hanging out backstage, listening to us rehearse and mess around, as out front.

Must have been at the Apollo that I played behind Jackie Moms Mabley. She was doing her bit—acting like an old lady who wants to be loved by a young man—and she cracked me up. I played piano behind her when she sang her songs. Things like "My Man."

I also met the other great comics playing the black theaters back then—fabulous cats like Pigmeat Markham, Redd Foxx, Slappy

White, and Clay Tyson. In those days their material was raunchy and rough and funny enough to make you weep and pee in your pants at the same time.

All this time, I still didn't have anyone taking care of me. I was on my own. Even when I was in New York for the first time, I knew how to get around. If you wanted to show me where the restaurant was, fine. But if you were too busy, I'd find it by myself. Hell, if I was hungry and wanted some food, I didn't have to wait on you; I could get off my ass and find the place, sit down, and wait for the waitress. I knew she was going to ask me what I wanted.

"I don't know, honey," I'd say, "what's on the menu?" And of course she'd tell me.

I figured out all the basics. I knew I'd have to find a restaurant, 'cause I had to eat. I knew I'd have to find my gig, 'cause I had to work. I knew I'd have to find my hotel, 'cause I had to sleep. That simple.

As I moved from town to town, I also put together my address book —with people's phone numbers and other information—on a deck of cards. I punched out the numbers with my little stylus, and I was able to get three or four people on each card. Soon I had numbers for cats —and many women—all over the country.

My relationships with women never suffered that much, and certainly not during this period of my life. It was easy meeting them— being a musician and touring the country—and I had enough to keep me busy and satisfied. Once in a while, though, I got myself in trouble.

There was this time in Oakland when I almost got myself killed. And if it wasn't for my dear friend Dug, I probably wouldn't be here to tell the story.

Dug was a dude I met through Lowell. He was one of these people you didn't have to worry about: If he liked you, he'd die for you. The other thing about Dug was his size; he was big. Not fat, but huge, and strong as a bull. Ain't no one gonna mess with you if he was your partner.

Well, I had this gal I was going with up in Oakland. Her name was

Maybelle, and she was married. Her old man was called Fox, and he was a notorious dude, one of these people who would cut you if he got mad.

On this particular day Maybelle and I go to Dug's girlfriend's house. We've just finished fucking and we're both buck naked when we hear a knock at the door. We look out the window and our hearts nearly stop beating.

"Oh, shit," Maybelle says, "it's Fox."

Dug goes to the door. Like I said, he's big, but Fox is one of these mean-acting cats. He's a bad motherfucker.

"Have you seen my old lady?" Fox asks.

"No," Dug answers, guarding the door. "Why would you think she'd be here?"

In the meantime, while this little conversation is going on, Maybelle and I are in the bed. And the bedroom is mighty close to the front door. If Fox turns a certain way, he can practically see us.

Maybelle and I get so close that you don't see no two heads or no two bodies; just one. We're sure-enough tight-knit.

Meanwhile Fox is still pressing:

"Sure you ain't seen my woman?"

"Ain't seen her."

"Well, they told me on the street that Maybelle had come up here."

Fox knows that Maybelle and Dug are friends, but he also knows that they ain't lovers. Dug's the type of guy who knows lots of people. And all the men understand that Dug can be trusted. If he takes out your wife, and if he likes you, you don't have to worry about him getting no pussy from her. If he's your friend, then your wife can't do shit for him.

So Dug keeps repeating, "No, she ain't here."

And Fox keeps asking, "You sure, now? You absolutely sure?"

Finally Dug lets him have it:

"Look, didn't I tell you, goddammit, she ain't here? You know me. If I tell you she ain't here, she ain't here."

"Okay, man, I'm sorry. Didn't mean no harm." And with that, Fox splits.

That's it.

You talk about two scared souls! You talk about relief! Me and Maybelle were so shook we were still shaking, even after Fox was long gone.

"I was scared too," Dug said afterward, "but I sure as hell wasn't going to let him through."

That's the kind of friend Dug was. And the man's my partner to this day.

Some other strange shit happened to me when I was on the road with Lowell, and not all of it was pleasant:

We were around El Paso when Lowell and the cats decided to go to Juarez to buy some pussy. I went along for the ride, though I didn't go inside with them. Funny thing, as much as I love women, I've never been able to get into buying pussy. I can't get that thing together. I have a friend who always argues with me about it.

"What do you do when you want a good steak?" he'll ask.

"Buy it," I'll have to answer.

"What do you do when you want a good stereo?"

"Buy it."

"Well, pussy's the same."

Of course it ain't, and he knows it. It's just that some cats prefer to pay for it so they can skip the preliminary work. Maybe I've been blessed, 'cause I've always been able to find women who would give me some without demanding direct payment.

Well, the guys in the band were inside with the women while I was outside in the car. And this particular night was freezing cold. The little heater in the car only put out so much, and soon I started thinking that I was Frosty the Snowman.

I happened to have a bottle of Southern Comfort with me, and I figured that drinking it might warm me up a bit. So I gulped down the whole bottle, and before I knew it, I couldn't feel the heat. I couldn't feel nothing.

When we got back to the hotel someone had to carry me to my bedroom and, let me tell you, I never felt worse in my life. I was dying.

My head started a-swimming and a-swirling. The room started closing in on me, and the ceiling was a-swaying back and forth. Man, I was hurting.

Good God, I prayed, if you just let me get over this one, I will never —I mean *never*—touch that Southern Comfort again. I promise you, Lord. Just let me off this one time.

On another trip we were playing up and down the Carolina coast. We had an afternoon off and Lowell, me, and the boys decided to go to the beach and mess around.

We started running footraces and I surprised the cats. I could beat nearly all of 'em. (At school, I loved to run, and I was a pretty good sprinter. You might beat me on the long distances, but I'd give you hell for a hundred yards. I learned to run with my body erect and in a perfectly straight line so I wouldn't waste any steps or time.)

On this particular afternoon we were tired after running and just relaxing out there—this is in Myrtle Beach, South Carolina—when I decided to go for a swim. (That's something else I learned in Greensville. We had ponds back there and one day someone pushed me into one. I decided that was a good time to figure out how to swim.)

The water was cool off Myrtle Beach and I was having a ball, splashing in the ocean like a baby in a bath. I kept swimming further and further out when suddenly I heard one of the cats screaming, "Hey, Ray, come back, man. Come back!"

I thought I had simply gone out too far and that the cats were worried about me drowning. But that wasn't it.

"Wow, we caught you just in time," one of the guys said when I got back to shore.

"What you talkin' 'bout?"

"You were about to go over to the white side, man!"

White side! Shit. Who ever knew of such a thing? I couldn't figure out how the ocean could have a white side and a black side. It struck me as being funny—not funny-funny, but funny-ridiculous, funny-sad.

My race consciousness was something which was just starting to develop. I'm not trying to give you any liberal bullshit. This was just how my mind worked. Awareness of race came late to me; I simply couldn't see it.

I remember the first time I ever made love to a white woman was in Seattle. But I never thought much of it. That's when Louise had left town and I was especially loose. The color thing didn't matter and didn't make much of an impression on me one way or another.

In much the same way my blindness kept me from getting nervous when I went out onstage: I couldn't see the people looking back at me. So I just tried to please myself. I figured if I could please Ray, that was good enough.

But touring the South with Lowell gave me eyes I hadn't had before. All of a sudden I had a new point of view. I had drifted away from home, been to Seattle, been to L.A., seen that the world didn't have to be the way it was in Greensville. That had an impact on me. I had something to compare to the South; I was witnessing something a little better.

When I first lived in Florida, no one talked about race. It was no big thing. I never heard expressions like blue-eyed devils or pigs. I never heard of the NAACP and no one seemed very excited about anything. We were all just living. But coming back to my home turf, I was aware of the ugliness of prejudice for the first time.

Making my way through the South in 1951, I suddenly saw the divisions: It was white toilets and black toilets; it was white restaurants and black restaurants; it was white hotels and black rooming houses.

Not that Seattle or L.A. had been perfect. Far from it. There were places in California when I arrived in '49 or '50 where blacks couldn't go. Many places. So it wasn't any Garden of Eden out there. It was just a little more sensible than the Deep South.

Traveling with Lowell, the cats told me about signs that said, "No Jews, dogs or niggers allowed." And that might have been when I first realized that Jews and blacks were lumped in the same category. Those Jewish people must be in pretty bad shape too, I thought. And that made me feel a certain kinship with them; they were hated just like us.

But to tell the truth, I'm not sure I even knew what a Jew was until I got to be twenty-four or so, around 1954. Even when I first met Billy

Shaw and Jerry Wexler, cats I worked with, I didn't think of them as Jews. Back in the country, I only knew that there were blacks and whites.

All these things were new revelations for me. I was losing my innocence. My little country town of Greensville was so quiet, so peaceful, so backwards that I grew up without any idea that there was actual hatred between the races. The system was whatever it was. And as far as I could see, people were cool with it.

You could run free in the woods, the air was clean, and people weren't piled on top of each other, like in New York or Chicago. There was room to breathe, and, at least when I was coming up, not much cause for animosity.

Call me naive, and I suppose I was. I just accepted things for what they were. I had no squawks, had no reason to be angry, no one had attacked or harmed me. Oh, there might have been an incident or two when I was a kid. At school, I remember a white kid once called me nigger and I knocked the shit out of him. But that wasn't because he was white. I would have done the same thing to a black kid if he had used the word. I had been raised to believe that nigger was obscene language, and that no one should use it—me included.

We went back to L.A. from time to time and I had a chance to do a little more recording. This was in 1950 and 1951. I remember a couple of dates with a band which included some of the heaviest players around then: Jack McVea, Marshall Royal, Maurice Simon—musicians with very big reputations. To me, being with these cats on a record date was a major event.

I wrote the charts for those sessions and I also wrote a lot of the tunes. But something else happened around this time which was even more important: I started changing my style.

Now I've been telling you all this time how I loved—and how I imitated—Nat Cole and Charles Brown. I had been stealing their licks and singing and playing like them for seven years—maybe even longer.

Two days didn't go by without someone saying, "Ray, you sound *exactly* like Nat Cole." Or, "Ray, your voice is the *spittin' image* of

Charles Brown." At first that delighted me. They were bad cats—those two—and I was proud to be confused with them.

But after a while these comments started getting to me. I thought it'd be nice if people began to recognize *me*, if they'd tell me I sounded like Ray Charles. So I started experimenting with a different voice. Strangely enough, that voice turned out to be *mine*. I really didn't have to do anything except be myself.

I did some tunes for Jack—"The Snow Is Falling" and "Kissa Me, Baby"—which were about the first ones I'd ever tried without consciously trying to imitate anyone. These songs were the prototype of me.

This didn't just happen overnight. Like I said, it was an experiment; I was trying to get a pulse. But I was still cautious. After all, I'd had my first hit with a Charles Brown–influenced number—"Baby, Let Me Hold Your Hand."

Slowly I began to wean myself and come into my own. Still trying to be my own man, but not about to give up what I already had. Matter of fact, even after I changed record companies—from Swingtime to Atlantic in 1952—I was still doing Nat Cole and Charles Brown–type numbers.

But by 1951, I had ever so slowly edged away from what I had been doing for so long. I was trying to be accepted as me.

Jack Lauderdale remained my friend all this time, although I never saw any royalty money for "Baby, Let Me Hold Your Hand." Can't blame Jack, though. I didn't know what I was doing and, as I mentioned before, business details didn't mean much to me. I was so thrilled to be recording that nothing else mattered.

Besides, I found a sly way to get money from Jack. When he was gambling with other people around him, I came up and asked him for bread. I always made sure that it was done in public. Usually he'd hand over $300 or $400. I'd gamble with maybe $30 or $40 and put the rest in my pocket. This happened every six months or so, and it was the best method—really the only method—I had of getting paid.

Jack also promoted me some. I can recall one day when we went to meet Joe Adams who was a big-time disc jockey with a show on KOWL from noon to three that everybody in L.A. listened to. We were pushing, "Baby, Let Me Hold Your Hand" or maybe "Kissa Me, Baby."

About ten years later, Adams wound up working for me, but to this day he claims not to remember meeting me back in 1951. Guess I didn't make much of an impression.

Even though I was still tight with Loretta, I also had several other girlfriends by this time. I especially remember Madeline—another girl I met through Jack and his girlfriend Betty. Then, like now, I was pouring all the energy I had into women and music.

When I went out on the road again with Lowell in 1951, I decided to get my own transportation. I bought a used Rocket 98 Olds—a 1950 model—and this was the first car I had ever owned.

Does that sound strange to you? A blind cat buying a car? Well, to me it made a lot of sense. I found a guy, Al Curry, who drove for me, and having these wheels really made my life easier. Meant I could be more independent. All I needed to know was the location of the gig, and I'd be there on time. Afterwards, I was able to go off and do what I wanted. This way I called the shots.

I was used to having radios and electronic devices around me, and now with my own car I could play with all this stuff, make it as loud as I wanted without disturbing anyone. Pretty early on, with my first bread, I bought a Zenith Trans-Oceanic radio. It was something I could play with all day long to make the dusty road a bit shorter.

So here I was: running round America, up one coast and down the other, playing nasty blues licks behind Lowell and getting to refine my own strange style at the same time.

I liked being on the move—I've always liked forward motion—and it was another period of heavy learning. I saw how many of the big stars performed in public, and I got a taste of what the road was like. I saw it was something I could handle. It might be tedious, but the road wasn't ever going to break me.

When we played Atlanta, I got to run home and visit all the folk in Greensville. It was about three hundred miles away and in those days —specially with my own car—that was nothing. I was always anxious to see what was happening back in Florida. Plus, back on my old stompin' grounds, I could usually find some purr tongue. (That's the word us country boys used for clitoris.)

Right around in here, I also decided to get married. Now I know that sounds sudden, but believe me, that's how it happened. I've always been one to do something on the spur of the moment.

Eileen was a beautician in Columbus, Ohio, in these years. I met her through my friend Billy Brooks, who had just started playing trumpet with Lowell. Billy came from Cincinnati, and back then he was going with a chick named T who came from Columbus.

Well, Billy married T and that got me to thinking: Why not me? Billy and I were running together a lot and it seemed like a good idea. Besides, Eileen was really a lovely chick and we had a very smooth relationship. So when the band went to Atlanta, Eileen came along, and she made me very happy; I always liked the idea of having a wife and a family, and this seemed like the right moment for the thing to get started.

It wasn't. We weren't together for very long. A couple of months after we got married, I decided to quit Lowell's band and go on my own. And because I was on the road so much, the marriage was doomed from the start.

Maybe I should have known that you can't tell enough about a person after three weeks to decide about something as serious as marriage. But I was the kind of cat who followed his own instincts. And back then it seemed like a pretty hip idea.

We found a place in Columbus on East Lang Street. We lived with a lady who owned a big house, and we stayed in the upstairs part. I wasn't there more than a couple of weeks, though, when it was time to hit the road again.

As best I can tell, the marriage broke down for two reasons: First,

I just wasn't there. And there ain't no substitute for being with the one you love. Eileen couldn't travel with me because she had this good gig as a beautician. She had her own following of customers—they loved her—and there was no reason to give 'em up. So we literally drifted apart.

The other thing was her drinking. She started doing it in a big way. When I'd get home—maybe once or twice every six months—I'd see her boozing and I didn't dig it. Just never liked to see women drink.

Mary Jane used to drink when I was with her in Greensville. And as much as I loved that woman, it still bothered me. My attitude is hypocritical, I know. I drink. So where do I get off telling women what they should or shouldn't do?

If I find a woman is doing a lot of drinking, I don't complain and I don't try to change her ways. I just split. Maybe that's a strange attitude, but that's how I think.

With Eileen, it could be that I actually contributed to her drinking. Being gone for so long must have made her lonely. But in my mind, I didn't have any choice. I was worrying about eating. There were still periods when I couldn't find work. So if I was lucky enough to have nineteen straight gigs in nineteen straight days, I played nineteen straight gigs in nineteen straight days. That was my life.

Eileen and I didn't officially get divorced till sometime later—1953 or so—but the thing didn't last more than twelve or sixteen months.

Before that, something else broke up: my thing with Lowell. Now Lowell was a very likable dude, and I dug him in many ways. Like Mr. Pit or Jack Lauderdale, he was one of the cats who encouraged me and helped me on my way. Our relationship was always good, and that's why I quit—I wanted to keep it that way.

Lowell was a flashy, flamboyant cat back then, and he loved having people around him. He knew how to party, and that was fine by me. I'd always been more of a loner, but I could understand Lowell's attitude. He was a big star, and he got a kick out of playing the part.

We were pretty tight. He knew he could trust me. I got along with most everyone, and I think that's 'cause I understood how to keep things to myself. Mama taught me that. She taught me to keep my mouth shut.

"The most vicious weapon is the tongue," Mama said, "and it can hurt *you* worse than anyone."

Mama also said, "A dog who will bring a bone, will carry one."

So I didn't forget my country learning, and I was able to form nice friendships with many cats in the band. Especially Lowell. We could confide in each other and know it wouldn't go any further.

But at a certain point—long round 1952—Lowell and I began to have our difficulties over bread. That was a touchy subject, and rather than jeopardize the good feelings between us, I decided to cool it on out. That way we could remain friends. That's what happened, and to this day I can truthfully say that I love Lowell.

When something turns bad for me, I tend to get angry. And that's a state I should always avoid. If a cat wrongs me, and if I haven't had time to free myself from the situation, then the guy is as good as dead as far as I'm concerned.

You could come tell me that a certain cat who did me wrong has been run over by a truck. I won't be glad, I won't be sad. It won't mean nothing to me. When I cancel a person, that's it. Like a canceled check. They become grains of sand; I just don't pay them any mind.

A few cats who have worked for me have done some raunchy shit. I've canned them. If they return to me in three or four months and tell me that they need their gig back to keep their mama from dying, I still don't budge. Once my mind's made up, that's it. So I always try to dance around those nasty confrontations. If you wash yourself in anger, you never have clean hands.

I told you how I had played behind T-Bone Walker and Joe Turner. I saw that those guys were singles. When I met them, they were using Lowell's band because we happened to share the gig with them. And they'd use whatever musicians were around town. They'd pick up what they needed.

In my own foolhardy, half-crazy way, I figured I could do the same.

Funny thing about me: I believed I could do whatever I set my mind on. Didn't occur to me that these were heavy dudes who had already made it. No, I was hell-bent on trying it for myself. I wanted to be a single and travel alone.

So that's what I did. I'm not sure how, but the Billy Shaw Agency in New York started representing me. Lowell might have told them about me, since they were also booking him. Or it might have been through Howard Lewis, the big promoter in Texas. Anyway, they signed me up and I was soon on my way, more alone than ever before.

Being alone was nothing new. I never had a roommate when I was with Lowell—not unless I was forced to—'cause I wanted to be able to entertain women friends whenever I wanted. It was important that I stay flexible.

Being with Lowell taught me how to take care of myself under new sets of circumstances. And that came first. It had to. I knew that when you broke it down, no one cared about me as much as I cared about myself.

Now I was about to take this new step, to go for broke on my own. Sure, I had these apprehensions and doubts. But I hated the idea of falling on my ass and making a fool of myself so much that I knew I'd find a way to avoid it.

I met a gal in Atlanta who was a taxi driver and got her to drive for me—another impulsive act on my part. Little by little, we started hitting some towns and clubs and theaters—the Showboat in Philadelphia, the Flame Showbar in Detroit, the Apollo in New York.

For the most part, I was still broke, but I was also free to romp and play—free to starve, but also free to survive.

Struggling as a Single

I came up at a strange time in music. I was caught right in the middle. The swing era had blossomed when I was a kid, but as I became a man, modern jazz was appealing more and more to young musicians, cats who were really interested in playing.

The early fifties were a good time to be alive, a good era for music. It was something like a baseball team: You had the youngsters whc were eager and full of enthusiasm and new ideas, and you had the veterans who couldn't run as fast as the kids, but who could sure as hell outthink them.

No one was giving us any real breaks. Back then you didn't find the kind of money in the music business—at least not on the black side— that there is today. We had to make our own breaks, force our own way, scratch and scuffle any way we could.

Sometimes I think I made it 'cause I was stupid; I just didn't know anything better than to keep at it. This single act, for example, was probably something I shouldn't have done until much later. I had a secure gig with Lowell, and there was no way I could tell how I was going to do alone. But I loved the idea of working for myself. And being pigheaded, I figured I could now lead my own life with no questions asked.

I'd never give such advice to anyone else. In fact, I always say that you shouldn't haul off and cuss out your landlord until you're sure you have another place to go; the landlord might put your ass on the street.

I mentioned to you that I hooked up with the Billy Shaw Agency in New York. That was in '51 or '52. And I can still remember that first meeting with Billy when he laid it on the line with me; he told me something which scared me, but it was something which I'll never forget:

"Look, kid, any time the Shaw Agency doesn't fulfill its duties towards you, you don't need the Shaw Agency. But any time you don't perform for us, we don't need you."

This was some pretty cold-blooded shit. I was only twenty-one or twenty-two then and the business world was all so new and strange to me. But I loved hearing it; I understood—right off the bat—that the man was talking truthfully.

I wouldn't want to characterize my relationship with the Shaw Agency as all business. Far from it. Billy's wife, Lee, also worked there, and I've never known a kinder or sweeter woman. She was like a mother to me, and I can't tell you how I adored that lady.

She brought me Jewish candy called halvah from her neighborhood which was so rich and delicious that I ate it till my stomach ached. Outside of Mama and Mary Jane, I can't think of a warmer, more genuine woman.

It was also in New York—right around this time—that I signed with Atlantic Records. The thing with Jack and Swingtime had been funny for some time. I'm not sure what happened. But now Jack was about to close up his recording operation, and I was more or less on the loose.

I was staying at the Braddock Hotel at 126th and Eighth Avenue in Harlem when Herb Abramson and Ahmet Ertegun came to see me about making records for them. Atlantic was a tiny label then. There was hardly anyone except Ahmet, Herb, Herb's wife, Miriam, and a doctor who was a silent partner.

I can't remember the terms—if there were any—and I can't remember the details. I was just happy to have someone else interested in letting me record. There wasn't much to talk about. They must have heard a couple of my things—maybe "Baby, Let Me Hold Your Hand" or "Kissa Me, Baby"—and now they wanted me to sing for them.

The relationship with Atlantic Records proved to be one of the happiest in my life. They were people who understood me, and what we had was much, much more than a business agreement.

Later in 1952 and a couple of times in '53, I cut my first records for Atlantic. I still hadn't given up the Nat Cole/Charles Brown thing completely, and some of those tunes—"Funny, But I Still Love You"—were in the old vein. Others—especially "Mess Around," which Ahmet wrote—sounded more like me. And there were also throwbacks to my Swingtime items: "It Should Have Been Me," done on one of those early Atlantic dates, reminded me of my old "Kissa Me, Baby."

But I still didn't have my own band yet, and most of the songs and charts were not mine; Jesse Stone, who worked for Atlantic, wrote the arrangements.

New York never became my home. I didn't have a home—not after splitting from Eileen. I just lived in one hotel or another. When someone wanted to write me or send me something, I gave them 565 Fifth Avenue as my address—the Shaw Agency.

I still wasn't earning big money—especially compared to the white artists who had a hit record or two. With Lowell, when I was getting $50 a night, I might have made $12,000 in a year. As a single, sometimes I got $75 a night, but my yearly income remained more or less the same because I wasn't working as often.

The struggling hadn't stopped—not by a long shot. There'd still be long, long droughts before the rainfall, and money was something which continued to worry the hell out of me.

This was also a period in my life when I spent some time in New Orleans—several months at a time. I lived at the Foster Hotel, which was only a couple of blocks away from the Dew Drop Inn—Frank Painia's place, the heart of all the musical activities.

There were good sounds in New Orleans back then—this was 1953 —and I sat in with as many of the cats as I could. The blues were brewing down there, and the stew was plenty nasty. I was experimenting with my own voice and doing fewer and fewer imitations.

I made a record with Guitar Slim, and that turned out to be a big smash, though at the time it was just another gig, another way to earn some pocket change.

Guitar Slim—whose real name was Eddie Jones—played extremely good blues on the electric guitar, and he sang too. He was a country boy, and I liked him very much. One day he mentioned that he had a record date and asked whether I would like to play piano on it. Course I would.

Well, I wound up producing the tunes and writing the charts off the top of my head. The hit was called "The Things That I Used to Do," and someone later told me it wound up selling a million records. We also did a song called "Well, I Done Got Over It."

Maybe "producing" is too big a word. What happened was really this: We got in the studio and I took over. Wasn't anything I had planned. It evolved naturally. We needed some riffs, we needed some ideas, and everyone was pleased to let me lead the way.

Around this same time, I recorded one of Guitar's tunes—"Feelin' Sad"—on my own, so we both gave each other something of ourselves.

Five or six years later, Guitar was dead. It happened in a way which shook me up. He had played a gig in Lake Charles and driven all the way back to New Orleans. That was common in those days. I had done it with many cats, many, many times. After a job, we just piled in the car and drove all the night long till we could hardly see.

Well, Guitar made it back to New Orleans and was only four blocks from his home when he fell asleep at the wheel and ran into a bulldozer. That was it.

I wasn't exactly prospering in New Orleans, but I was making out. I had a fine girlfriend whose name was Rudell. And I was working from time to time, though nothing spectacular was happening.

I had one record session with Atlantic while I was there. Jerry Wexler and Ahmet Ertegun came in town and recorded me with a pickup band. We did some blues, as I remember, and a tune called "Don't You Know, Baby?" By this time I was much more aggressively into my own style. I still didn't have my own band, though, and that kept me from being able to completely express myself.

I had seen a couple of my records sell, but you could hardly call me well-known. I was still searching, still on the streets, still after any work I could nail down.

My social life centered around finding gigs. I can't really say that I ever hung out with anyone. If I went to a club, it was in the hopes of sitting in and maybe finding work. I always had a purpose and a motive. Loud parties, large crowds, being out with the gang—none of these things interested me. And the same's true today. I'm still alone.

Of all the people I've met in my life, I'd have to struggle hard to find five I'd call my friends, people I can really count on. And that's my doing. I'm just not the type to have scores of long-lasting, intimate friendships.

Touring the country and playing singles had its nice moments. The grind was wicked, the drives endless, but there were also some laughs and pleasures:

I remember one night in Hattiesburg, Mississippi, when T-Bone Walker and I happen to be on the same bill. After the gig, we go back to our rooms. And you know we ain't staying in no Sheraton or no Hilton. We're in a rooming house owned by an elderly lady.

T-Bone and I get into a friendly game of blackjack which lasts all night. By the time the sun comes up, I've won just about all of T-Bone's money—maybe a couple of thousand dollars. He only has $80 left, and they're all in ones. This is bread he's been sitting on. All the bills are flat and wet from his sweat.

"All right, man," he says, "let's go with this."

And he puts his last $80 on the table.

I feel the money and can see that it's a lot. But I don't bother to count. What difference does it make? I've been winning all night.

I deal. I'm cool at 20. T-Bone has something like a tre and a deuce to start with. Then I hit him with another tre. Then a four. Then another four.

And at the precise moment I hit him with a five—just enough to make 21—the landlady walks through the door. She's an elderly Christian-type woman, very kind, and wanting to know if she can fix us breakfast. She sees T-Bone taking the money from me and she starts into scolding him:

"Son, I got to tell you something. The Lord ain't going to bless you. No, he's not. Taking money from a blind man like that. You going to be sorry one of these days. It's a shame 'fore God."

Now T-Bone's so frustrated he really wants to say something like, "Look, bitch, this man done beat me out of thousands of dollars and you going to come here and give me a hard time!" But he doesn't. And that's one of the reasons I respect T-Bone. He treats this elderly lady right.

"No, ma'am, I'm not taking his money. He's won a few dollars from me."

"Well, maybe so," she says, "but to take from the blind is something that just ain't right."

When she leaves the room, T-Bone starts yelling like an innocent man trapped on death row: "She come in here and tell me that the Lord ain't going to bless *me!* Hell, he ain't been blessing me all goddamn night!"

So I say, "I'm gonna write a song about it."

"Well, you need to," T-Bone shoots back.

And I do. I call it "Blackjack," and sometime later I record it for Atlantic:

> *Now let me tell you people about this*
> *Blackjack game,*
> *It's caused me nothing but trouble,*

And I've only myself to blame.
Hey hey yeah, how unlucky can one man be,
Every quarter I get, Blackjack takes away from me.

My friends don't come around me because
I've been so blind,
Can't even borrow a nickel
Now I've almost lost my mind.

I sat there with two tens, I thought I'd have some fun,
The dealer hit sixteen with a five
Just enough to make twenty-one.
Hey hey yeah, how unlucky can one man be,
Every quarter I get, Blackjack takes away from me.

This blackjack game was one of the ways I got to know T-Bone real well. Many other times we were on the same bill and stayed at the same rooming houses. After a while, I'd be singing a couple of T-Bone's old blues songs.

There was one, I remember, which they called "Mr. Charles' Blues" that I recorded in New Orleans for Atlantic. The title is misleading, 'cause it was really T-Bone's tune.

Later on, I also made a record of "I Want a Little Girl," a blues ballad I'd been listening to ever since I was a kid. It was T-Bone and Pee Wee Crayton's versions which made lasting impressions on me, and when I sang the song myself, I tried to put as much feeling behind it as they did.

Around this time—when I was out as a single—I happened to be in Kansas City for a week or so between gigs. I had some spare time to go out looking for sessions.

I met up with Miles Davis. He was playing a club three blocks down from my hotel, and he invited me to sit in. We jammed all night long. Miles turned out to be a nice cat, and I liked listening to his growling, crackling voice. Course I'd always loved the way he played trumpet. For the period, he was into very modern music, and that suited me fine.

I hooked up with Al Hibbler, who's also blind, and there's a funny little story to tell you about him and me in Chicago. I've heard the incident told some other ways. But that's true of many things which have happened to me; the stories get twisted.

Someone once told me a story of how I walked in a bar and set everyone up, bragging that I was going to buy a drink for every man and woman in the joint. I'm here to tell you that I ain't ever done that in my life, and I never will. Now back to Hibbler.

Al and me were staying at the same hotel—the Persian at Sixty-third and Cottage Grove—and I went to hear him sing at the Chez Paree. Afterward we all decided to get a bite to eat, and at about four or five in the morning we came back to the hotel. Al asked me up to his room.

There were two girls up there with Al, and neither one of 'em belonged to me. Now Al happened to have a few trophies sitting on the dresser and, by accident, one of the girls knocked one to the floor.

"Hey, man, get away from there," Al said to me.

I was over by the dresser, so I could understand why Al assumed it was me. I waited for the girl to speak up, but she didn't.

"No, man, I haven't touched no trophy," I finally had to say.

Few seconds later she knocked over another trophy, this time on purpose. I suppose she was curious to see how two blind cats might fuck up each other in a fight. Can't say. But it was a rotten thing for her to do.

This time Al was steaming.

"I'm going to kick your ass," he screamed at me.

"No need for you to do that," I said.

But there was no calming him down. He couldn't see, and I couldn't convince him that it wasn't me. I tried to stay on the lookout. I could hear Al picking up a chair and coming after me, so I moved from the dresser to the door. He chased me into the hallway with the chair, and I reached the elevator before he did.

Now if you had asked me, "Ray, are you scared?" I'd have said, "Yeah, I'm scared." I ain't one of those cats who claim to be brave.

I suddenly remembered something that a friend had told me about this elevator. And it was something which, in the heat of the moment, I was certain Al had forgotten. If you pressed the button, the elevator door would open, but there wouldn't be any car there. Just the empty shaft. So I pressed the button. And I knew when Al heard the doors open he'd think I was getting on the elevator and he'd get on and try to smash the chair over my head. My plan was to step aside as the door opened and let Al fall down the shaft.

Fortunately, Al's girl—the chick who started all this—followed him into the hallway and stopped him just in time. But I must confess that I would have let him go. I knew Al had been drinking, and I understood that. But at the same time, when someone's trying to hurt me, I lose my sense of restraint. I wasn't mad; in fact, not being enraged was what enabled me to plan my strategy.

If Mama knew this story, she'd rise from her grave to scold me. I know it gives you a bad impression of me, but it's a truthful reflection of how I'm prone to take care of myself in unusual situations.

Later on, Al and I laughed about it and agreed that we had both been stupid.

There's another story about me and elevators which happened many years later. It's another reason why I always put one foot in an elevator before I actually walk inside.

We were in Buenos Aires this time and one of the promoter's assistants—a very kind man—was escorting me to the gig. The concert hall was housed in a building which had the type of service elevator that could only be opened with a key.

My Argentinian friend opened the doors to the elevator all right, but he failed to see that the car wasn't there. I was standing next to him when he stepped into the elevator and then vanished; he fell four or five floors to the basement.

My valet and I ran downstairs to the bottom to try to get him out. We were afraid that someone might get on the elevator, take it to the basement, and crush him. We didn't know any Spanish, but by yelling "Elevator! Elevator!" we finally got to him and saw that he was unconscious, a mess of broken bones.

I went to see him in the hospital. He'd survived the fall. And the thing which broke me up—I mean this really tore into me—were his first words when he came to:

"How is Ray? Was Ray hurt?"

Well, I couldn't take that. I broke down and cried like a baby.

But back in the early fifties I was trying to avoid other kinds of falls, just trying to stay alive as a single. That's why I was so happy to get a gig playing piano in a band led by Joe Morris, a trumpeter.

Now Joe had a big hit then, a tune called "Anytime, Anyplace, Anywhere," sung by Laurie Tate. So they sent him and Laurie and his band out on the road. Man, I learned a lot on that trip.

I thought the tour was going to be real smooth and slick. After all, the man had a big record. But don't you believe it. They gave this poor cat such bum equipment that most every day something broke down —either the bus or his own car. It was a rough tour—out to Utah and New Mexico, over to Alabama and Georgia. Nothing seemed to work.

Joe was as sweet as he could be, and even though I didn't have shit, I felt sorry for him, so I wrote some charts for the band and from time to time loaned him some bread. And that taught me something. You might have a smash on the charts, but that didn't mean nothing. You still had to haul your ass out on the road. You still had to live like a dog. You still had to scuffle.

Maybe some of the white artists with hits were living pretty good. I don't know. But believe me: Cats like Joe Morris were hurting bad.

Sometime later in 1954, after three years on the road by myself, I found myself playing a gig in Philadelphia. As usual, I was forced to use any band which happened to be there. Usually it took me a day or so to whip one in shape, but this group was impossible. It just wasn't working; the cats were so off they literally hurt my ears. I struggled with them for two days, trying to straighten them out, but I might as well have been trying to drive a truck through a brick wall. That was punishment. I was disgusted and discouraged.

I like music to be precise. I like it right. Even if I met up with cats who could play, it always took two grueling days for them to get used to my moves. Meanwhile, I was suffering. I was living with frustration of wrong notes and missed cues. And that aggravation stayed with me, ate at me, gnawed at me until I became sick.

I knew that with my own band I could impose my own musical discipline and get to hear my music the way I knew it *must* sound. Pickup bands were too painful, and this one in Philly was the last straw. So I called the Shaw Agency and told them I wanted to form a band of my own.

"What?"

"You heard right. My own band."

"You realize the cost? You understand the problems? You're barely making enough for you to eat, much less a whole band."

"Doesn't matter. I think I can do it. Fact, I know I can."

So it went, back and forth. Finally, they saw how sincere I was and mumbled something about Ruth Brown, who had some big hits then. She didn't have a band, and Shaw said maybe if I got one together I could tour with her.

So on the small promise of doing a little work with Ruth Brown, I went down to Texas to put together a group. My very first.

Texas

Two important things happened to me in Texas: I got my own band and I got married again. First, the romance.

In 1953 I was in Houston for a gig, and I was invited to a radio station where a disc jockey—a cat named King B—interviewed me. He happened to ask who my favorite gospel groups were. "Guess what?" I said, "one of my favorites comes from right here in Houston—Cecil Shaw and the Cecil Shaw Singers."

One of the Cecil Shaw singers was listening, and when the show was over she called the station to thank me for the plug. Would I like to meet Cecil, she wanted to know. I said sure.

Cecil came to see me at the Crystal Hotel. We had a nice visit and before he left he asked if I'd like to meet the young lady who had called me. A few days later he introduced us.

Her name was Della. I called her B 'cause her middle name was Beatrice. And I liked her right away. She was a singer, a quiet lady who didn't smoke or drink, very shy. I liked that in her. Gabby women drive me nuts.

I had to split town for other gigs, but I kept up the courtship over the phone and through the mails. I called her several times, and I wrote her several letters on the portable typewriter I always carried with me —the same kind sighted people use.

The thing got hotter and hotter, and finally I convinced B to move along with me to Dallas. B had an enormous family in Houston and I knew I had to get her out of town. The ordeal with Louise and her folks was still a fresh memory inside my brain. I didn't want a repeat performance of that nightmare; couldn't deal with even the possibility of being hassled.

There were other reasons Houston didn't appeal to me. Back in '52, David Newman and I had a nasty incident there.

Early in my career, when I was still touring with Lowell, I met David Newman, the cat everyone calls Fathead. He and I became fast friends. He had one of the kindest, sweetest dispositions of anyone I'd ever known. Later on, he joined my band and was with me—playing tenor in his own wonderful style—for nearly twenty years. But while I was out doing singles, he'd sometimes come along with me and drive my car—not as my driver, but as my pal.

On this particular night in Houston the cops decided to stop us. They gave no reason, though soon we saw it was because they didn't like David's hair. He had a conk, or a do. And they thought he was trying to look white.

Anyway, they kicked me out of the car.

"You blind, boy?" one of the cops asked.

"Yeah," I said.

"Well, you better find a way back, 'cause we're taking this other nigger and his fucked-up hairdo down to the station."

They took Fathead to headquarters and roughed him up. And they left me alone on the side of the road with my car, a '52 98 Olds, the first brand-new car I ever had.

Well, I managed to find a way to the police station because I knew that, if I didn't, David wasn't going to get out. I paid $25 and they let him go, without ever telling us what the charges were—if there really were any.

Back then they didn't need no charges. They'd bust you if they felt like it. They'd call you nigger, motherfucker, or anything else which tickled their fancy. And the worst thing you could do was talk back. Try to explain, try to defend yourself, try to reason—that's all the excuse the cops needed to bust you upside the head. If you didn't want to get fucked up, you just kept quiet and bit your tongue.

In those days it was even worse if you were arrested by a black cop, because many of those cats had been brainwashed. If a so-called brother busted you, he might drag your ass down to the station and call you nigger in front of the white cops. And that made you want to kill him that much worse.

So Houston wasn't my favorite city. It always seemed wet and muggy, and so much other raunchy shit had happened there. A promoter slapped Little Richard onstage; Johnny Ace blew his brains out playing Russian roulette there. There was just something about the town that didn't seem right to me, although I might have just been looking for excuses to get away from B's family.

I got my way. B and I—still unmarried—moved to Dallas. I knew the town and I dug it. I had been there a lot and stayed at the Green Acres Motel, just behind the Empire Room where I used to play. And I had several friends in Dallas besides David—John Dee and Rayfield who drove cab, and Buster Smith, who played some of the filthiest alto you'd ever care to hear.

Another guy, Jeff Brown, who had been Lowell's bus driver, was also driving cab in Dallas, and once my band was formed he became my manager.

Even though there wasn't a hell of a lot of money to live on, we managed. During our early days there B went out and got a job at a drugstore to help pay our bills. And I was happy to have her all to myself, away from her family.

My first band was a bitch, one of the tightest little bands around—only seven pieces. I loved it. I got to do everything I wanted. It tapped all my resources. I wrote songs, wrote arrangements, played alto and piano, and sang. In a band that small there was no skating. Everyone could hear everyone else. Each man literally had to be on his toes. We all stood, and we all played our asses off.

David was on baritone—later he switched to tenor; a cat named A.D. also played tenor; Joe Bridgewater and Clanky White played trumpet; Jimmy Bell was on bass and Bill Peeples on drums.

That gave me five horns when I was playing alto, four horns when I was singing and playing piano. This was the sound I'd been looking for. I knew I needed a tenor, a baritone, an alto, and two trumpets. I didn't want to use a trombone; I figured that the fast runs I liked to write would be too tough for most trombonists to cut.

My theory was this: If I found cats who could play jazz, I could fix it so they could play my other little items—the rhythm-and-blues things. If a guy can handle jazz, that means he's a good musician, and it's easy for him to switch over to less complicated styles.

Each of my horn players had to be able to stretch out on jazz tunes, play a lot of complicated figures and also have that basic, bluesy, down-home sound. Sometimes the band would be burning, but other times it'd be moaning.

I didn't know any other group with this exact setup. Tiny Bradshaw and Louis Jordan both had superb little bands, but the instrumentation was different than mine.

Yeah, this was a new thrill for me. Finally I was shaping my entire musical environment, from top to bottom.

These are the years—'53, '54, '55—when I became myself. I opened up the floodgates, let myself do things I hadn't done before, created sounds which, people told me afterward, had never been created before. If I was inventing something new, I wasn't aware of it. In my mind, I was just bringing out more of me. I started taking gospel lines and turning them into regular songs.

Now, I'd been singing spirituals since I was three, and I'd been hearing the blues for just as long. These were my two main musical currents. So what could be more natural than to combine them? It didn't take any thinking, didn't take any calculating. All the sounds were there, right at the top of my head.

Many of those first tunes were adaptations of spirituals I had sung in quartets back in school. "You Better Leave That Woman Alone" was originally something called "You Better Leave That Liar Alone." "Lonely Avenue" was based on a spiritual that Jess Whitaker used to sing with the Pilgrim Travelers. "Talkin' 'Bout You" was another song which I had been singing my whole life in another form.

None of the spirituals had copyrights. How could they? Black folk had been singing 'em through the hollow logs as far back as anyone could remember. And often my new tunes would be based on three or four gospel numbers—not just one.

But the basic line, the basic structure, the basic chord changes were throwbacks to the earliest part of my life on earth. Nothing was more familiar to me, nothing more natural.

Imitating Nat Cole had required a certain calculation on my part. I had to gird myself; I had to fix my voice into position. I loved doing it, but it certainly wasn't effortless. This new combination of blues and gospel was. It required nothing of me but being true to my very first music.

Now with my band I could rebuild my own little musical world that I first heard in Greensville. In fact, this was the heaviest writing period of my life. When Ahmet Ertegun or Jerry Wexler at Atlantic sent me songs they thought I should record, I often didn't like them. That inspired me to begin writing more tunes of my own.

Atlantic let me record anything I wanted to. They never said, "No, do our songs, not yours." They trusted me and left me alone.

The same thing had been true with Jack Lauderdale when I was recording for Swingtime. And it would be no different years later when I would start making records for ABC.

I've never had what they call a producer to oversee me. I've always produced myself. And during my Atlantic days, I always came into the studio with the tunes already picked and the arrangements already written. There was nothing left for a producer to do.

You might ask: How could a young kid like me—at twenty-two or twenty-three or twenty-four—have that kind of power? I still wasn't much of a name. And I certainly didn't have any right to go round demanding or dictating a goddamn thing. Well, these record people saw that I was developing and that I needed space to find myself. Even though I was young and tender, they let me make my own mistakes, let me produce my own small triumphs.

Only one time at Atlantic—and that was a very minor incident— did one of the cats suggest that I listen to Fats Domino and maybe do something on the style of "Blueberry Hill." I told the guy that I was *for* Fats, but that I wasn't Fats. I was Brother Ray. That quieted him down.

I looked on Jack Lauderdale, Ahmet and Neshui Ertegun, Jerry Wexler, and later the folks at ABC like I looked on Mr. Pit back in Greensville. He could have made me get up from that stool when I was trying to bang the piano at age three. "Get away from me, kid," he could have said. But he didn't. He saw the love and the music inside my eyes. And he helped me. Instead of chasing me away, he made me feel good. He sat me down. He said, "This is a piano, boy. Just play it."

So I was lucky. Lucky to have my own band at this point in my career. Lucky to be able to construct my musical building to my exact specifications. And lucky in another way:

While I was stomping around New Orleans, I had met a trumpeter named Renolds Richard who by this time was in my band. One day he brought me some words to a song. I dressed them up a little and put them to music. The tune was called "I Got a Woman," and it was another one of those spirituals which I refashioned in my own way.

"I Got a Woman" was my first real smash, much bigger than "Baby, Let Me Hold Your Hand." This spiritual-and-blues combination of mine was starting to hit.

But even though this record, made toward the end of 1954, was very big, that didn't mean I was making very big money. It was like that story I told before about Joe Morris. He had a hit, but he still had to hustle like crazy. Well, now *I* was Joe Morris. The success of my record meant I'd get to work more often. But the black promoters—the men I dealt with—still paid very little. And as for royalties, well, they took a long, long time to start coming in, and when they did I used the money for things like new tires for the car.

At the time this was happening, not everyone approved. I got letters accusing me of bastardizing God's work. A big-time preacher in New York scolded me before his congregation. Many folks saw my music as sacrilegious. They said I was taking church songs and making people dance to 'em in bars and nightclubs.

Must tell you that none of those reactions bothered me. I'd always thought that the blues and spirituals were close—close musically, close emotionally—and I was happy to hook 'em up. I was determined to go all out and just be natural. Everything else would spring from that. I really didn't give a shit about that kind of criticism.

"Everyone has a point of view," Mama used to say to me, "and everyone is entitled to one. So, don't judge them. Leave them alone."

I knew well in advance of any controversy that nothing was going to bother me. I wouldn't have done it if I had believed it was wrong. My first concern was seeing whether Ray Charles as Ray Charles—not as Nat Cole or as Charles Brown—was going to work.

Besides, the church was something which couldn't be taken out of my voice even if I had wanted to take it out. Once I decided to be natural, I was gone. It's like Aretha: She could do "Stardust," but if she did *her* thing on it, you'd hear the church all over the place.

On the other hand, I've always believed in separating religious music and popular music as far as my own recordings go. I could never do both simultaneously. In fact, I once turned down a nice little piece of change by refusing to do an album of spirituals.

I don't put down other singers who record commercially in both fields. (I always dug Sam Cooke, for instance; dug his gospel work and dug his pop songs.) What they do is their business. I respect them, and

I respect their art. But I was raised to believe that you can't serve two gods.

I might do a spiritual album someday, but if I do, I'll give the money away—to a church or a charity—unless I decide to change careers and earn my living exclusively as a gospel singer.

As I told you, I wasn't what you would call religious as a boy. But I did believe in God and I was taught to say the Lord's Prayer every night. I still do.

This was the happiest period of my life so far. Not that this was the pinnacle. As I achieved one thing, I started formulating other goals in my mind. Doing my gospel-and-blues stuff wasn't the answer to all my prayers.

I began thinking: One day it'd be nice to play Carnegie Hall. One day it'd be nice to record a country song. I'd also secretly held the hope that I'd get to sing with violins and cellos ever since I'd heard Frank Sinatra do "Nancy (With the Laughing Face)." I was crazy about that song; the strings sounded so lush and beautiful. And I knew it'd be a thrill to hear all those romantic instruments behind me.

There weren't that many black singers back then who recorded with strings. I remember Nat Cole doing "Nature Boy," but us rhythm-and-blues musicians had had a label slapped on us—strings were out.

So I had my private goals. I didn't discuss them with anyone. I didn't let them eat at me or drive me crazy. And I'm not sure I really expected to see them come true. But they were there.

Roughing It

My career never zoomed, so don't wait for the page when I'm going to tell you: Baby, this was the day it happened. No, my progress was slow. Steady, but very, very slow.

That summertime of '54 in Texas wasn't any picnic. I remember leaving Houston at 6:00 A.M. one morning for El Paso, seven hundred miles away, where we had a gig backing up Ruth Brown. I had bought two new cars for the band—a two-door Ford and a De Soto Firedome station wagon. We drove like maniacs, even though you weren't supposed to drive new cars too fast because of the thin oil. We had to be at the gig by nine that night, and we made it, in spite of all kinds of car trouble. But there was no time to shower or eat, just barely enough time to put a little water where it would do the most good.

We rushed to the bandstand, set up, and hit at 9:45. For about fifteen minutes I did my own shit and then Ruth Brown came out and sang her big record—"Mama, He Treats Your Daughter Mean"—and we backed her up, playing that song for the first time. Everything else she did was new for us, and yet I do believe we got the music right.

I had the kind of band which could knock out a good riff once it was set for them. And most of the material being sung was simple variations on blues changes. So we were able to fall right into the groove.

Within nine days or so, we played six or seven dates with Ruth. The next night after El Paso we were booked in Alexandria, Louisiana, which was about a thousand miles away. Well, after working a four-hour dance we didn't get to our hotel till two-thirty. We didn't get to sleep till three or four, and the next morning we were up at eight. We grabbed something to eat and were on the road by nine. We drove all that day—till nine that night—and we still couldn't make it to Alexandria in time for the gig. Damn if we didn't try.

The grind was really a bitch. We didn't have a driver who could sleep while we played. Cats in the band did the driving, alternating among themselves. And we were always uptight about being picked up by small-town cops and getting hauled off to the constable.

I was being tested in this period. In 1954 the Shaw Agency was looking to see how I'd be accepted with the public around the country. I was a so-called artist now. I had my little songs out. Nothing as big as "Mama, He Treats Your Daughter Mean," but I did have "Mess Around" and "It Should Have Been Me" and "Funny, But I Still Love You" and "Heartbreaker." "I Got a Woman" hadn't come out quite yet.

Strange thing about my hits: I never tried for them. They happened or they didn't. I've never consciously made a single, for example, with a "hit side" in mind and then a "backup side."

Naturally, I wanted each tune I did to be a hit. And I liked each song I recorded or I wouldn't have sung it. When a record reached the stores and when we played at dances and clubs, I started seeing the reaction, and I concentrated on those numbers everyone seemed to like best.

To this day, I haven't really understood why some music clicks while other stuff just dies as far as the public goes. Course lots of it has nothing to do with notes. It's promotion and payola, but that was something in the mid-fifties which I knew nothing about.

In the recording studio I simply went for the throat every time. I approached each song like it was a winner, and I sang it and played it with all the conviction in my soul.

My money was still funny. Say a gig was worth $250. The Shaw Agency got 15 percent. Each of the cats would get $20. There were six other musicians besides me, plus my manager, Jeff Brown. That meant the cats were supposed to get $140 with $72.50 left over for me. But out of my $72.50 I had to pay all the expenses—the gas, the upkeep on the cars, all the extras. Many times there'd be nothing left.

On some nights, when the promoter didn't come through, we didn't get paid at all. But I still felt an obligation to pay the fellas. I gave them their $20, even though I might have asked to borrow it right back. But I always put the bread in my musicians' hands first. Then they had a choice of whether to lend it to me or not.

I never wanted to owe musicians money. I know some people think I'm tight—and I guess I am—but I'd be surprised if there's anyone who would claim that I beat him out of a dime.

Affluence separates people. Poverty knits 'em together.

You got some sugar and I don't; I borrow some of yours. Next month you might not have any flour; well, I'll give you some of mine.

That's how my band made it. We swam through a lot of shit together, we swallowed a lot of pride, but we managed to do what we needed to do.

Once in a while, there'd be a surprise on the road. I remember the time in San Antonio when we lost our tenor player. James Moody happened to be in town. He came by our gig and played with us all night, just for the fun of it. We had a ball, and he wouldn't even let me pay him. He was almost incensed that I offered. That's the kind of people he is.

I was still meeting musicians I had heard about and listened to— gospel singers like Alex Bradford, piano players like Amos Milburn, vocal groups like the Clovers.

Somewhere in the middle of the fifties, the pace started to pick up, and often it got furious. We were running from town to town without time to catch our breath. There was also something frantic about our music.

We were playing a lot of dances in this period and, as a result, a lot of things could explode in our faces. Some cat steps on another dude's foot without apologizing and boom—a fight. Someone calls someone else a motherfucker. Some woman comes in and sees another woman dry-fucking her man. Drunks. Knives. Razor blades. The whole bit.

And when fights started, the joint might erupt and everyone start swinging just for the hell of it. Course I was particularly edgy since I couldn't see if a punch or a knife or a bottle was heading my way. At the first sign of serious trouble, I'd duck by the side of the piano or even throw myself out a window. A piano's a pretty good thing to hide behind; you're protected by steel and wood. If a bullet can tear through that, well, your number's up anyway.

One day in Daytona Beach, Florida, the action got pretty wicked. A fight started, and a woman who was sitting right in front of me stood up to leave. Just at that instant she got clobbered by a bottle. Next thing I knew, her blood was flowing all over me and my piano. Not a pretty sight.

In Pittsburgh once, someone started a ruckus, and this time the police made a mistake. A cop fired his pistol in the air to calm the people down. Naturally, it had the opposite effect. The folk went berserk. They panicked. They stampeded. They started flying out windows and running for the doors like rats deserting a ship. It was wild. One poor lady fell down and got trampled by the others. When she was finally able to get up and managed to crawl through a window, her shoe got caught. Later, the owners of the joint sealed up the window —with the woman's shoe still in it—to remind everyone of what had happened. Never will forget that.

It was sometime around '59 that I played a dance for the last time. I knew this was the last one 'cause I promised myself if I got out alive, I'd never work a dance again. I was that scared.

There was a huge army base outside of Fayetteville, North Carolina, and on the first or the fifteenth of the month, we played our gig. That's when the boys got paid. The soldiers came into the city, and the money and the juice started to flow. These cats got pretty wild. They'd been caged up, and when you let 'em out, you'd better watch out.

A fight started. Two guys began firing shots at each other. An innocent bystander was shot in the leg. One of the two guys who began the brawl was shot dead in the mouth. The police arrived. And then someone stole a pistol from one of the cops. That enraged the police and they closed off the place—wouldn't let anyone leave—until they got their gun back. Meanwhile, we were corralled in there till they made a thorough search. They finally found the gun and we were allowed to split. Man, it was a wicked night. Being that afraid ain't good for nobody.

I've never used music as a stimulus to get crowds crazed with nervous energy. I realize that a lot of my music is hot and rhythmic, and of course I understand that people want to dance. But there's a difference between giving folks pleasure and driving 'em into a frenzy.

I've heard about performers who get crowds stirred up and then drop a handkerchief so everyone will fight over it. Never did that. Never wanted anyone to rip my clothes off or run up on the bandstand.

It's bad enough when it's calm. People always talk and joke among themselves. I can't make them stop chattering entirely, though I always want to. I want my show to be about music—not a bunch of bullshit surrounding the music. I want the attention paid to me, to what I'm singing and what me and my band are playing. I don't like distractions, and I'll never do anything to encourage a violent outburst of any kind. They scare me.

In the early days, many of the dives where we had gigs were just too rough to tame. All you could do was play and pray.

Family Dreams

When I married B, I was twenty-four or twenty-five, and I'd been fooling around for years. Don't want to be bragging, but the simple truth is that my relationships had been many. Being a musician and a jive-ass celebrity meant that I was exposed to girls every night. That was all right, but I was beginning to want something better—a sweeter, more sensible life.

What had all these women gotten me anyway? Many heavenly times —that's for sure. But now I wanted to feel something deeper. Something permanent. Something solid.

Around this time I lost the last member of my original family. In 1954 Mary Jane passed. She'd been sick for a long time, and I'd gone home and put her in a decent hospital near Greensville. I did all I could, but it was not enough.

I went home to her funeral, and it hurt me so bad. I loved that woman. If any man could claim two mamas, I could. Two women who had been devoted to me, who had given me all their finest feelings. So I went to Greensville to kiss Mary Jane good-bye. There was no way —not with flowers or with gifts—that I could ever tell her what she had meant. Like Mama, she gave me all her love.

Now I wanted many things I had never known: I wanted my own house; I wanted to come home to the same woman every night. I wanted to raise some kids, have someone carry on my name. I wanted to see me grow up again.

When I married, I was as genuine as any man. I wanted it to work. It wasn't a joke to me; it was for real. I told B about my other girl-friends. At some point, we talked about Louise, my daughter Evelyn, and my previous marriage to Eileen. These weren't things I washed her face with; no woman enjoys hearing about her man's other ladies. I simply told her that I'd seal off the past as best I could.

I let my girlfriends know B was now my woman, that we were together, so please not to contact me. I made a point of getting in touch with the ones in Dallas and Houston. I didn't want them to call the house; I didn't want them to send me letters.

I told B: "This is my part of the dresser; these are my drawers. That's your part over there; those drawers are yours. Let's respect each other's privacy. If one of those seals has a crack and something gets through, I want you to know that it won't be my doing. Let's say you happen to see a letter someone sends to me. The hippest thing you can do is leave it alone. Don't open it. Let's not go looking for trouble."

So we had an understanding: The past was the past. We put all our chips on the present.

A year or so after we were married, Ray, Jr., was born. The pregnancy wasn't easy. B had to stay in bed 60 or 70 percent of the time, and she was very weak. But we didn't want to lose the baby, and she took care of herself.

When little Ray was born, I was out of town, playing a gig some-where in Texas. A couple of days later, I came home to see my son. I was afraid to hold him. He was so small I was scared I'd hurt him. The doctor said that he was tender, but not *that* tender. Didn't make any difference. He felt like the most delicate creature I had ever touched.

By the time he was two or three months old, I got over my fear. And slowly I got into playing with him and roughing him around. He liked that as much as I liked being papa. And B was happy too. She had something to do besides sitting home and worrying about what I was doing or not doing out on the road.

B and I had a good twelve or thirteen years of marriage. Sometimes when I think about it, I'm surprised that we managed that long. The pressures on us both were very heavy, and yet we endured them for a long spell. When we were together, we were together. I give her a great deal of credit for putting up with me and my strange ways.

B may have thought my touring was going to be something like she had done with Cecil Shaw where they'd go out for a week or two and then be home for a couple of months. But that wasn't the case with me and my band in 1954.

I needed every gig I could get. If I was playing Chicago for one or two nights, I might not have another job for a week or two. But I still couldn't jump in the car and race down to Dallas. There wasn't enough time, and the bread wasn't there.

So B waited back home, in our little house on 2642 Eugene Street. She worried, I'm certain, and the hurt must have been painful and long-lasting.

The other tremendous burden on her was my drug habit. When we were first married, she didn't know about it. I never told my first wife Eileen, and I didn't see any need to tell B either. It would have just upset her, and, besides, I've always seen dope as a private matter.

B and I spent more time together than I had spent with Eileen or Louise. And in '54 and '55, I was doing more dope than I did in '48 and '49.

It wasn't long before she discovered what I was up to. I can't remember how. Could be that she found something unusual in the bathroom like a cotton ball lying in a burnt spoon, something left there by one of my partners who had come over to give me a fix.

But whatever it was, I know she didn't like it. She never forced the issue and she was never hard on my case. But I know it hurt her. She was at a loss and didn't know how to deal with it. She didn't bug me, but it had to be bugging her. Still, she stuck with me.

My life was what it was. Whatever it became, I made it so. Now I had a wife. I had a child. I was the leader of a little band. I was a blues singer, a rhythm-and-blues singer—or whatever the hell they were calling me—a recording artist of modest stature. I was also a man who still loved women and who enjoyed getting high.

Leading

I began writing more and more tunes, not usually out of inspiration, but out of necessity. I needed material to record and I needed stuff which suited me. Jerry and Ahmet would send me songs, but often I didn't like them so I'd work up something of my own. That's how most of my hits came to be written.

I always tried to get the lyrics first. That was the hardest part for me. If I could get my words straight, then I knew I could find a melody somewhere. If I liked a tune, I'd record it. I never believed in testing a song before the public. I couldn't expect the public to like something I didn't. That's why I always began with me.

In 1954, Jerry and Ahmet came down to Atlanta, since I didn't have any dates around New York, and I made my first recording with a band of my own. That's when we did "I Got a Woman," "Blackjack," and "Greenbacks." We used the equipment at a radio station, and every time they had to do the news, we had to stop playing.

Our session in Miami was scheduled after a gig, and we didn't get started recording till four in the morning. I had been singing all night, so my voice was hoarse as hell. Turned out all right, though: I did "A Fool for You," which became another small hit of mine and earned me a few pennies.

My head still wasn't into business at that point. I remember that the Atlantic people asked me if I wanted to give them the right to publish my songs. I said yes, sure, but I was really surprised to be asked. I had been assuming that they had the right all along. Basically, I was still wide-eyed and innocent about all the finer points of finance. Still, I was able to keep myself and my band together.

I never thought much about being a leader and, looking back, I think it happened naturally. I guess the other cats had some respect for me because I worked as hard or maybe harder than anyone else.

Discipline in those years wasn't a problem 99 percent of the time. Maybe once in a while someone would lumber up to the bandstand juiced and fall out during a set. When that happened, I wouldn't deal with the cat that night. I didn't believe in talking to people who were drunk or smashed. I'd be too upset and they'd be too messed up, and there was no real chance of getting my message across. I'd wait till the next day when all was calm. Then I'd make my point—slowly and deliberately:

"If that ever happens again," I'd say, "you're out. No questions, no discussions, no pleading, no second chances."

My voice would be low when I'd say that, and the cat would know —especially since it was the next day and the heat of the moment had passed—that I was for real.

That's just how Mama had done it with me.

Obviously I liked getting high in those days myself, so it wasn't a question of being too strict or sticking my nose in the other guys' personal business. They could do whatever they liked—just as I did my stuff—as long as it didn't fuck up their ability to play the way I wanted 'em to play.

My band was really shaping up. I found me three or four real motherfuckers, guys who could hold their own with anyone, anywhere.

I've already told you about Fathead; he practically became part of my own sound—that's how close we were. Donald Wilkerson, another tenor player, joined us, and, like Fathead, he was one of the best musicians I'd ever heard.

We played the famous circuit of black theaters for years and years —the Apollo in New York, the Regal in Chicago, the Royal in Baltimore, the Howard in Washington, D.C. But we were spending most of our time in the South, performing before strictly black audiences.

Traveling those Southern states, we were forced to live through some funny social situations. After all, we were a black band, and America wasn't exactly embracing us with love, affection, and equal opportunity.

We could be driving for hours and never find a gas station which would let us use the bathroom. If we stopped by the side of the road, we stood a chance of getting busted, so we'd open both doors of the car and piss between them. We could be hungry as bears and go half a day before we'd find a joint that would serve us. The race thing hit us where it hurt—in the stomach and in the balls.

Soon the wickedness started creeping into our professional life, and I found that I wasn't the right one to tolerate it.

There were a couple of ugly encounters in the middle fifties. One took place in Augusta, Georgia: A promoter insisted that a date we were about to play be segregated: the blacks upstairs and the whites downstairs. This was a concert-type situation. We hadn't faced the problem before, just because we'd mostly been playing dances.

I told the promoter that I didn't object to segregation, except that he had it backwards. I suggested the whites go upstairs and the blacks sit downstairs, in the so-called best seats. After all, I was black and it only made sense to have the black folk close to me.

Mama had always told me: "Don't burn the bridge that brought you over." No, I told the man, if he wanted to segregate, he'd have to do it the right way—*my* way.

Whatever little name I had, I'd earned by playing in front of black people. They were the ones who'd been supporting me, and I wasn't about to insult them.

Course he refused. And he threatened to sue. I didn't have much money, but I figured if a man wants to sue you, there ain't much you can do. Let him sue. But fuck it, I wasn't going to play.

And I didn't. And he sued. And I lost.

We went to court in Atlanta and it cost me $1500 or $2000 for breach of contract, plus his advertising and promotion expenses. That griped my ass, but at least the fucker didn't make me go against myself.

Around that time I also refused to play a segregated job up in Nashville. In this case, though, the promoter backed down and decided to let blacks and whites mingle.

Years later—in '62—it happened again in Baton Rouge. We demanded that the concert be integrated, and it was. Afterward I even got a call from the governor of Louisiana, Jimmy Davis. (He happened to be the same guy who wrote a song I did on one of my country-and-western albums, "You Are My Sunshine.")

"I am proud to say the Negroes acted better than the whites," the governor told me.

"All right, man. Whatever's fair," was all I could say in reply.

I don't go round shouting about it, but I was one of the first cats to get sued for refusing to play a Jim Crow job. And I think we were the first band to integrate music events in places like Nashville and Baton Rouge.

The more I saw, the more I realized how my own personal movement was limited. And the North was only a hair better than the South. Up there the hatred and prejudice was a bit more subtle, the hypocrisy a little slicker. You could change the lyrics, but the song was still the same everywhere you went.

Don't get me wrong: I never blamed all the white people in America. I didn't fault all of *any* one group. Lots of white cats were afraid if they served blacks at their lunch counters or let blacks use the bathrooms in their gas stations, they might lose their whole business. After all, there were actual laws on the books against integration of any kind.

Then there were the pressures of their friends. If a white dude was nice to a black, his partner might scream at him, "You a nigger lover or something? Next thing you know your daughter will be fucking a coon!"

On the other hand, I understood that the big Supreme Court decisions which were changing the laws about segregated schools were being made by white judges.

Still, every day I began to see that we were just starting to talk about getting certain things—freedom to go to a school, to eat in a truck stop, to piss in a bathroom—that should have been ours all along.

Like my musical career, my sense of social or racial conflict was something slow to build. It was a little item here, something else over there, until after a while it couldn't be ignored.

As a child, my country upbringing gave me one view of the world. In some ways, that view was distorted. And being blind kept me from having to look at the differences. Even though that earlier world was now being shattered, I knew enough to hold on to my country ways. I knew that being blind was suddenly an aid. I never learned to stop at the skin. If I looked at a man or woman, I wanted to see inside. Being distracted by shading or coloring is stupid. It gets in the way. It's something I just can't see.

The Girls

I was playing in Kentucky in 1955 when a promoter told me about a vocalist named Mary Ann Fisher who was gigging around Louisville and Fort Knox. I caught her act, liked her style, and decided to try out a little experiment. I asked her to join my band.

Immediately I started writing some material for her. I remember doing a chart of Ellington's "I Got It Bad," and there was also "What Kind of Man Are You?"—a tune of mine which we recorded a couple of years later.

I wrote another song—"This Little Girl of Mine"—and had Donald Wilkerson and Fathead form a vocal trio with Mary Ann. They sang backup to my lead, and in some ways this was an indication of things to come.

Mary Ann was a good singer. I used her the way Charlie Brantley or Lowell had used me—as a featured vocalist. She did mostly sentimental and torch songs, and she added a lot to our program. But I wanted more. I was like the cat who says, "I loved the greens, but I'd still like a little dessert." I wanted to hear several female voices behind me—a strong feminine sound to enhance my vocals. The end of "Drown in My Own Tears," done toward the end of 1955, was the first time I used female voices, but that was just for the recording.

I'd always liked the sound of girls' gospel groups. Albertina Walker —who had James Cleveland playing piano for her in those days—was a favorite of mine. And the Davis Sisters were also highly satisfying spiritual artists.

I could have had four men and formed a regular all-male gospel quartet, the kind I sang with back at school. But instead I wanted the flavor of a man's voice—my voice—set against women. I hadn't heard anyone do that with popular music before, and I didn't really care whether it was an old idea or a new one; I just knew that was what I was searching for.

One night in 1957 I happened to be playing Philadelphia and, after my gig, decided to catch the Lionel Hampton band at the Uptown Theatre. It was a band I'd always dug. I didn't know Hamp personally, but I did know one of his trumpet players—Benny Bailey—and I wanted to see how he was doing.

Chuck Willis—the cat who did "What Am I Living For?" and "C. C. Rider"—also happened to be on the bill. He had these three girls backing him up, and right away their singing got to me. They were called the Cookies. They blended so tightly together that I couldn't help but sit up and take notice. They used just one mike, and yet I could hear every part clearly, without any one of the chicks sticking out and drowning out the others. They had their program together.

In those days I was gutsy. I simply walked backstage and introduced myself to them. The lead singer for the group was Margie Hendrix, and she seemed to be the one in charge.

"How you doing, sweetheart? I'm Brother Ray, and I like y'all. In fact, I'd like y'all to record with me if you're free."

"Why sure," Margie said.

I didn't know it at the time, but all three girls lived in New York, and that turned out to be another plus for me. While we were recording, I figured I'd have a chance to probe deeper and see if they wanted to hook up with me permanently. My plan was to hire all three.

Before the recording date in New York, I didn't have that I'm-sure-I-got-them feeling. I didn't even know what kind of arrangement they had with Chuck Willis. Didn't have any idea what they were being paid and what they wanted.

I knew I might get a no for an answer. But so what? I had gotten noes before. Another one wasn't going to kill me. So I decided to hit on them. Two of them said yes—Margie Hendrix and Darlene MacRae. The third lady couldn't leave New York, but Margie knew another young girl by the name of Pat Mosley which gave me three. Pat was only fifteen so I had to get her mother's permission, which I did. But that's another story that I'll tell later.

I had their name already picked out. The Cookies were no longer the Cookies; now they were the Raeletts.

I was very pleased. I had put together my own band and molded the sound I wanted; now I could do the same with the girls. I could write their parts and have them accompany me every day. I liked that male/female friction, and once I had it, I never let it go.

Margie was really something. She sang even better than I had guessed. I tried her out on different things and she knocked me out. Had that growling, churchy feeling in her voice that I couldn't resist. I wrote something for each of the girls to do in a feature spot, and for the first year or so Mary Ann Fisher stayed on and became the fourth Raelett.

It was three weeks or so after that recording date that the girls joined me, and suddenly our eight-member band grew to eleven. Mary Ann had always ridden with me in my car, and now the other three girls joined her. (When Mary Ann left—I think it was around the beginning of 1958—a girl by the name of Betty Smith, who we called Betty Boo, made the transition for a few months and then Gwen Berry, who we called Squatty Roo, took her place.)

When the girls arrived on the scene, there was suddenly more perfume in the air. And I had to think about how I was going to deal with the boy/girl undercurrents in the band.

Just as with everything else, I decided to start with myself. How was I going to handle my own case? Everyone has certain indulgences, certain habits. Some are clothes fanatics; others chase money, power, or position. My obsession centers on women—did then and does now. I can't leave them alone.

So I didn't—and don't—have a policy against hanky-panky among the girls and boys in the band. How could I, as much as I loved to fuck? I'd look like a fool and I'd be a hypocrite. The guys were adults and so were the women. They could decide what they wanted, who they wanted, and when they wanted it. I had only three main rules:

One: I didn't put up with any fights where a chick might get hurt or hit upside the head. I didn't want everyone in the band looking scratched or bruised with puffy eyes and swollen jaws. I didn't want the organization to look raunchy and tattered. Do what you want to do, I said, but don't do any damage to each other.

Two: As far as I was concerned, I let the chicks know that they were there to sing. That came first. Stern as I was about getting my music sung right, nothing could interfere with that.

And three: Since Pat, the youngest Raelett, was only fifteen and therefore under age, the fellas had to stay away from her. (But somehow, my manager didn't quite get the message, 'cause two years later I was the last one to discover that he and Pat were keeping house.)

Many years later, I remember going to a banquet where I was being roasted. No one had much on me except one dude, and he was very cute:

"Now Ray Charles is a fine man. He digs his music and he takes it seriously. He also digs his Raeletts. He selects the gals real carefully. First, they need to know how to sing. Next, they have to be looking good. And finally, in order to be a Raelett, you first must let Ray."

Well, that was a funny line, but not exactly true. Certainly I've gotten next to many, many of the Raeletts. But I've never insisted that *any* woman sleep with me. When sex happens between me and one of the Raeletts, it happens naturally. It doesn't concern her pay or her music. I never allow those two currents—lovemaking and music—to cross each other.

I'd never want to make love to a woman thinking that the only reason she agrees is because I'm her boss. I can't feature that. I have to feel that she wants me as much as I want her. And I look for the signs. You can always tell—a slight touch on the shoulder, something in the way she shakes your hand or takes your arm, all those small gestures which say, "Maybe if you ask me, I just might give you a little."

I also have another personal sex policy: If a girl's with another guy in the band, I leave her alone. I don't want my cats thinking that I'm interfering with their business or their love life. I don't want one of the musicians believing that he has a girl already made and then suddenly swooped up and stolen by the boss. I couldn't live with that.

If a chick wants to get with me, and if I want to get with her, we'll work it out. Sometimes I'll have to wait. I'll have to be certain that she ain't messing with anyone in the band. But time, you know, is a bitch; it can be your enemy or it can be your friend—I learned that early in life. Patience will usually give you what you want.

Time both creates the problems and solves them. You go out on the road with the best intentions. But by the third week, you start hurting a little. And if you're working a period when you don't get near your home for two or three months, watch out.

If you're a girl, someone's always hitting on you. Little by little, all resistance wears away and you forget those little reasons which tell you not to do what feels right. Finally, everyone starts pairing off and the band gets hip to who belongs to who.

Course there were eight guys and only four chicks in those days. If all four of the gals were going with someone in the band, the other four cats had to do some more struggling. They'd wait till a girl changed, hoping that they'd have better luck with the new one.

Yeah, I let everybody be who he or she wanted to be. And that included me. But in spite of the escapades, there was very little shacking up—where a man and a woman from my organization would actually check into a hotel together. It happened sometimes, but not often. Usually the girls liked to keep their separate rooms.

No one flaunted these affairs, and they weren't any big things that we discussed or gossiped about for hours. They were just part of life on the road. I saw and found myself part of many different relationships. Sometimes you'd get locked in; other times it'd be casual and pleasant; once in a while you'd be searching out someone you could just talk to; and often you'd get through playing your music at some ridiculous hour and find yourself all high and ready to romp.

It's like a doctor and his nurse working late for a legitimate reason. They find themselves together and alone, let's say, at midnight. Somehow they touch, and there's a spark. Same thing might happen to a teacher and a student or two people staying overtime in an office.

Music can get you worked up. The atmosphere can be hot, the rhythms and the lyrics and the feelings are physical, not just musical. And in my own case, a large part of my music relates to the troubles and the ecstasies between men and women. In this situation, it just makes sense that sex is going to happen.

We were a young and a healthy band, living and playing and singing as much as we could. We had energy. When I think back on some of our schedules, I can hardly believe it. But I wanted it that way. I didn't like the idea of working only a day or two a week. Cats would hang around and get nervous. The bad undercurrents would start flowing. So, I tried to keep us working four or five days a week. Early on, I saw that idleness caused more damage than pleasure.

We didn't have to worry about being lazy, though. The work came. And it seemed to come in torrents after the Raeletts joined us. Once it started, it didn't stop. Things got hectic. We ran like we'd never run before. Gigs everyplace. After all this time, we were generating our own heat. Twelve or thirteen years after I had broken away from Greensville, it was finally about to happen.

Was I thrilled? Was I happy? Was I a brand-new man?

No. I didn't have time to think about it. I was too busy burning up the highways, trying to make the next gig on time.

Fooling, Drowning, Hallelujahing

After "I Got a Woman," my three big records were "A Fool for You," "Drown in My Own Tears" and "Hallelujah, I Love Her So." These were the songs which caught on, the tunes which kept me working.

"Hallelujah" was probably the most important. I did it in late 1955, at the same session as "Drown," and, as far as I was concerned, it was just another number I'd written. I didn't ascribe any great importance to it, and actually the lyrics were a little more lighthearted than the ones I usually wrote.

When I was writing songs, I concentrated on problems or feelings everyone could understand. I wouldn't call the tunes biographical; I just made 'em up. But I always tried to stick to common themes—love heartaches, money heartaches, pleasures of the flesh and pleasures of the soul.

"Hallelujah" clicked. It sold big among blacks, and I guess it was my first record to enjoy some popularity among whites.

If these early hits sold two hundred thousand copies, I was pleased.

That was almost all in one market—the black market—and two hundred thousand were a lot of records in those days. Oh, sure, there'd be whites who bought my sides—even *sneak* and buy 'em if they had to —but up until "Hallelujah," the overwhelming majority of those listening to me were black.

When I stopped imitating Nat Cole and slid into my own voice, I saw that my successes were exclusively at black clubs and black dances. My music had roots which I'd dug up from my own childhood, musical roots buried in the darkest soil. Naturally it was music blacks could immediately take to heart.

Little by little, though, beginning around 1956, I saw that my music had appeal beyond my own people. I saw it breaking through to other markets, and now and then there'd be a date in a city auditorium where whites would come along with blacks. It probably took me longer to digest this gradual change than it would have taken someone else. I couldn't see the increasing number of white faces.

It meant more work and more money. But it wasn't going to change my music, and it wasn't going to change me. The more people there were who liked my stuff, the happier I was. But at this point in my life that only convinced me to stick to my guns and follow my program.

Most of the material the band was playing was our own. Ninety-five percent of everything we did in those years was written by me. There were the original songs—maybe fifteen or twenty that we played. And there were also Latin numbers and hard-driving jazz tunes which I arranged. I remember writing a chart of Dizzy's "Manteca," and we also did a bolero thing on "In a Little Spanish Town" and "Frenesi."

I might write arrangements on ballads like "Funny Valentine" or "If I Had You." I loved old standards and always had them in the book. From the first days the band was together, we played a mixture of the different music I found myself drawn to.

The cats in the band could play the blues. That came first. Show me a guy who can't play the blues and I'm through with him before he can get started. If you can't get nasty and grovel down in the gutter, something's missing.

It's not that the blues are complicated. They're not; they're basic.

There are hundreds of versions of the same blues—the same changes, the same patterns—just as there are hundreds of versions of the same spirituals. The music is simple. But the feeling—the low-down gut-bucket feeling—has to be there or it's all for nothing.

My cats could also play serious jazz. Donald Wilkerson, for example, could kick the ass of almost any tenor player in the country. For my money, he's one of the best saxophonists of the century. Fathead was right there next to him, playing with a lyricism and a sweetness which Donald lacked. Fathead didn't have Donald's speed and maybe not as much fire, but he could make his sax sing the song like no one else.

In this period, I loved to watch Donald attack Fathead on the stand. Course that was good for David, and it brought out the best in both cats. When someone tries to stomp on you, naturally you're going to respond. And together—blowing out in front of the band—they'd be burning up the place.

Most of my original compositions—the ones with my own words and my own music—found their way to the recording studio, but I'd guess there must have been three times that number of songs—maybe as many as a hundred—which I arranged and never recorded.

I like to think I'm a half-ass composer. I ain't no Duke Ellington, but I *can* write. There isn't that much to making a song—jazz or otherwise. There are lyrics, and then there are notes, melody lines which you set up.

As I told you before, I could write on demand—especially when we were about to go into the studio. And I suspect that if you asked me tonight to write you a song, and if I wasn't too sleepy, I'd have it done by morning.

In the fifties, I kept up with all the music around me, especially jazz and gospel. I'd never abandon my favorite spiritual musicians—Mahalia Jackson (Lord, she was a singing lady!), Jeter, Whitaker, Ira Tucker, Archie Brownlee, Albertina Walker, Edna Gallmon Cooke—and I listened to my old jazz favorites as much as I ever had.

Jazz was going through some changes about now. I heard what West Coast cats like Gerry Mulligan or Brubeck or Kenton were doing, and it was good music. But my heart was really with the East Coast dudes. They were harder cats and had a grittier sound. I'm talkin' 'bout Art Blakey's band or Horace Silver's or the Max Roach/Clifford Brown outfit. There was more blues in their playing, the approach was tougher, and my own band, when we did jazz, played more in that mold.

Even today, some twenty years later, I still hear something different about the way the cats play back East. They're pushier, more aggressive. They got a certain stink that the guys in L.A. lack.

California musicians are pure and clean. They play correctly—almost virginlike. But I miss the filth—the East Coast filth—that you hear on the streets and in the recording studios of New York City.

Everyone was talkin' 'bout Bud Powell back then, and he was a fine pianist. But I actually preferred Hank Jones. I liked his touch, and I had a great feeling for his solo work. He reminded me of Nat Cole—with all that wonderful taste.

Phineas Newborn was one of the best young pianists of the period, and of course I still had tremendous admiration for the real masters—cats like Oscar Peterson and Erroll Garner.

I noticed some interesting developments in popular music. White singers were picking up on black songs on a much more widespread basis. They had always done it, but now it was happening much more frequently. Georgia Gibbs and Pat Boone and Carl Perkins and Elvis were doing tunes which originally had been rhythm-and-blues hits.

It didn't bother me. It was just one of those American things. I've said before that I believe in mixed musical marriages, and there's no way to copyright a feeling or a rhythm or a style of singing. Besides, it meant that White America was getting hipper.

Something else happened in this time slot: rock 'n' roll. I have a hard time defining schools of music, and I've never been one to even try. I've been arguing against labels my whole life—I hate it when they're slapped on me—but finally they become so popular that even I have to use them.

I never considered myself part of rock 'n' roll. I didn't believe that I was among the forerunners of the music, and I've never given myself a lick of credit for either inventing it or having anything to do with its birth.

When I think of the true rock 'n' roll, cats like Chuck Berry and Little Richard and Bo Diddley come to mind. I think they're the main men. And there's a towering difference between their music and mine. My stuff was more adult. It was more difficult for teenagers to relate to; so much of my music was sad or down.

A tune like Little Richard's "Tutti Frutti" was fun. Less serious. And the kids could identify with it a lot easier than my "A Fool for You" or "Drown in My Own Tears."

I don't want to put down the others, and I don't want to butter myself up. Richard and Chuck and Bo sold millions of records, and they helped the whole industry. They did some spirited music and it broke through some thick barriers. Those guys sold a hell of a lot more records than I did back then. They sold to whites by the truckloads. Fats Domino had huge hits in the white market—"Blueberry Hill" and "Ain't It a Shame"—and I wasn't even in the same league.

Rock 'n' roll was also music that the teenagers were able to play themselves. Little Richard's or Jerry Lee Lewis's piano style—taking your thumb and scraping all the way up the keyboard—had a flare and a sound that the kids loved. And which they could duplicate.

I sang some happy songs, and I played tunes with tempos that moved. But if you compare, let's say, my "Don't You Know, Baby?" to Little Richard's "Long Tall Sally," you'll hear the difference; my music is more serious, filled with more despair than anything you'd associate with rock 'n' roll.

Since I couldn't see people dancing, the dance crazes passed me by. I didn't try to write any jitterbugs or twists. I wrote rhythms which moved me and figured they'd also make other folk move.

I've heard the Beatles say that they listened to me when they were coming up. I believe them, but I also think that my influence on them wasn't nearly as great as these other artists. I was really in a different world, and if any description of me comes close, it's the tag "rhythm-and-blues." I've fooled around in the same way that blacks have been doing for years—playing the blues to different rhythms.

That style requires pure heart singing. Later on they'd call it soul music. But the names don't matter. It's the same mixture of gospel and blues with maybe a sweet melody thrown in for good measure. It's the sort of music where you can't fake the feeling.

Something else separated me from these other cats: I played jazz. In fact, right in the middle of the rock 'n' roll craze, I made my first jazz records. Not that I hadn't played jazz on records before. My Nat Cole things always had little jazz solos. But this was something new. This time I recorded with the best jazz musicians in the country.

Neshui Ertegun set up the sessions at Atlantic and hired these other musicians. Over a period of two years—1956 through 1958—we had three or four different dates. I was playing with cats like Oscar Pettiford, the great bassist, Skeeter Best, Billy Mitchell, Connie Kay, Kenny Burrell, Percy Heath. And there were two fine sessions with Milt Jackson. (This is where I played alto on some tunes.)

I hadn't met these guys before, though I knew them by reputation. Yet it was like we had always known each other. The sessions turned out to be little jams, everybody doing what came naturally, everyone having a ball.

"What do ya' wanna play, Ray?" one of the cats would ask.

"You name it."

"How 'bout a little 'Man I Love'?"

"Suits me fine."

"What key, Ray?"

"Whatever's comfortable for you, baby. They're all on the piano."

And so it went. With good musicians there's never any hassle.

I'll always have a soft spot in my heart for the Atlantic people who arranged these sessions—Jerry, Neshui, Ahmet, Tommy Dowd who was the engineer, Herb and Miriam Abramson. They never denied me anything I wanted along musical lines, and they genuinely loved my musical talents.

My recording sessions were just brief intermissions from the main show—the one we were playing on the road. That never stopped. I don't suppose I believe in relaxation or vacations. I always feel like I'm getting paid to do what I love, and as long as someone is willing to pay, I'm willing to play.

There wasn't much time for my wife and child back home in Dallas. Schedules wouldn't permit it; my music wouldn't permit it. When I started making a little more bread, maybe I'd fly to Texas for a few days, but that was rare.

By the time 1956 came around, we might be working 300 or 315 days a year. And from then on, the pace didn't slacken. Our runs from city to city were more and more hurried, the dates more jammed together, our life more frantic.

In 1955 I bought my first Cadillac, and for the next five years— through 1960—I'd buy a new Cadillac every twelve months. I've wound up with all kinds of cars in my life. I've had a Corvette 'cause I dug shifting the gears; I've had an Olds, a Mercedes, and a Volkswagen—all at different times. But nothing has flipped me like that 1960 Cadillac. Man, I loved those long lines and those big fins; I thought it was the prettiest short I had ever seen. Back then, Caddies were *the* cars to have. They held up all right, and for me that was a necessity: I'd put a hundred thousand miles a year on the things.

In 1956 I heard about a place in the Midwest which would be willing to make two Chevrolet sedans into one long, limo-looking contraption with four doors and four rows of seats. So I got rid of my old De Soto Firedome and bought one. The cats in the band called it the Wiener.

That was us in those years: the Caddie and the Wiener, rolling, running, and rocking from gig to gig, all of us, jammed together inside, sweating and freezing our way to the promised land.

Whiskey
and Watermelon

They used to tell me that whiskey and watermelon don't mix. Maybe so. But the mixture ain't ever bothered me. Maybe I'm crazy. Maybe I'm just different. I don't know, but I've mixed up all kinds of elements together and somehow gotten away with it. I'm not making recommendations, and I don't want anyone to follow my lead, but if I'm going to describe my life accurately, I got to tell you how my drug habit affected me.

I don't think it really held me back.

Anyway, around 1958, I was going strong. This was when I was shooting up every day, but it was also when I was writing music continually, working every day as hard as I could.

Hank Crawford had joined our band. He played baritone and took down songs and arrangements which I dictated to him. I was writing the same then as I do now, the same way I wrote for Joe Anderson in Florida, the only way I know how: I see and hear the chords in my mind. I don't use Braille music. I just call out the notes—instrument by instrument—for everyone in the band. I keep a sound picture in my head.

Writing arrangements is something like shaving. You might have trouble getting started; you might even dread the work. The fun only comes when you get to feel your clean face. Or when you get to sit back and listen to what you've done. It's like growing flowers. A little seed starts blossoming, and it's all because you put it there.

Charts often begin with just a simple thought. But when it's all written up and the band's playing it, that thought comes back to face you. It's thrilling to be able to say to yourself, Hey, that's really *me*.

Soon Hank learned exactly how I work. He played very good jazz and blues himself, and he turned out to be my first musical director. But that came later.

On the road, there wasn't that much to do during the days, so I'd call Hank about noon. Figured that gave him enough time to get up and eat. He'd come to my room and we'd sit there—maybe till two or three the next morning, if we didn't have a gig that night—writing music.

Sure, I was getting high. And naturally I was not denying myself the pleasure of female company. But none of this kept me from working. I always put first things first. On the other hand, smack didn't increase my productivity or stimulate my creativity. I doubt if anything outside of myself really helped or hurt my music.

One important thing about me and dope: I never lost myself, even just after I shot up. From time to time, I watched cats fall down drunk or hit themselves with so much smack that they couldn't walk straight. Well, that wasn't me. I made my gigs, I sang my songs. I tried to please my audience. I played my music. I never wanted to lose control. I didn't see the point.

I've never been one of those dudes who got so strung out or so fucked up that he didn't know where he was or what he was doing. Grass, booze, heroin—it didn't matter. I never did more than get my buzz. Then back to work.

I'm sure there are many people—maybe most people—who can't do what I did while I was still a junkie. I think it has a lot to do with metabolism. And everyone is different.

My thing with dope was peculiar. I knew it was poison, I knew it could make you sick enough to die or crazy enough to steal—not to mention death from an overdose. I was hip to drugs from every angle. But my situation was different than most. I never let it drive me anywhere I didn't want to go. In fact, it didn't drive me at all; I never let go of the steering wheel.

When I started making more money, I bought more smack, just the way I bought better cars and nicer clothes. If I made less money, I'd buy less. But high prices for anything—and that included drugs—have always restrained me. I never had an excessively expensive habit, even at its height, when I was hitting myself every day. During this period, I might get high in the morning and then maybe take a little pinch before or after a gig at night. That was what it took to keep me cool.

I never liked hunting for pushers up the streets or down the alleys. I let them come to me if I could manage it. And I bought fairly large quantities—maybe four ounces at a whack—so I could cut down the amount of contact I had with these folk. They lived a low life which didn't appeal to me.

My bottom line, though, wasn't drugs. It was money. If I had it, I spent it. If I didn't, I wouldn't. I only became a daily user when the bread was there. I let myself increase the frequency strictly according to my financial situation.

I've heard there are many people whose need for heroin becomes greater and greater until it cannot be contained. Their bodies are ruined, their minds are rotted, and their lives end pitifully early.

But my story didn't go like that.

I know people say I was relatively cool with drugs because I could afford them. They might have a point. Money helps, God knows. But much later I stopped shooting smack when I could most afford it. I stopped because I wanted to. I quit for several specific reasons, and they had nothing to do with money.

Sometimes a reporter will ask me what I have to say to kids about dope. I don't have anything to say. I'm not in the business of guiding other people's lives. Ministers and counselors and rabbis can do that. All I say is that when I was a little boy, I would pee in my bed. But when I saw how it irritated my skin and how cold I got when the freezing air hit me, I stopped.

In Philadelphia, in 1958, dope got me in trouble. I suppose it had just been a question of time.

We had just played a dance and were sitting around the dressing room when the cops barged in, screaming, "Nobody move!" and hauled our asses off to jail. They found a little grass in the corner.

Funny thing about that bust: I heard later that the promoter—who was a disc jockey—had caught someone smoking a reefer in the dressing room and called the fuzz. He was one of those cats who literally despised drugs.

But believe it or not,, this time we happened to be straight. I was really clean. We were sharing the dressing room with another band. It was actually their shit and we were just there, waiting to go on.

Didn't matter, 'cause the charges were dropped. When they found the grass, it was all by itself, just sitting there and attached to no one in particular. So they couldn't prove who it belonged to.

Naturally it made the papers—RAY CHARLES BUSTED!—but that didn't bother me none. In fact, the whole episode didn't shake me as much as you might guess. If anything, it pissed me off and left me more hostile toward the law and maybe a tad more defiant. I don't mean I went around smoking grass in public or cooking up heroin onstage. But the experience didn't cool me out either. I figured whatever I did was my business—as long as it didn't hurt no one else. I believe that people even have the right to commit suicide, if that's what they want.

The police should police laws that keep people from fucking up other people. If a cat breaks in and robs my building, I want the cops to catch him and put him in jail. But if the cops think I'm doing something which is bad for me—for me and for no one else—then I want them to leave me alone.

Hell, there are dozens of crazy laws. I understand in some places it's forbidden to suck your wife's pussy. Well, they can't enforce that one, but if they could, wouldn't it be a bitch?

In my own mind, if I was hurting anyone it was only me. And I'm still not convinced that I was being hurt.

At some point, the press got on me. Not on any large scale, but now I was made aware of their little barbs. I'm afraid that the public understanding of me became warped. And I'm not certain it was all the fault of the press. It's a complicated matter.

First of all, I never tried to hide my habit. I didn't flaunt it, but at the same time I knew that certain gestures and mannerisms were making people suspicious, if not out-and-out certain that I was a junkie. Heroin can make you scratch, for example. And when I itched, I scratched.

I couldn't watch myself walking or talking or playing the piano. I let my body react whichever way it wanted. I had nothing to compare it to. I didn't know how John or Mary walked or scratched or nodded, and I didn't care.

But my being blind confused folk even more. They had to believe that someone—my manager, my agent, my friends—was getting me the stuff and forcing me to take it. They saw me as the victim, a helpless puppy dog being led on a leash.

Bullshit.

Some people can't believe that I can shave myself. And when I tell them I sometimes use a straight razor, they nearly faint. I wonder: How do they think I got around when I first hit the road by myself? How do they think I found the hotels? The restaurants? The gigs? How do they think I picked out my clothes? How do they think I managed my life?

If I could fix my own plumbing, fool with light switches, and do repairs on my TV and stereo equipment, I sure as hell could find a way to put a little dope in my veins. Or to put it another way: I can thread a needle.

Other people have asked me how I could trust any of the dope, since

I couldn't see it. Well, how do the sighted folks know what kind of weed they're smoking or what kind of coke they're snorting? Nine out of ten times they rely on the cat who copped it for them. They don't put the shit under a microscope and examine it. Unfortunately, there are no government regulations so we might be able to know something about what we're smoking. Blindness has nothing to do with it; we all go into drugs blind.

So many of the writers and people observing me just didn't understand that I knew what I was doing. I was conscious, I was alive, I was making the decisions.

In fact, my manager, Jeff Brown, hated dope. Jeff and I were very close in those years—he was like my brother—I was with him every day, and yet I never shot up in his presence just 'cause I knew it disturbed him.

Same went for the people at the Shaw Agency or Atlantic Records. They didn't condone my habit. No one was making sure I stay loaded. They just put up with it 'cause it was part of me.

All the bullshit in the press only seemed to attract more people to my dates. Made them curious and kept them thinking about me, rightly or wrongly. I began to see what living in a glass house was like.

My dope thing probably hurt B more than anyone. I regretted that the most, but not enough to make me quit. So I tried to keep it away from her. During this period we were already set on two different courses, though we were still in love with each other.

In 1958 my second son, David, was born. Naturally I was very happy, and yet I still couldn't spend much time at home. If we had a week-long gig at a club, I'd send for B and sometimes she'd come. But traveling with little babies was difficult, and she wasn't a great lover of the road.

She had chosen to stay home. If she had wanted to come with me —even to sing, as I later suggested—I would have welcomed it. But B was a lady who loved home life, and she loved her little boys. She didn't want anyone raising them except her. And she felt they needed a stable life at home. I didn't argue.

A couple of months after David was born, we moved to Los Angeles, but that didn't change our arrangement much. I was still living on the road for the most part, and B still stuck to the house.

I had been out to California sometime before and heard about a house on 3910 Hepburn Avenue. I went over to see it, checked out a few items, decided I could handle the payments, and bought it. Cost maybe $30,000 or $35,000.

B was pleased to move out there. She liked the climate as much as I did. I suppose ever since I first went to L.A. in the late forties I'd thought about coming back. It reminded me of my home back in Florida. Southern California is warm. There's sleet and ice and freezing rains in Dallas, and I hated that. In California, I'd get to ride my motor scooter around the backyard any time of the year.

I tried to keep my drugs and my women away from B. I'd fix it so she wouldn't be getting phone calls or letters. I respected the home she had built up for us. On the other hand, I didn't stay there for long. I had worked my whole life to be in a position where people would be coming to hear my music. Now that they were actually paying decent money, I couldn't turn it down.

B understood. She left me alone. And I left her alone. We made our choices, we followed our own instincts. And in some ways, those instincts sent us out in such different directions that neither one of us was willing to turn around. You'll see what I mean later.

The road was my life. It still is. I'll follow it for as long as it pays. I've shared the good times and risked the dangers along with every other entertainer who's gone the same way.

One incident that happened in 1959 made me realize just how risky the business could be. I had hired a driver named Charles Shackleford. He was a nice guy, but he always wanted to be around when we were playing a gig. That wasn't too cool with me. I wanted him to be getting his sleep back at the hotel so he'd be able to drive when the gig was over.

But not Charles. He liked to be with the guys 'cause during a break they be trying to cop some pussy, and he figured there might be some for him. I always told him to get his rest, but Charles never paid me no mind.

A couple of times when he was driving I noticed the car swerving. That woke me instantly. Strange, because bumps—even bad ones—never woke me. But when the car started going from side to side, I snapped to attention. Probably due to my fear of death.

Anyway, after some incidents like that I let Charles go. I couldn't get him to do right. And about four or five weeks later I learned that he'd found a gig driving for another singer, Jesse Belvin. One night in Arkansas when Charles was driving, he got into a wreck and he and Jesse were killed.

That hurt me bad. Charles was a very decent cat and Jesse was just getting started. Jesse would have been very big, maybe even as big as Nat Cole. He was a fine singer, with a warm, sexy sound, and it was a crime that he had to cut out so early. But the road can mow you down like that. You got to keep your eyes peeled and look where you're going.

Once in a while, though, you could let the good times roll.

Carnegie Hall in 1959 stands out in my mind as one good stop along the way. I'd heard so much about the place and had promised myself I'd play there one day.

The night was especially memorable 'cause we happened to be appearing with Billie Holiday. I hadn't met Lady Day before. This was the very end of her life, and three or four months after this gig she'd be dead.

Her voice was very tired. I could hear how it had deteriorated. But she was a veteran, one of the best singers ever, and she could still whip your ass just from her experience. Yeah, old pros have their long lives to rely on, and even in the end, Lady had wisdom and dignity inside her singing; she could still make you cry like a child.

As for me, I didn't have butterflies or shakes the way some folk do, but I was still pleased to be at Carnegie Hall. I had dreamed this might happen, and now I could check it off my list.

I had been on the same bill with one of the best singers in the world,

Lady Day. And only a few months before I had played some gigs with another legendary singing lady, Miss Dinah Washington.

A lot of my dreams were coming true, but there were still others. They might have been crazy, but they were dreams, and dreams, if they're any good, are always a little crazy.

Widening
the Range

I mentioned to you that by 1959 I was ready to put the era of dances behind me. Some of my nasty experiences had given me the nerve to tell the Shaw Agency that I wouldn't play gigs like that anymore. Now I was banking on my ability to get decent concert jobs and nightclub engagements.

I no longer wanted to take the chance of getting clubbed or shot—I didn't need that kind of shit. Now, more than ever, I was interested in protecting *me*. I figured the Lord had been good to me so far and maybe I should quit while I was one step ahead.

Self-preservation wasn't the only reason, though, that I quit playing dance halls. I also felt it was having a bad effect on my music. I often wouldn't play my trio numbers at those places because the pianos were so pathetic. I've seen some incredible instruments, pianos so shoddy and flat that I had to play C-sharp instead of C to be in the same key as the band.

Actually, that's how I learned to play in all keys. I was forced to in order to match the band. But even that might not do the trick. Two or three keys in the middle of the piano wouldn't work at all, or would keep ringing after you'd strike 'em.

Some promoters just didn't give a shit. They stuck your name outside and hoped that the bodies would flow in. Others took the time to make sure your playing conditions were decent.

It's not just the ratty dance halls that have bad conditions. Even in the so-called fancy supper clubs I've seen dressing rooms so filthy that you wouldn't let a dog use 'em. I can't stand my own filth, much less anyone else's. (I remember playing a high-class club in New York once where the facilities for the artists were so dirty that I had to rent a hotel room next door for me to change my clothes.)

But at age twenty-eight I was still innocent enough to think that conditions were really going to get better. I wanted to upgrade my act. My money wasn't as funny as it had been. In 1954 I might have been making $200 or $250 a job; by '58 or '59 that had increased to $500 or $600, and a good night brought $800.

Newport and Carnegie Hall became early proof that I could reach different audiences in different arenas. I saw that as a compliment and a challenge, though I wasn't *that* overwhelmed by the experiences themselves.

I've always played to people, not to places. Maybe that's because I can't physically see those places. I'm not certain. Either way, I've never been impressed by the idea of performing in a club or a concert hall with a fancy-sounding name. After Carnegie Hall, I've been more or less nonchalant about all the others.

Earlier I was telling you how I never test songs on the public before I record them. I've always been my own private testing service. But there was one exception to this rule, even though I didn't mean for it to happen the way it did. I'm talking about the accidental birth of "What I Say."

We happened to be playing one of my last dances—somewhere in the Midwest—and I had another twelve minutes to kill before the set closed. A typical gig of that kind lasted four hours, including a thirty-minute intermission. We played from 9:00 till 11:30, took a half-hour break, and then did the final hour.

It was nearly 1:00 A.M., I remember, and we had played our whole book. There was nothing left that I could think of, so I finally said to the band and the Raeletts, "Listen, I'm going to fool around and y'all just follow me."

So I began noodling. Just a little riff which floated up into my head. It felt good and I kept on going. One thing led to another, and suddenly I found myself singing and wanting the girls to repeat after me. So I told 'em, "Now!"

Then I could feel the whole room bouncing and shaking and carrying on something fierce. So I kept the thing going, tightening it up a little here, adding a dash of Latin rhythm there. When I got through, folk came up and asked where they could buy the record. "Ain't no record," I said, "just something I made up to kill a little time."

The next night I started fooling with it again, adding a few more lyrics and refining the riffs for the band. I did that for several straight evenings until the song froze into place. And each time I sang it, the reaction was wild.

I called Jerry Wexler from the road and told him that I was coming to New York with something new to record. "I've been playing it," I said, "and it's pretty nice." That was further than I usually went with Jerry. I don't believe in giving myself advance notices, but I figured this song merited it.

We made the record in 1959, and it became my biggest hit to date. Like "Hallelujah," it sold to whites and blacks alike, although not everyone dug it. It was banned by several radio stations. They said it was suggestive. Well, I agreed. I'm not one to interpret my own songs, but if you can't figure out "What I Say," then something's wrong. Either that, or you're not accustomed to the sweet sounds of love.

Later on, I saw that many of the stations which had banned the tune started playing it when it was covered by white artists. That seemed strange to me, as though white sex was cleaner than black sex. But once they began playing the white version, they lifted the ban and also played the original.

These bans didn't bother me none, mainly 'cause I could see, feel, and smell the royalties rolling in. At this point, it was bread I really needed.

A few years before "What I Say"—sometime in 1956—I recorded my first album. I had made dozens of singles by that time, but I hadn't put together an album of my own with a concept and tunes that related to each other.

I used my own band and arrangements by my partner Quincy Jones and me. By then, Fats Webb—the cat I knew in Jacksonville—had come and gone from my band, and John Hunt had taken his place on trumpet. Joe Bridgewater also played trumpet on the session. We did an instrumental version of "A Fool for You" called "Sweet Sixteen Bars," and Quincy had charts on "Doodlin'," "Undecided," and a song he wrote for me, "The Ray." There were no vocals, just straight-ahead jazz.

It made sense that my first real album would be devoted to jazz. To my mind, the average listener doesn't appreciate the technical feats of most jazz artists. I've heard people say what a bitch Mozart was, and yet in the same breath they'll tell me they can't hear what Charlie Parker was doing. Or other folk might claim that Beethoven and Bach were so heavy. Meanwhile, they're unaware of the cats just crosstown who might be playing music even more complicated.

I dig classical music. So much of it is moving and beautiful, and I love listening to it. But I'm not sure that classical music—as so many people think—is the last word. I like to use the differences between golf and baseball as an illustration:

The golfer is like a classical musician. He's got this elegant stick in his hand, and he wants—he demands—that everyone be quiet so he can concentrate. The fans must not whisper and the birds must not sing. He's addressing the ball, and nothing can disturb him.

The jazz player is like a batter at home plate. Some motherfucker is going to throw a ball at him at a hundred miles an hour. It might come in straight, it might curve, it might break inside or break outside. Everyone's screaming at him—the catcher, the fans, the coaches—and this poor slob has got to decide in a split second whether to swing at the ball or let it go by. Now if that don't take concentration, what does?

Classical music is already written. It's a matter of interpretation. But with jazz—oh yes—with jazz you got to compose as you go. And you're supposed to be following the chord changes along the way.

I suppose that's why I'm always proud that I can play jazz and why it isn't any accident that I've always wanted to make jazz records and have a true-to-life jazz band.

But that wasn't all I wanted in the last half of the fifties. Remember how I was talking earlier about singing with strings behind me? Well, that idea was something I would hold on to. The sweet love songs with lush violin backgrounds I'd heard as a boy never left my memory. I could still hear Axel Stordahl's beautiful string charts for Frank Sinatra's early music, and I grew as romantic and enchanted behind those arrangements as anyone else. It was something I could hear myself doing.

In those days you didn't see many artists—if any—dabbling in both areas. You sang rhythm and blues—that was one field. Or you sang standards or love songs with strings—that was another. But you did not combine the two which, of course, was exactly what I had in mind.

I had been playing standards—mainly to feed the kitty when I was working white clubs—ever since I was a teenager. And I was wild for those songs. I reasoned this way: I had already proven myself in the rhythm-and-blues field. I didn't want to give up that material; I did it originally because I felt it was me. Now I just wanted to expand upon it, add to it, build on top of it.

It's one thing to have an idea, it's another to make it go. I might say I want to bake a cake, but if I don't have the right ingredients, the thing will collapse in the oven. I didn't want my idea to fall apart, so I let it cook a while.

Atlantic sent me material they were recording of their other artists, and that's how I got a certain Chris Connor release. She had an album which I remember putting on the box while I was still living in Dallas. I was particularly struck by the strings. So next time I talked to my friends at Atlantic in New York I asked them: Who wrote the strings for the Chris Connor record? Ralph Burns, they said. Ralph Burns! That was the same cat who had done so many swinging things for Woody Herman's band. That did it; he was the man I wanted to write *my* string arrangements.

Yes, Lord, it was time to do it! I had lived with the thought long enough—it was already 1959—and in my head I started selecting tunes: "Am I Blue?" "Just for a Thrill," "Come Rain or Come Shine," a tune I used to love to hear Louis Jordan sing called "Don't Let the Sun Catch You Crying," an old Charles Brown number, "Tell Me You'll Wait for Me" and "You Won't Let Me Go," which I had heard Buddy Johnson do when I was still a kid.

On the other side of the album, I wanted to do brassy stuff with a big band—sixteen or seventeen pieces—something I hadn't done before. I decided to incorporate my own small band into the larger one, and I had Quincy write some arrangements.

There were also charts by Al Cohn and Ernie Wilkins. And Johnny Acea arranged "Two Years of Torture," a song by a friend of mine, Percy Mayfield, who I had met years before when I was with Lowell Fulson. Also did another tune associated in my mind with Louis Jordan —"Let the Good Times Roll."

In driving into new areas—string arrangements, big-band charts, and later country songs—I was careful to pick vehicles which were well-worn and proven, vehicles I had been testing and riding in for a long, long time.

You might think that Atlantic would have balked at this idea. But they didn't. I suppose by then you could say I had a good track record, but this had been their attitude with me even from the beginning, before I had built up a name.

I've worked closely with every arranger I've had. That's always been my style, and it's the only way these sessions work out. I more or less tell the arranger what I'm hearing in my head and what I want to hear in the studio. If he can come close to that—and usually he can—there's no trouble. If he can't, I wind up rearranging the charts myself—but that's costly. Studio time is high, especially when thirty musicians are waiting around for me to get through a rewrite.

But those first string sessions were little trouble and great pleasure. I sang the ballads as I had planned, and I loved working with a big band. Both settings felt perfectly natural, and from then on they became part of me. Once I had them, I couldn't ever let them go.

Atlantic called this album *The Genius of Ray Charles*. I had been called other names—the High Priest, the Reverend, the Right Reverend, Brother Ray; but it was the boys at Atlantic who started using the genius label.

It wasn't my idea. Calling someone a genius is some heavy shit, and I'd never have used the word in regard to myself. I think I'm pretty good at what I do, but I've never considered myself a genius. Yet between Atlantic and the public, the name stuck—that and Brother Ray. I saw it as a high compliment, and I certainly didn't complain. If the public accepted that, fine. On the other hand, I tried very hard not to let myself feel pressure; I didn't want to feel compelled to live up to the name. And I haven't thought of myself as a genius before or since. I go by Brother Ray.

I didn't stop turning out the blues-and-gospel sounds. A little earlier than this I had done readaptations, in my style, of strange songs like "Swanee River," "My Bonnie," and "Yes Indeed." These were melodies I had been hearing my whole life, and I wanted to see if I could do 'em over. ("Yes Indeed", another childhood memory of mine, was an old-fashioned swing song done by arranger Sy Oliver for Tommy Dorsey.)

By now my band had a good snap to it. In one configuration or another, we had been together since 1954, and I was getting the sound I wanted. Once in a while I used other musicians in the studio for a single record, though it was usually my own crew.

I remember the conga player Jerry Wexler hired—a cat called Mongo Santamaria—to help us with "Swanee River Rock" and "I Had a Dream." He didn't speak much English, I didn't speak any Spanish, and it was tough getting our rhythms straight. He was playing tick-a-TOCK. I wanted tock-a-TICK. I had to have that old backwoods backbeat. Finally, we just talked a little jungle talk to each other—ticky-a-tock, tocky-a-tick—and before long we got the thing straight.

The last session I did for Atlantic, in the summer of 1959, sticks in my memory because of two songs:

"I Believe to My Soul" caused me all kinds of fits. On this particular day, the Raeletts couldn't get their parts together. We did it what seemed like a hundred times, and each time one of the gals goofed. I was impatient—sometimes I get that way—and I finally told 'em to go home; I'd do it myself.

I did all four parts, one at a time, singing in falsetto. They made a tape of each one and then put them together; that way I had my own four-part harmony. And in front of that, I sang my part—the lead—in my normal voice.

Incidentally, I also played electric piano on that tune, just as I had on "What I Say." Back then, the musicians would tease me, "Hey, man, what you doin' with that toy?" but it didn't bother me none. I had been fooling with electric pianos and celestes since my days up in Seattle, and I was always looking for new or old combinations of sounds.

"I'm Movin' On" was another tune we did that day. That's a Hank Snow song, and it became the first country-and-western number I ever recorded. I wanted Chet Atkins to play his country guitar on the date, but he was already booked up that afternoon.

I would have liked "I'm Movin' On" to have become a hit, but it was put on the flip side of "I Believe to My Soul," and, as best I remember, "I Believe" was the one more people asked for and listened to.

This completed an era for me. By the end of 1959, I had changed labels, left Atlantic and gone with ABC. It was a tough move for me—I loved the Atlantic people—but it was probably the smartest money decision of my life.

ABC made an offer to my manager and booking agent which was hard to pass up. They told me that in addition to 5 percent of the royalties—high for the time—they'd give me 7½ cents of every dime's worth of profit for my services as producer of my own material. And I also had the guarantee that I would ultimately own all my master tapes which I recorded for the label.

I had someone from the Shaw Agency prepare me a piece of paper with the main points of the ABC deal written plainly. I studied them, and I brought the paper with me when I went to see Ahmet Ertegun. I didn't want to leave Atlantic—they had treated me wonderfully—and yet I didn't want to hurt myself. This was a hell of a deal I was being offered.

I told Ahmet simply that if he would match the offer, I'd stay. He said it was a little rich for his blood, and, though he wished me well, he decided to pass.

ABC had a rhythm-and-blues gap which they were counting on me to fill. I didn't plan to do that exactly. I was feeling comfortable about growing into these other areas—love songs with strings, big-band jazz, and the little country tune by Hank Snow. I didn't tell anyone what was rattling round inside my head, but I did have a few thoughts of my own.

Meanwhile, I also had some trouble from the law.

Busted Again

In 1961 I'm sound asleep in a hotel room in Indianapolis. And when I sleep, baby, I *sleep*. Nothing wakes me. I've slept through electrical storms on planes and earthquakes on the ground. But this morning someone's banging and banging and banging at my door so goddamn hard that my head's about to split open. Usually I don't open the door for nobody. Can't see who it is and don't like to take chances. But I'm half-asleep, half-crazy.

"Who is it?"

"Western Union."

If I'd been awake, I would have told the cat to slip the telegram under the door. But my mind was still foggy with dreams. Like a fool, I opened the door.

Boom.

Cops stormed in, stomping round like they were on TV, opening drawers, looking under the bed and in the closet, pulling the mattress back, going into the medicine cabinet where they found heroin. They rushed me down to the police station, took my fingerprints, and asked me a bunch of questions.

I was brought in around eleven. By twelve-thirty I was out. And three or four months later, the charges were dismissed. Illegal entry or search without a warrant—something like that got me off.

I was even able to make my gig the night of the bust—that's how fast the lawyers worked.

Did this fuck me up or get me scared? Did I haul off and promise myself never to shoot up again? Did I reform and change my ways before something *really* bad happened? No. I just carried on with business as usual. Fact is, like the Philadelphia bust, it made me even angrier.

The incident in Indianapolis was serious. This time they found smack. But to my mind, the situation was the same. I was being hassled for something I viewed as no one's business but my own. I got out of it all right, but only because I had bread.

At this point in my life I had long since lost respect for the law. I had already seen too much shit—in the name of the law—which made me sick to my stomach. I don't see the police as black or white. I see them as the law. And it was the law who I once saw, earlier in my career, pull a guy from his car in a parking lot outside a dance hall and scream in his face, "Nigger, didn't you see that goddamn stoplight back there?" When the man attempted to answer, the law slapped him upside the head with their billy clubs and said, "Keep your mouth shut while we're talking, nigger." That was the law. It's one thing to watch a bunch of hoodlums acting that way. It's another when the law is doing it.

Here's how I reason:

If the law is so particular about drugs, why don't they bust the cats doing all the heavy trading? They say they know who's doing it. They say they've been investigating these deals for years.

Why pick on some poor cat who probably had to steal five dollars to feed his sickness? He's just reacting to what's available. But no; the cops will follow him back home, watch him crawl into his crib, peel off his shirt, and—just as he's about to hit himself—they'll bust down his

door and stick his ass in jail. Only a public defender—if one's around
—will help him.

But the cops are overjoyed. They got themselves a pigeon. They done
nabbed this little cat, and now they can tell the churches, they can tell
the better business bureau, they can tell the city council what a fucking
good job they're doing. Now they be shouting, "Look at all these dope
addicts we've picked up!"

This is the injustice in justice. It's kicking the weak and protecting
the strong. It's ass backwards, and it don't make no sense. It's corrupt
—it's deeply corrupt—and I still can't get the thing straight in my
brain.

My desire, my whole notion of life, is simple: I leave people alone.
And I want them to leave me alone. Why do we need laws which tell
me what I can or can't put into my own body? Yeah, I might be busted
on a Monday, and then I read in the papers on a Tuesday how the
government is subsidizing tobacco companies while forcing them to
stick little warnings on cigarette packs that say that the shit is bad for
you. You figure it out.

I'm not sure that justice can be entirely bought, but money don't
hurt none. I saw that for myself. I'm not saying that our lawyer paid
off the DA or the judge. No one told me that, and I never assumed
it to be true. But I do know that I was in and out of the police station
within an hour and a half, and the average person—the average junkie
—just can't get that kind of drive-in, drive-out treatment.

Good lawyers, like good doctors, don't come cheap, and if you can
pay, your chances of surviving the crisis start improving at the first sign
of those new green bills.

Just like you can buy grades of silk, you can buy grades of justice.
You can buy the so-called best minds, and the best minds—the best
legal research—might be the very thing which saves your ass. Doesn't
seem right. I understand justice to mean that every individual will get
exactly the same treatment. And I understand justice to mean that the
punishment will fit the crime—and that the same punishment must
apply to everyone.

None of this is sour grapes. After all, I *did* get out, I *didn't* have to serve time, I *wasn't* hassled beyond that first morning in my hotel. I *could* pay. I just want to express my disgust for a system which goes around hounding poor-ass junkies while the fat cats and syndicators are left alone to rake in the millions which they can use to keep the law at arm's length.

So my habit continued, even beyond this miserable morning in Indianapolis. I'm stubborn, and I usually go on doing what I like.

My music was going well—that was the most important thing—and I didn't see how the dope was hurting. I don't mean I wasn't sick now and then in those years, 'cause I was. I'd hit a dry period and go through the same convulsions as any other junkie. I'd try to plan ahead, try to keep my supply in good shape. When the cup would be a quarter empty, I'd make arrangements to fill it up again. But that wasn't always possible, and there were days when I just sat and suffered. For the most part, though, I had myself under control. There wasn't anything which I could see destroying me, not as long as I was still managing my own affairs and able to play my music.

Actually, the only time I got sure-enough messed up really didn't have much to do with drugs, although I'm sure that sometime during that day—like all days—I had my little fix, and maybe it was stronger than usual.

Hank Crawford came to my house in L.A. and we were going to write some music. This was in the early sixties. I had been up for a couple of days—I did that kind of crap all the time—and I still felt like working. If I kept working, I could stay up for a long, long time. But if I'd stop, I'd fall out. Hank had to leave to buy some paper and pens, and meanwhile I went upstairs to nap.

I collapsed from the fatigue. And somehow, in my state of unconsciousness, I slammed my hand against a glass table top and sliced it to ribbons. None of this woke me up, though, and the cuts merely numbed my hand. I continued to sleep, bleeding like a hog.

It was my son, Ray, Jr., who saved me. He happened to wander upstairs and noticed all the blood. He ran down and told his mother.

By then Hank had returned, and he and B threw me in a car and rushed me to Dr. Foster's office where I finally came to.

I was bleeding profusely. They soaked up two huge beach towels with my blood—two quarts worth. At this point my partner Hank passed out from the sight of all this gushing blood. By the following morning I was having convulsions, so B took me to the hospital where I was given a transfusion.

Later, Doc Foster told me I had cut an artery and a tendon in my left hand. He instructed me not to work for a while. Naturally, I refused and went right back on the road, even though I could only play one-handed piano.

Bob Foster, who is one of the dearest people I've ever known, insisted that he go on the road with me, in case the hand got infected. That proved to be a wise move. He put a cast on the hand, and everyone I met couldn't resist touching it or shaking it. The hand did get infected, but Bob was there to keep me straight.

I must say something about Bob, though, before anyone gets the wrong idea. Although he was my personal friend, and although he traveled with me for about ten days during the time my hand was in the cast, I never let him do anything illegal for me. I liked him too well for that. If you really love a person, you won't get him involved in something which might hurt him.

Bob's a marvelous surgeon. He sewed up my hand so smoothly that you can barely detect the cuts today. He's the man who got me through the crisis with my hand, and for a piano player, that's some serious business.

Other stuff wasn't so serious. Sometimes my life on the road could take a funny turn, even though the joke might be at my own expense. One crazy example:

I checked into the Park-Sheraton Hotel in New York one night so tired that I could barely put one foot in front of another. I got to my room, fell asleep, and drifted off to another planet. I mean, I was out.

When I woke up the next morning, I was still in the twilight zone, neither here nor there. I opened the door and stepped inside the bathroom to pee when I suddenly heard the door slam behind me. I realized I wasn't in the bathroom at all. The bathroom door didn't have no spring to it. I was in the hallway. And I was stark naked. I tried to open the door, but it was locked tight.

You fool, is all I could say to myself, you goddamn fool. You out in the middle of the hall of the Sheraton Hotel in New York City, and you buck naked. Now what you going to do?

If guests had started popping out, Lord knows what they'd have thought. Streaking hadn't become popular yet. But I lucked out. I heard a maid somewhere on the floor.

"Oh, maid," I cried, "maid, can you come here, please?"

"Yes, sir," she answered, far off in the distance, "I'm coming, sir," she repeated as she approached my room. "Here I am, sir . . . sir . . . my GOD, *SIR!*"

"Now look, honey, I don't have time to debate it with you. You can see I've locked myself out of my room and I got to pee. Open the door, sweetheart, before I have an accident right here."

Since that time, I've been more careful about looking before I leap.

Keeping Track
of the Change

Once I was by myself. Then there was a trio. Then I was by myself again. Then I worked for other cats. Then I had a little band of my own—first with four horns, then with a girl singer, then with three churchy backup singers, then with a fifth horn.

When I look at my career as a musician, I see that I believe in accumulation. I never really gave anything up except the Nat Cole and Charles Brown imitations. Everything else I developed I just threw on top of the pile.

When I got to ABC nothing really changed, and people who think the label switch made a difference with my music are way off base. ABC was like Atlantic—they left me alone—and so I continued to call the shots. The microphones didn't know what label they belonged to and, in the truest sense, neither did I. I continued my program as though nothing had happened.

By this time I wanted to hear another horn behind me while I was playing piano. I told you how I'd get up and play alto, becoming the fifth horn myself. Well, by 1959 I figured I was making enough bread to hire that horn and keep myself rooted at the keyboard.

While I was still living in Dallas, the cats used to take me to a Sunday jam session where many musicians would be romping, including students from North Texas State. Of all the guys I heard, one stood out in particular—a baritone saxophonist named Leroy Cooper. Sometimes they called him Hog.

Leroy was an amazing player and—as with Don Wilkerson and Fathead—there were very few if any limitations to what he could do. Hog played fast, like Bird, when he wanted to. He played blues—very filthy blues. And he could romp and wail with as much old-fashioned spirit as Harry Carney. So when I decided to add another horn, I told Fathead to call down to Dallas and tell Leroy that he was our man.

There were dozens of personnel changes in the small band, and unfortunately I've forgotten many of the cats. There were carloads of swinging musicians who passed through—people like Wilbur Hogan, the drummer, or my wonderful bass player, Edgar Willis.

I often hired on the spot. Whenever I heard something or someone who moved me, I made my move. Phil Guilbeau was a cat I spotted playing first trumpet for the house band at the Howard Theatre in Washington, D.C. He could play—I heard that instantly—so I hit on him and hired him immediately. Turned out to be one of my most expressive musicians.

I was still writing songs and turning out singles when I went to ABC, and some of them—"Them That Got," "Who You Gonna Love?" "My Baby"—were small successes. Others—like Percy Mayfield's "Hit the Road, Jack" or "Sticks and Stones" or "Unchain My Heart"—turned out to be big hits.

For a while, I continued to integrate my small band into a bigger orchestra when I recorded. That wasn't as good as having my own big band, but it worked on the records and I got the sound I wanted. I loved my small band to the drawers, but my heart was set on something bigger.

It was still with this same small group that I went to Europe for the first time. This was 1960. And just around then we did our first national

TV shots—Dinah Shore and Ed Sullivan. I wasn't seeing stars, but I was very anxious to expand. I began calculating ways to beef up my repertoire and my band.

It was around September of 1961 that I finally stopped the dreaming and did the doing: I put together a big band. I could see that my bread had grown to the place where I could afford it. I don't want to give you the wrong idea. I still wasn't getting rich, but the money was flowing in steadily. Back in 1959, for example, I saw where I could afford a plane, and I bought one—a Cessna 310, a small, twin-engine job. I bought it used from two gals for around $25,000.

Might sound extravagant to you, but I never consider anything I really need or want to be extravagant. In fact, people close to me often think I'm cheap—or economical, to use the nicer word. They're right. I only buy what I need. And I only employ people who have jobs to do. I don't believe in excess fat.

I can honestly live on around $250 or $300 a week—and that's true today. Of course, I don't have to pay rent or make a house payment —that's all taken care of—but I still don't require much. A warm bed, food to put in my mouth, a car, phonograph, TV, and, Lord help me, a decent piece of pussy to set off my day.

It don't take much, and that's 'cause I started with nothing. I learned how to live with little. And I haven't forgotten. The reason I bought a plane had nothing to do with showing off or acting like a big shot. I thought it'd be helpful for me—and also healthy—not to have to ride around all night and day in a car, running from gig to gig.

The Cessna was a simple plane, but I loved it very much. I sat right up there next to the pilot, and I fooled with everything. I've said before that I'm a gadget man. And it seemed like the most wonderful invention I had ever toyed with. This was when I first got hooked on planes and started learning something about how they function—the radios, the fuel mixtures, the prop adjustments.

By 1961 I knew my money was straight. I probably could have made the big-band move earlier, but I'm cautious by nature, and adding an additional eight or ten folks to the payroll gave me a lot to think over.

I might have been grossing $100,000 or $150,000 a year in the early sixties, but I doubt if I was netting more than $15,000 or $20,000 for myself. No efficiency expert will ever tell you to tour with a big band. It took no more than three or four days to select the cats I wanted. But I was blessed; I had some marvelous help from my dear friend Quincy Jones who was just disbanding his band. He gave me a whole trunkload of his music and told me to take whatever I wanted. So I chose ten or twelve of Quincy's charts, wrote a few arrangements of my own, and had some done by other people. In no time, my book was together.

Don't bet any money on this, but I believe I can reconstruct the band fairly accurately:

On trumpets—Marcus Belgrave, John Hunt, E. V. Perry, Lamar Wright.

On trombones—James Harpert, Grachan Moncur III, Calvin Jones, Henderson Chambers.

On saxes—David Newman, Donald Wilkerson, Leroy Cooper, Rudy Powell, and Hank Crawford who was now my musical director and helped me with most of the charts.

Milt Turner was the drummer, Edgar Willis, the bassist, Sonny Forrest—who I got from the Coasters—the guitarist.

Before very long, Keg Johnson joined on bass trombone, and from then on the personnel changed too often for me to even hope to remember.

But there it was: a real-life big band. I was proud, but I also soon became aware of another problem which I had tasted before only in small portions—discipline.

I know I've been called a shrewd businessman and also a ridiculously strict disciplinarian. To my mind, neither label comes close to the truth. I have my own attitudes about these things. I'll explain how I feel and you judge for yourself.

For example, I can't remember any brilliant business moves I've made. The ABC deal came to me. I didn't plan it, and I didn't arrange it. I knew it was good, Atlantic wouldn't meet it, so I took it. That's all.

I put my big band together when I thought I could afford it. I had no magic formula, no scheme for it to make me money. I wanted music in my ears that only a big band could provide. And that's the whole story.

From the get-go, my progress has been slow and steady. I never woke up one morning at 0 and went to bed that night at 1000. That ain't me. I've got some common sense. I've got a certain mother wit. But I'm not a schemer and I'm not a high-powered negotiator. I just sit there and listen to what the other person has to say. If I don't have to give away too much, and if the deal makes sense for me, I take it.

There are certain points I won't negotiate. I won't let anyone make me sing or record music which I can't feel. I won't let anyone own me.

I know I can sell anything I set my mind on. And I love to sell, but only when I'm dealing with something I like. When I sing, for example, I'm really selling a song.

In business, I stick to the essentials. I get down to brass tacks right away. I started out knowing nothing about finance, but I learned as I went along. I'm not one of those persons so loose that I don't pay attention to what's happening around me. I may not know something now, but if I see it, I'll remember it.

I can also figure out the numbers—in the most basic sense. I can add, subtract, multiply, and divide. And I can do a lot of it without any pencil. But I depend on others to do the detailed business dealings for me. Not that I don't make the final decisions—I do—it's just that I'm not crazy about all the preliminary discussions. I'll know all the points, and I'll study the issues. Then I'll decide what to do.

For years, Jeff Brown was my trusted friend and manager. And in the early sixties, Hal Zeigler, the promoter, used Joe Adams to emcee some of our shows. Joe was the disc jockey I'd met in L.A. years before. I discovered that he was a very competent businessman with an uncanny memory for small details.

By 1964, he was handling my business affairs and Jeff left to go out on his own. I worked well with both these guys, because they complemented me. I could be the good cop and they were the bad cops. I tended to be Brother Ray, someone the cats in the band could talk to. And Jeff and Joe were authority figures who were resented, because if they saw that a musician was late or out of uniform, they'd tell me.

I must say, though, that Jeff was much softer and more subtle than Joe. The cats could get away with some stuff. But once Joe joined me the slipping stopped. Joe's as hard-nosed as they come.

Course the final blame should be placed with me. I was the one telling Jeff or Joe what to do. I was the one who saw the need for discipline and order in the band. And more or less, here are my terms:

If a cat works for me, I tell him what I expect beforehand. He has to be backstage a half hour before the first note is to be played. That gives him time to get ready. If he's late, I can fine him $50. (It used to be $5 or $10, but I learned that didn't do any good. It didn't sting.) The fine is at my discretion, and I don't always use it. I might wait and see if it happens again. If a cat is chronic—late three or four times— I fire him. That saves me future aggravation.

I don't want the money from the fines for my personal use. It's recycled back into the band for such things like cleaning uniforms or repairing equipment. But it's an effective deterrent.

I'd rather not fine anyone. But I expect to get what I'm paying for —nothing more, nothing less. (I once paid someone to fly from Los Angeles to our gig in Mexico City to pay my cats in cash when I could have given them checks.) I figure I do my part. And I expect the same of them.

When I played with Joe Anderson down in Orlando, he told us he wasn't going to put up with any smoking on the bandstand. So I didn't smoke on the bandstand. It was his band, he gave me the gig, and I figured it was his shot to call. That's how I came up. And that's how I am.

So when my band was formed, I tried to follow the advice of the Bible. I put away childish things. Now I had a large organization, and I knew it had to be run smoothly. Too much money was involved not to take it seriously. I expected everyone to be in uniform. If I could wear a coat and a tie and suffer my way through, so could they. What they did off the bandstand was their business. I had my own indulgences, and I let them have theirs. But as far as the music went, the thing had to be tight.

Now I didn't mind the musicians using words like "damn" or "hell" around the Raeletts. But I didn't want them to use the real heavy curse words—like "motherfucker" or "kiss my ass." I reminded the guys that the Raeletts were women like their own sisters and mothers. And I told them that they should show some respect and restraint for them as they would for their own.

I had no patience at all for musicians who showed up juiced. If someone couldn't play—or couldn't sing—I had no use for them. I might put up with it for a month or two, but no longer.

Jeff and Joe became my eyes. I wanted it that way because I was convinced that if I could see, there'd be less funny stuff on the bandstand. They reported back to me what I couldn't catch, and then I decided how to respond.

I've read where one ex-sideman of mine has said that my band was like the army, that everyone had to be in uniform and exactly on time. Well, I've heard that the army has a few more demands than that—but he sure got the rules straight.

My attitude toward clubowners is no different. I expect them to do what they promise—pay me. And I do what I'm being paid for. If I'm getting $35,000 and see that the club is doing $350,000 in business, I don't expect another penny. On the other hand, if we play to an empty house, I demand my bread just the same.

The first couple of years with the big band weren't easy. It didn't make no difference whether it was the sly old veterans or the wild new cats; I was having more trouble with all of them than it seemed to be worth.

I struggled with it—putting up with lateness, drunkenness, rowdiness—but around 1963 I got fed up and decided to disband the whole bunch, right in the middle of the season. Fuck it; that was my attitude.

There were two really punctual cats in the band, though; Henderson Chambers—who we called Mr. Chambers—and Keg Johnson. And right after I decided to cancel the entire band, Keg took me aside and gave me a little talk:

"Brother Ray, you've worked your whole life to have a big band. Don't you think it's dumb to let five or six cats mess up the works? Now that don't make sense."

Naturally Keg was making sense. He was a good soul, and he really turned me around. I decided instead to can the cats who were running wild and hire new people in their place. In essence, though, I formed a new band.

Other times I've been very protective of my cats. I don't let anyone discipline them except me, and they understand that I'm always the one who will hire or fire them. I don't believe in delegating that authority.

Years later there was a cute confrontation about the band between me and Norman Granz who had booked us into Munich. For some unavoidable reason, we got to this gig late and Norman was all excited and up in arms. While I went to get dressed, Norman cornered Leroy Cooper, who was then my director, and told him that the cats had to go on the bandstand immediately—without changing—and start playing.

Hog knew that wasn't my style, so he came and told me what Norman had said. I told Leroy to instruct the guys to get in their uniforms as fast as humanly possible, and then to go to the bandstand.

Norman found out that his orders had been undermined and he charged into my dressing room. He was on fire. I mean, the cat was steaming:

"What the hell are you doing? All these people have been waiting all this time, and you tell your guys to get dressed? Are you crazy? Are you out of your mind?"

He went on for three or four minutes. All I said was, "Norm, I hear this city has marvelous sausages, and I've always wanted to try them."

Now he lost his senses.

"Sausages! *Sausages!* Man, screw the sausages! Why do I give a goddamn about sausages while your fucking band is farting around with their shirts and ties?"

He wouldn't let up until I finally interrupted him again:

"Quiet, Norman," I said, "I'm trying to listen to my cats."

"What?" he said.

"Quiet, man," I answered, "my band's playing and I want to hear."

Sure enough, they had begun to play. Norman left without saying another word, and after the show he returned with the biggest sack of sausages I'd ever seen in my life.

"Stick 'em up your ass," Norman said.

"No, Norm, I ain't going to stick 'em up my ass. I'm going to eat these sausages."

And ever since that night, Mr. Granz and I have been the best of friends.

Ray Charles at the piano, early 1960s. (*Harrah's Hotels and Casinos, Reno and Lake Tahoe*)

The Apollo, the early 1950s. Upper left, from left: Leroy Cooper, Fathead Newman, Rick Harper, Walter Miller, unidentified trombonist. Lower left, from left: Edgar Willis, Leroy Cooper, Bill Peeples (on drums), Fathead Newman, Mary Ann Fisher, Rick Harper, Walter Miller. Upper right: the Apollo marquee. Lower right: Ray at the piano. Center: Fathead Newman.

One of the first big bands, the early 1960s. Lower row, from left: Hank Crawford, Edgar Willis (bass), Sonny Forrest (guitar), Fathead Newman, Rudy Powell, Donald Wilkerson, Leroy Cooper. Middle row, from left: Bruno Carr (drums), Leon Comegee, Henderson Chambers, James Harbert. Top row, from left: Marcus Belgrave, Wallace Davenport, John Hunt (not shown, Philip Guilbeau).

On the band bus, mid-1960s, Ray Charles plays chess with trombonist Fred Morrell. Looking over Morrell's shoulder is critic Leonard Feather and behind him, keyboardist Billy Preston. (*Earl Fowler*)

The Raelets. (*Maurice Seymour*)

Ray Charles with Billy Davis, ad agency executive, and Aretha Franklin during recording session for Coca-Cola commercials, 1966. (*Howard Morehead*)

Ray Charles's sons, 1965.
From left: Robert, David,
Ray, Jr.

Ray Charles's daughter Evelyn.

Della Robinson (B).

From left, Joe Bridgewater, Donald Wilkerson, Ray, Fathead Newman.

Ray Charles

Clydie King

Merry Clayton

Alex Brown

Gwen Berry

Ray Charles climbs into his Cessna 310, early 1960s. (*George Pelling*)

Ray Charles with his Raelettes, late 1960s. From top: Clydie King, Merry Clayton, Alexandra Brown, Gwen Berry. (*Maurice Seymour*)

Zubin Mehta and Ray Charles during taping of 1970 NBC special, "Switched-On Symphony," backed by Los Angeles Philharmonic and the Roger Wagner Chorale. (*NBC*)

Ray Charles co-hosting the Mike Douglas show, early 1970s. (*CBS*)

Big band in Tel Aviv, December 1972. (*©1978 Sherry Suris*)

Ray Charles and David
Ben-Gurion, Israel, 1972.
(*Joe Adams*)

Ray Charles with Norman Granz during 1976 recording of *Porgy and Bess*.
(*Phil Stern*)

Ray Charles, 1976. (*Joe Adams*)

Too Close
for Comfort

In the early sixties, our style of travel changed. I mentioned my Cessna 310 to you. That's the plane that I personally hopped around on back then. For the first couple of years, I had a bus for the band, and then —in 1963 or so—I switched over to a plane—a Martin piston-driven job—which we set up to seat thirty people or so.

I love planes, and I figured everyone would be more comfortable in one. They were safer than ground transportation, and they got us to the gigs faster. By 1963, we were all up in the air.

That turned out to be a good move, and I've been going that way ever since. Later, I traded the Martin for a secondhand Viscount, and I've also been lucky enough to find superb pilots to fly for me.

I'm strict as hell about how the cats act on the plane. No dope is allowed, and if anyone's caught, he's automatically fired. I believe in safety. Even leaving an empty half-pint bottle on a seat can be trouble; if we hit turbulence the bottle can fly into someone's head.

The more I flew, the more I learned about planes, until I reached the point where I was convinced I could land one if I had to. I might tear off a wing, but I think I'd get the son of a bitch down. I figured that since my life depends upon the plane, I might as well know what makes the thing tick. Besides, just being around something every day will make me curious; I'll naturally want to learn all the mechanical mysteries for myself.

I've been told that flying can be a hundred hours of sheer boredom or thirty seconds of stark terror. Amen. And here's scripture and verse which prove the point:

It's the early sixties. We're flying my Cessna from Shreveport, Louisiana, to Oklahoma City. The plane holds five, but there are only three of us today—me, my pilot Tom McGarity—a black dude with an Irish-sounding name—and a magazine reporter who's following me around to do a story.

The weather's bad, but we figure, fuck it, we'll make it. We get up to 16,000 feet and we're above the soup. Nothing's going wrong, and we're having a pleasant enough time—happy, nonchalant, bullshitting, and sailing along.

Twenty-five miles from the Oklahoma City airport and still no problems. We call the tower and they give us clearance on ILS. That's Instrument Landing System. Simply means that because of the lousy weather and poor visibility, we'll have to use our instruments to guide us in. There's nothing around us but gray skies and muck.

It's snowing pretty heavy now, but still nothing unusual. We start coming down from 16,000 feet, 15,000, 14,000, 12, 10, 8, 7. Everything seems fine. But it isn't. We don't know it, we can't tell it, but our windshield is completely frozen over, covered and caked by a thick layer of ice.

Tom doesn't notice because there isn't anything to see outside but the lousy weather. And his eyes are peeled on the instruments which are telling us how to land.

Finally we are 250 feet off the ground, the absolute minimum altitude allowed. We still can't see the airport lights. And now we realize what's happened to the windshield. Our visibility is zero.

Apparently we turned on the windshield defroster too late, when we were a hundred miles or so outside Oklahoma City. By then the frost and freezing rain had already done their damage, and the windshield couldn't get hot enough to melt off those layers of ice.

Now Tom doesn't have a choice. We don't have enough fuel to make it to another airport because all those nearby—those within 150 miles of Oklahoma City—are also socked in. All Tom can do is circle the field. We can't see the ground; we can't see shit. We're literally flying blind, and it's much too risky to try to land. Cessnas—unlike Pipers—don't glide, and during those last few feet during landing, we could easily drift off the runway and crash.

So we're stuck, trapped inside this little plane with windows totally covered by ice too thick for anything but a chisel to chip.

Circling the field doesn't do us any good. It just creates more trouble. There isn't much turbulence, the plane isn't shaking or bouncing, but the freezing rain and the ragged ice are weighing us down and fighting the plane's lift.

Round ice isn't bad, but ragged ice—the sort of ice we're battling today—is downright negative. Planes get their lift from the wind blowing over the top of the wing, and ragged ice fights that process.

Now Tom's wrassling the plane to keep it level, but the Cessna's getting heavier and heavier. Now he's desperately trying to trim the plane—that's a way to keep tipping up the nose—but it's becoming nearly impossible. I mean things look bad. We're headed for a fall.

Our reporter friend—who's been strangely quiet—starts to make his presence known. He begins with a mild "Hail Mary, full of grace," but after a few minutes, the faint prayer becomes an all-out shout: "HAIL MARY, FULL OF GRACE . . ."

I'm not against praying, but I'm busy working the radio. I'm reporting to the tower what Tom is telling me. And even though Tom can hear the tower's instructions to us, I'm repeating them back to him to make sure he has understood. My mind is fixed on ways to keep us from crashing.

Finally, the Hail Marys get out of hand, and I turn to the cat and say, "Look, man. Don't know what kind of relationship you have with Mary, but whatever it is, tell her this one last time and then shut the fuck up."

So much for the reporter.

Tom keeps struggling with the goddamn plane, trying to keep it level. But the ice is building, building, building, and every time we make a turn, we lose altitude, altitude which we can never recover.

The defroster is on full blast, but it doesn't do a thing. We can blow hot air on the windshield, light a match under it, or put a blowtorch to it—nothing's going to melt this ice. It's there to stay.

"I think we can only make it around one more time," Tom says. Just like that. "Okay, man," I nod.

It's not that I ain't scared. I am. But I might be too scared to react to the fear. I have my hands full, explaining our plight to the tower and relaying instructions. Tom doesn't panic and neither do I. And that's how we go into this last turn, still trying to figure ways to keep from busting our ass, with little murmurs of Hail Marys coming from behind us.

It takes only five minutes or so to circle the field, but believe me, man, that's a lifetime. Our hearts are frozen stiff—just like the windshield. How the hell are we going to land? How the hell are we going to see? How the hell are we going to get out of this motherfucker alive?

I cannot explain what happens next. Even telling you about it now, I'm still amazed. Toward the end of this last turn, we notice something in the midst of the windshield—a tiny, clear circle no larger than a half-dollar piece. A peephole in the middle of the frost, just barely large enough for Tom to squint through and follow the strobe lights home.

That's how we came down safely—with Tom gazing through that tiny hole.

And Tom was beautiful throughout the ordeal. He had piloted the Cessna like a champ. But when the danger was over, the excitement finally got to him. As he climbed out of the plane, he fell down and nearly broke his neck. Only the snow on the ground saved him from being hurt.

Our reporter friend was still Hail Marying, and I felt sure he must have shit over himself. But I couldn't blame him. His prayers may have helped.

And even the cat from the control tower came out and inspected the plane. He couldn't believe it. It was as though someone's hand—the hand of God—had taken an ice pick and chipped away in that one spot. Everything around that circle was packed solid with frost. It looked like the windshield had been touched in this single spot by a magic wand.

I like scientific, logical explanations, and I usually look for one at times like this. But not today, baby. I could understand it if I saw a whole patch of melted ice. But there was nothing of the kind. Our path was cleared by someone or something which instruments cannot detect.

When I got on the ground, I had to feel that half-dollar circle for myself, and when I did, I knew that I was a blessed man on that particular day of my life.

There were other scary plane incidents. One time our pilot forgot to pull the flaps and we weren't climbing like we should have been. For some reason, I could feel the problem, I mentioned it and the flaps were pulled. We were okay.

Another time the tower gave us clearance for 11,000 feet. For whatever stupid reason, I had got the number 13,000 lodged in my brain, and I asked the pilot to check the flight plan. Sure enough, 13,000 it was. The controller had made a mistake. Maybe we would have had room to get over the mountains anyway (providing we didn't hit any drafts), but I ain't one to take chances.

I can also remember a day when Joe Adams and I were in New York. I had to go to Texas and he was headed back to L.A. when I asked him to fly with me. That's something I never do.

"There's no reason to, Ray," Joe said, "I'll fly nonstop to L.A."

"Man, I just think you should be with me."

I argued so long that he gave in. Switched planes and joined me. Didn't even have time to get his luggage which was already on the L.A. flight. That was the flight that crashed and burned, killing everyone aboard.

Don't ask me for explanations.

The road can be a bitch all right. It's killed many cats I've known —Guitar Slim, Jesse Belvin—and that time in Oklahoma, it nearly got me. I escaped with my life, but sometimes I got to shake my head with wonder when I think of those wicked twists and turns which could've tripped me up . . . and didn't.

Back to the Country

Sam Clark was president of ABC when I got there and a sweet guy named Sid Feller was in charge of what's called A & R—artists and repertoire. Sid became a friend of mine and one of my tightest musical associates. We still work together today, although both of us have long since left ABC. Our chemistry always clicks, and he's someone who understands the way I like to operate.

When I joined ABC, I formed a publishing company and called it Tangerine, after my favorite fruit. Atlantic had handled my songs through their Progressive Publishing Company, but once I switched labels I decided to begin my own firm so I could keep the publishing profits for myself.

This was a good move, even though by 1961 I was writing fewer original songs and arrangements. I had always written out of necessity. I understand writing and I liked it, but it wasn't like playing or singing. Those are things that I don't have to gird myself up for. I just do them naturally.

Writing's another matter. It requires discipline, putting yourself in the right frame of mind. As long as I had to, I wrote. But when the need passed, I stopped. By this time, I had people bringing me arrangements and songs and had built up a large book for my band. There was no longer any pressure for me to generate my own material.

Once in a while I'd hear something in the middle of the night and call a cat from the band to write it down for me. I still compose at least one arrangement a year for my big band—just to make sure I can still do it. But I got to be in the right mood. In contrast, I'm *always* in the mood to sing.

Before I left my writing behind, though, I did an album for the new ABC jazz subsidiary—Impulse. Ralph Burns and Quincy Jones wrote the charts for a big band which included some of the heaviest cats around. The album was called *Genius Plus Soul Equals Jazz.* I played Hammond organ—just to do something different—and wrote three of the tunes. We had a couple of big records off the album—"One Mint Julep" and "I've Got News For You," which was something I remembered Woody Herman singing.

Another tune—"Outskirts of Town"—was something I had heard Louis Jordan do years before, and "Stompin' Room Only" was a simple swing song I had loved as a child. I think Glen Gray had done it.

On this album, like so many others I'd soon record, I found myself in the fortunate position of being able to reconstruct bits and pieces from my childhood—from all those years spent listening to the jukebox at Mr. Pit's and listening to the radio at school.

Quincy put together the band, and I brought along my own trumpet player, Phil Guilbeau, to do his nasty little business behind me. I was pleased with the results, and in many ways the record became a continuation of what we had begun on the big-band side of the *Genius* album for Atlantic.

By this time, I was involved in planning albums. In addition to playing dominoes or shooting craps when I was on the road with extra time on my hands, I dreamt up concepts.

On *The Genius Hits the Road,* I picked out twelve tunes for twelve states. Many people—and some critics—were surprised to see me doing "Alabamy Bound."

I remember one cat saying to me, "Come on, Ray, you ain't doing *that* tune?"

"That's nothing," I said, "I'm also singing 'Mississippi Mud.' "

These were numbers I had always liked, and I saw no reason not to interpret them my own way. I had Ralph Burns write the charts. And one of the songs from the album, something I had heard Hoagy Carmichael do, became a tremendous hit and earned me a great deal of bread. That was "Georgia on My Mind." When I recorded it, I had no plans to release it as a single. That was something ABC did, with my approval.

I've never known a lady named Georgia—other than Mr. Pit's wife—and I wasn't dreaming of the state when I recorded the song, even though I was born there. It was just a beautiful, romantic melody, and I still sing it most nights when I'm performing.

There were other concept albums which struck some people as being funny. To me, though, they were just little jive ideas I wanted to try out.

In 1960, just after *The Genius Hits the Road*, we did *Dedicated to You*. I chose twelve songs with girls' names in them, and one of the girls—"Ruby"—also became a big seller. This time Marty Paich did the arrangements, and I continued to use strings and choral backgrounds. That was the album, by the way, where I finally got to do "Nancy," the song I had loved for so long.

I also kept on producing singles with my small band. The big band wasn't put together till the last part of 1961, and my last small group—the one with five horns—did "Sticks and Stones," "Unchain My Heart" and "Hit the Road, Jack."

The bulk of my musical energy, though, was put into touring and planning albums. This is the period when I did those duets with Betty Carter. I know people still ask for that album and I believe there was something special about the music we made together.

I had first heard Betty the night I ran into the Cookies back in Philadelphia. She was singing with Hamp's band, and I was impressed.

She's a hell of a singer. I like to compare her to Sarah Vaughan, which is like comparing Benny Goodman to Artie Shaw. Sarah's like Benny. She has unbelievable technique and deserves all the praise she's gotten. She's a master. But Betty's like Artie. She's a marvelous technical singer, but she's also got that old feeling—that raw feeling—that destroys me.

The biggest of the concept albums involved country-and-western music. And it came about because I had been planning it for years. If I had remained on Atlantic, I would have done the country thing a year or two earlier. I knew, however, that ABC thought of me as a rhythm-and-blues singer, and I didn't want to shock the label too badly or too quickly. So I waited till the beginning of 1962. That seemed like a reasonable time.

My contract was up for its three-year renewal and, to my way of thinking, I had done well for ABC. They hadn't hassled me before, and I had no reason to believe they would bother me now. Still, my country music idea might have hit them as half-cocked and completely crazy.

What better time to test their faith in me? If they were really behind me, they'd let me do what I wanted. And if they weren't with me all the way, I'd get to learn that right now.

I called Sid Feller and asked him to gather up the great country hits of all time. He sounded a little bewildered, but he was nice enough to do what I asked. Later on, the ABC executives mildly protested—but all in good taste.

They told me how this might injure my career. They told me how all my fans had been loyal to me. They explained how I might irritate some people, how I might lose my following. And even though I listened and understood what they were saying, I ignored them and made the record anyway. We had no contract problems.

I didn't plan on making a killing on the country stuff; I had no commercial scheme in mind. I just wanted to try my hand at hillbilly music. After all, the Grand Ole Opry had been performing inside my head since I was a kid in the country.

To show you how naive I was about the sales potential of this material, I put "I Can't Stop Loving You" as the fifth song on the B side. I called the album *Modern Sounds in Country and Western Music.*

I had no special plans for the arrangements. In fact, I set some of the songs against strings with a choir, the way I was doing much of my material then. Other tunes were done with a big band—my big band —which had just been formed.

I was only interested in two things: being true to myself and being true to the music. I wasn't trying to be the first black country singer. I only wanted to take country songs and sing them my way, not the country way. I wasn't aware of any bold act on my part or any big breakthrough.

It was just blind luck that the tunes—"I Can't Stop Loving You," "Born to Lose," and later, "Take These Chains," "You Are My Sunshine," "Busted," and "You Don't Know Me"—hit with such impact. These country hits wound up giving me a bigger white audience than black, and today when I play concerts, there are still usually more whites than blacks.

At the same time, "I Can't Stop Loving You" was a big song among blacks. It didn't get the initial air play that it might have, but that's 'cause it wasn't the kind of song black jocks normally programmed. And also I was led to believe by some of these cats that they just didn't like ABC. They told me that they played my songs only because it was me. Finally, "I Can't Stop Loving You" made the black stations simply 'cause they had no choice; the record was too important to be ignored.

I'm not sure what was at the root of the problem. I met deejays from time to time, but I never found out how the system worked. I wouldn't accuse anyone of either giving or taking payola, though I know damn well that it's something—like prostitution—which ain't ever going away.

Whenever one person—a jock or a program director—has control, and whenever the record companies have the money to pursue that person, you know something's got to happen. Don't ask any questions, though, 'cause everyone will deny it.

You might offer someone at a radio station $50, and all of a sudden he'll get mad and start cussing you: "What! You kidding? Forget it, man! I don't want to hear from nothing." Make it a grand, though, and you know he's just *gotta* think about it. Oh, he's going to think about it all right.

Maybe you could change the system by having the stations choose the music by committee and not just by single individuals. Maybe it can't ever be changed. I ain't sure.

I believe that talent will finally win out in this business. But Jesus could be coming tomorrow, and if no one knew, it wouldn't mean anything. Not even God can afford to ignore promotion.

Later on, when I began my own record company, I still didn't get involved in buying favors. Sometimes I had to wonder whether that cost me a hit every now and then. I'll never know.

I don't want to sound high and mighty about it. I'm not saying I'm above such practices. It's just that my little company has never had that kind of bread to throw around. If the money was there, I'm not sure what I'd do.

After the country sessions, I went back on the road and forgot about those tunes. Then one day—I think I was in California—Sam Clark called from New York:

"Listen, Ray. We just heard that Tab Hunter has put out a single of 'I Can't Stop Loving You' which copies your version to the letter. I want to release yours as a single, and I want to do it tonight. I'm calling for your permission."

Naturally I gave it to him. Sid Feller and I discussed the editing, and a single version was sent right out. We smothered the Hunter rendition and sold millions of copies of the song. Even the album went gold.

"Born to Lose" was on the other side, and it became a hit on its own. If we had known what was going to happen, we would never have put them back to back.

But I have no complaints. Sam and the other ABC executives always consulted with me first, and I appreciated the respect they showed me. I usually went along with their business decisions—especially about what songs to pull from albums as single releases—'cause that was their special area, just as producing and making the music was mine.

Years later, my own company had audits done on Atlantic and ABC which showed that both labels owed me some bread. They paid and everything was cool. I never thought twice about it. The respect they gave me as an artist was more important than the accuracy of their accounting.

Many people are confused about my decision to do country music. They think ABC dictated to me. They think ABC produced these albums for me. Not true. For better or worse, the records were my ideas. Anyone who knows me understands that I really like this music. Not for show, not for shock, but for my own pleasure.

Once in a while I heard voices—from friends or from writers—about how I had gone commercial. I really didn't know what that meant. I thought I had *always* been commercial. I had always been in the business of playing music for money.

Writers or critics never bother me. Sometimes I'll clip a bad review, frame it, and hang it on the wall—just for the fun of it. I believe everyone can say what he or she wants to say. I only get mad when opinion is passed off as fact.

A cat can say, "I saw Ray Charles last night and he stunk"—that's one thing—but if he says, "I saw Ray Charles last night, he stunk and no one dug him," he sure as hell better talk to a lot of people in the audience before he draws that conclusion.

Other musicians will also drop you hints about how they think you're doing. That's fine. But artists got to remember that writers and musicians aren't known for buying thousands of tickets and thousands of records. That's why I stick with me and the public as the first and last measures of how I'm faring.

The only musician whose opinion ever mattered to me was Lucky Millinder. He was the cat who told me I wasn't good enough for his band. They were negative words, but I'd come to cherish them. They made me realize I had to head back to the woodshed. Aside from that experience, I use sales, rather than what other musicians say, as a guide.

I gauge how I'm doing by how many folk come to my concerts and buy my records. And my fans make up their own minds.

People buy what they like. Period. I don't believe, for example, that I lost any black fans by doing country music; I just gained a lot of white fans. There were people—black and white—who were upset with my country songs. Some thought they were an abomination; others even called me sacrilegious. I got a lot of reaction. But this was nothing new.

I heard the same kind of bellyaching when I did my first gospel/blues songs. The critics said this or the critics said that. Called it shit or called it the most original invention since the cotton gin.

In both instances—with my early hits and my country hits—I just happened to hit some good timing. By chance, no one had tried these things before in quite my way. So it was new, different, and—for reasons I don't fully understand—appealing to what turned out to be a whole world of listeners.

If someone had said to me, "Ray, you can make a million by singing country, you got to do it," I'm sure I would have refused. I hate to be pushed into anything.

It's not that I'm against marketing. I think you should use any goddamn gimmick you can think of to sell records. Why not? It's a business, ain't it? But that's *after* the artist has already made the product. I don't believe in putting the gimmick in the product itself. After all, the product is me, and I don't see myself as a gimmick.

After "I Can't Stop Loving You," my royalties started mounting up. I was told that the tax consequences would be grave if I pulled my money out and treated it as income. So I followed the good advice of people around me, and I never touched it. In fact, all my record royalties at ABC just kept accumulating over there until the company and I went our separate ways in 1973.

From time to time, I borrowed against these moneys. In essence, I was borrowing against myself, but on paper the loans were being given to ABC. My interest rates were low—about 4 percent—and that way I was able to do a few things later on—buy some property, build an office building and a house—without disturbing the principal.

I wasn't interested in lavish purchases, and I was content to act like those royalties weren't even there. For the most part I lived off the bread I made performing on the road.

What did I really need? I could only sleep in one bed, eat one meal, and fuck one woman at a time.

I suppose that I became a big star at this point, but that really didn't change my attitude. I never cared much about being a headliner, and to tell the truth, I've never insisted on top billing. I've always let the promoter call his own shot. If he wanted me in the middle of the show, fine; or at the end, fine; or at the beginning, fine. Made me no difference.

Lots of stars take less bread in order to headline. Man, I've seen some crazy fights over billing. But my attitude is just the reverse: Gimme the bread and screw the billing. Besides, if the man gives me the kind of money I'm asking, I know he ain't going to bury my name.

I've always been a loner, and a lot of money and fame didn't change that. In my younger days, I went out to clubs only when I thought I could jam or find a gig. I had to be in circulation if other people were to hear me and hire me. But once that need passed, my nightlife came to a quick stop.

Oh, I go out now maybe once or twice a year. Folks say I'm private to the point of being antisocial, and I won't argue. I'll just say that since 1961 or so, I haven't been able to do what most people do: go to a restaurant, order my food, eat, and split. Many people—and 99 percent do it with love in their hearts—stop me and try to engage me in conversation. I'm not good in those situations. I withdraw into my little shell. Strange, because I love to perform in public. But performing and socializing are two different things.

I'm shy. I'm not relaxed with more than three or four people in a room, and if I don't know those people well, I'm really uncomfortable. If I'm in a public place and someone comes up to compliment me, I don't know what to say. I can't find the right words. I've never learned to be gracious or charming in those situations. I stutter and stammer and finally let loose with an, "Oh, thank you very much."

I know it's stupid, but I'm embarrassed by those sorts of friendly confrontations. So I avoid them. Even though I can print, I never sign autographs. That makes me uneasy and awkward. I don't discriminate about autographs either. I went to the White House when Nixon was there and he asked me for one. I turned him down. I wouldn't make an exception. Surest way to get folks pissed at you is to do something for Mary that you won't do for Jane.

If I go out—on that extremely rare occasion—it's almost always for music. Say Dizzy Gillespie or Oscar Peterson or Clark Terry is playing a club. I might sneak in and sneak out so no one knows I'm there. And if it won't cause a commotion, I'll go back after the set and say hi to the cats.

I've been known to catch a symphony orchestra concert, but if I go, I keep my profile real low. If I could manage it, I'd make myself invisible so I could concentrate on the music.

This is the bed that I made, and it's the one I gotta sleep in. I'm not griping about having fans. I'm just explaining why my true nature doesn't really permit me to mingle with them.

I've been this way since I was twenty. Over the years, I may have grown more mature in my judgment—least I hope so—but I've also grown even more adamant about my privacy.

So you can see why I didn't go hog-wild when my bread started to happen. And you can understand why I was content to let it rest over at ABC. I just didn't need it. My only habits were heroin and women, and I fixed those both where I could afford 'em in reasonable allotments.

I had climbed through years of hit records before this—some minor, some major—so having a bigger smash than I'd had before wasn't going to change me. Didn't require adjustment in my thinking or send me into orbits of ecstasy.

It was something like my going blind. That also happened gradually; the slow process permitted me time to grow accustomed to the darkness. If I had suddenly lost my sight at twenty, for example, it would have been rough. If I never had a single seller till "I Can't Stop Loving You," then maybe I'd have reacted less calmly.

I've heard stories about famous guys—cats I've followed my whole life—who had fortunes and blew 'em. One singer had a big house in L.A. which he was about to lose when his record label bailed him out. Tax problems. And as a result, he was committed to his record company —or so the story went—till the day he died.

I couldn't feature myself tied to any record company like that. And hearing about these guys—these heroes of mine—shook me. I could relate to their misfortunes, and I told myself it wasn't going to happen to me.

I don't believe in planning for the future. I believe in planning for now. You won't even have a future if you don't lay aside your bread for the tax man—and you got to do that as soon as you earn it.

But for all this money talk, I still wasn't making the kind of bread in a year that Tom Jones could make in a week. You got to remember: In 1962 and 1963, I was one of the few so-called rhythm-and-blues artists who was bringing the white populace over to my side. In the early sixties, there wasn't the kind of flow you have today.

In spite of my "Georgias" or my "Rubys," I still had a hard time breaking into the white pop market. That didn't happen till "I Can't Stop Loving You," and that was a highly unusual circumstance.

There were so many white pop artists that few blacks were readily accepted and bought by the great mass of whites. Of course Nat Cole was the exception. But look how good he had to be in order to achieve that. He had to have a fabulous voice, he had to have a unique sound, and he had to come up with consistently hot material.

Other examples exist—Louis Armstrong or Billy Eckstine. But a rhythm-and-blues singer, at least when I was coming up, was typecast, much like an actor. Even today I'm called "Ray Charles, the blues singer," or "Ray Charles, the soul singer." And this is after twenty years of singing damn near everything!

For the Love
of Women

I've always been wild when it comes to females, and I can see how my long line of love affairs finally busted up my marriage. I'll tell you more about that later, but now I want to set out the preamble to my constitution regarding women:

In spite of my old-fashioned attitudes, I believe that women have been the victims of society's oppression as much as anyone. They've been taught that they can't stand alone, they've been beaten down and treated like servants, they've been waiting on us men like slaves. I realize that, and I see the pity and the shame of it all.

On the other hand, I came up at a time when those attitudes were not argued—by men or by women. No one was challenging them, and I took them all for granted. In my middle age, I see the cracks in the old foundation—our thinking has certainly been fucked up—but I'm also a product of my time.

Women's lib is good to me, so I don't fight it. I want chicks to be more independent. I'm happy if they don't ask me for stuff. How can any right-minded man argue against that? But sometimes I wonder whether families can take too much competition between men and women.

A man has to feel like he's protecting something or somebody. If he doesn't, he's apt not to consider himself a man. That may be dumb, that may be ignorant, that may not be modern, but I bet you that 90 percent of the cats you meet on the street really feel that way.

It's been my experience that even strong gals finally lose respect for a man if he can be pushed around. They might go after you a little bit and test your ass, but when it gets down to the getting down, most of 'em still want you on top.

I'm one of those cats who looks at a cow pen and sees one bull; I look at a chicken house and see one rooster; I look at the lion's den and see one lion. But this bull has many cows, this rooster has many hens, this male lion has many females.

As far back as I can read, I see that man has been slipping around. The Bible talks about it time and again. And I do believe that deep down we've got a natural drive for more than one woman.

I recognize all the sexual differences—that there are men who lust for other men, women who dig other women, and people who go every which way. I respect those differences; I believe those desires are legitimate and wholesome, and what people do in their bedrooms is strictly their own business.

But there's a certain male drive—even though all males don't have it—which keeps us wanting more and more women: different kinds, different shapes, different sizes, with various voices, with sweet and salty smells and touches and feels which have us guessing and wondering and searching and switching.

I can see why, in the old days, a cat would pick out fifty or sixty women and put his seal on them. He was doing the same thing as a rooster or a bull, saying to the other cats, "Look, this is my territory, these are my women; hands off or I'll murder your ass."

Now I've never done that. But I have known more women than I can literally remember. I don't mean that as a brag, only as a fact. I don't ascribe it to anything unusual in me. In fact, I think that many,

many other cats would do exactly what I do if they had the chance. But I don't have to do much; often I just turn around and there she is.

There are lots of cats who do the same thing. They conceal it, though, with their money and power. You'll have to wait till they die before you're hipped to what's actually coming down. Actors, kings, prime ministers, chiefs, presidents—these are gentlemen with similar situations as mine. They're names. And they're exposed to many women who are willing, ready, and able to satisfy them at any given moment.

That's a lovely fate—at least it can be—and Lord knows I've taken full advantage of it. I wasn't cut out to discipline myself sexually; few human beings are, and when they are, watch out: They usually take out the frustrations on something or somebody else.

Having female singers around me also opens up many possibilities for me right at home. Don't get me wrong. If I was forced to look hard, I'd certainly look. I don't like to conclude a day without female companionship.

I'm probably a fatalist. I don't know if I have two more years to live, forty years, or another two hours. I've always felt that way. I don't want to be unhappy. Not if I can control it. Fate will lay enough unhappiness on me; I don't need to look for any of my own. So as long as I can generate my own good times, I'll be doing just that.

I meet a gal. She digs me. I dig her. The chemistry's right. She's clean, she talks nice, she's attractive, she's enticing, her voice is pleasing, and she's anxious to get down—well, that's enough for me.

My relationships with women have been loose. I've slipped in and out of many different situations, but I've tried to follow some rules:

I have no interest in trying to keep tabs on every move a woman of mine makes. If she tells me she's going to the store, fine. I ain't gonna follow her to see whether she's gonna meet some dude at the Holiday Inn. I don't want to aggravate myself.

Naturally, like everyone else, I'm jealous. I ain't made of stone. But if a chick says she's through with me, I don't argue and I don't try to talk her out of it.

I assume she's serious. It takes courage to say that, since some men will stick a knife in a woman for such statements. They'd rather have their ladies dead than fucking someone else.

In my young and foolish days, I might have popped a gal upside the head on a rare occasion. But that's when I was stupid. That don't solve nothing, and besides, if you're blind, you're really dumb to start that kind of shit. You don't know what's coming back at you, and there ain't no way you gonna duck in time. A gal can kill your ass.

I think everyone's jealous. Even God. The Bible says somewhere that God is love, but it also says that God is a jealous God. So even He's got those same feelings. Those two—love and jealousy—will be mixed together forever. The trick is learning to walk away from the bad feelings and say, "Hey, Mama, you got it. Shine it on. Do what you feel you have to do. But I don't think we need to destroy each other."

I'm the kind of cat, for example, who doesn't ask a lot of questions. If I'm gone for six months, I won't ask the little lady if she gave it to anyone. If she say no, I might not believe her. If she say yes, I don't want to hear it.

Or if I walk in on a lady friend balling some cat in my apartment, I ain't gonna kill the guy. I'm just gonna tell him to get his ass out. Ain't gonna kill her either, but I'll blame her more than him. She ought to have the sense to say, "Look, I'm gonna give you this pussy, but you going to have to take me somewhere. You sure ain't going to get it here." Certain amount of decency is due everyone—even a dog.

Oh, my nose has been open very wide. I can suffer at the hands of a woman. Cut me and I bleed as much as any man. If I dig a chick, I don't want it to end. There's something about the finale which is tragic—like death—and the pain will burn inside me for a long time.

That's why I believe in options. If a woman tells me she's through, I'll want to know two or three others who'll take me in. I got to be that way, since I'm not willing to tell any female, "That's okay, honey, let me tuck you under my wing and keep you there forever."

I can't characterize my love affairs as lighthearted or silly. They're often serious. Even when I was a kid I hung around older women. Maybe that's 'cause I was thrust into the world of adults so young. Or maybe it's just because I didn't like silly girls who giggled and acted the fool. I like to have fun, but I prefer women who are women—mature and worldly. Let me tell you about a few of such friends:

Margie Hendrix was a great lead singer, a great Raelett. She fitted very well with my own style. I thought she was a big talent. She was also a lovely and sweet lady.

There's one thing, though, that Margie had a hard time with: learning her harmony part. I'd have to take her aside and go over it with her for hours on end. She must have been trying *too* hard. But once she learned her part, she'd have it forever.

Anyway, because of those extra hours spent alone with Margie, she and I got closer and closer and one thing led to another. Soon we became lovers. We didn't live together—we always had separate hotel rooms on the road—but we saw each other often and grew especially tight.

Long 'bout 1959, she became pregnant. She told me about it and asked me what I thought she should do.

"What do *you* want to do?" I said.

"I think I want to have the baby."

"Well, that's what I want too."

And that was that. I'm not for or against abortions. That's the woman's business. So I would never—*ever*—even hint to a lady who I got pregnant that she should or shouldn't have an abortion. It's her decision. I'd never put any pressure on her one way or the other. I feel obliged to lend the kind of support that she wants.

Why should I do otherwise? I've never liked rubbers and therefore don't use 'em. So I certainly don't help prevent pregnancies. I feel obligated to live with the consequences.

Margie had a baby boy—Charles Wayne she called him—and I've supported him. I haven't seen him as much as my kids in California, but that doesn't mean I love him any less. I don't think one brother loses his love for another just because he lives far away. And that's how I feel about all my children. They are me.

Margie died a few years back, and it hurt me very deeply. We were together for a long while—up until she left the band in 1964—and there was something special about what we had. When you hear us sing together, you can tell how close-knit we were.

Today Charles lives with Margie's sister in New York, and I see him whenever it's possible.

I had a child with Louise, I had a child with Margie, I had three with my wife B, and there are four other times when I fathered kids.

Two of those times didn't result in any trouble. In the early fifties, a gal I was going with in Atlanta turned up pregnant. She had a little girl, and everything was cool. Same thing happened out here in California in the sixties. Another pregnancy, another baby girl.

I always made it plain that I'd support the children. I never denied being the father. How could I? My friends told me the babies looked like I'd spit 'em out. And besides, what man—married or single—really knows?

On the other hand, I didn't believe in supporting the child and also setting up mama in some luxurious crib with a Mercedes and two or three mink coats. No, sir. That ain't me. She wouldn't starve, and neither would the baby; but I didn't figure she was entitled to a lifetime of jewels and caviar.

That's how I got myself entangled in two nasty paternity suits. The first happened with a woman I knew in New York, and that's a story which is begging to be told:

If you remember, I met the mother of one of the younger Raeletts when I had to get her permission to have the girl join the band. This was when I was in New York so often that I even had an apartment at the Beaux Arts Hotel over on Third Avenue. From '59 through '63, all my business was in New York—my publishing firm, my lawyers, my booking agent, my accountant, most of the studios where I recorded, and ABC itself.

Well, this woman and I hit it off right away. I dug her so hard that

I rented us an apartment on Ninety-seventh Street and Central Park West. For me, that was a big commitment. Shows you how much I was into her.

Our relationship went on for some time. I couldn't live in New York —I've never wanted to live there—but I was there for long spells.

New York always seemed like an experiment some scientist dreamed up. Instead of rats, you crowd as many people together as you can, let them crawl over each other and live with their asses sticking in each other's face. You do that for a while and watch the results—wholesale craziness.

Anyway, my lady friend became pregnant in New York, and once again I didn't protest or encourage her to do anything but have the child. She did; she had a girl, and I was prepared to do what I had always done: support the baby. But my lady friend was listening to other folk. Friends started whispering in her ear:

"What, with all his bread! Well, listen here, if I was you—" That kind of chatter. She also talked to a lawyer, something which caused even more discord. Finally, she demanded more bread. *Demanded.* Well, I resent demands, especially when I think they're unreasonable. So I refused. She filed suit, it was later transferred to Los Angeles, and I lost. Again, I wasn't denying that I was the father. I was just denying that I was the Bank of America.

Exactly the same thing happened with a lady I had met in Ohio, who later came out to L.A. to work. She and I were very close for a while, she wound up pregnant, she had a little girl who looked just like me, and she demanded far more bread than I was willing to pay. Another paternity suit, another trial, another loss for me. By this time, you can see I wasn't exactly knocking 'em dead in the courts.

But that's not the point. I believe in doing what's fair and right. And it's very hard to threaten me. Even all the publicity and the embarrassment to my wife didn't make me budge. I considered those kinds of threats—"You gonna be exposed, Ray Charles"—blackmail, and I can't be blackmailed.

I've had fights with the musicians' union over the same kind of issue.

A cat once missed his flight with me and I was supposed to pay him back wages of $600. Screw it, I said, it's *his* fault. The union screamed bloody murder, put me on their blacklist, harassed my friends. Even my lawyer said it wasn't worth fighting, that the legal fees would be double the $600. Didn't matter, I said. It was the principle.

In the case of both paternity suits, I think the ladies now regret what they did. They see I've forgiven them, but I haven't forgotten. I pay exactly what the court ordered and not a dime more. If any of my children need help, I'm there. But except for emergencies, I do no more or no less than what the judge ruled.

If they had only cooled it and let the thing ride out naturally, they would have wound up with more bread. But they misunderstood, got a little greedy, started pushing, and found out I wasn't budging.

Now I don't believe in comparing women, and I don't believe in comparing my children. Every relationship is different. Naturally, I grew closer to the sons I had with B, because I was there more and got to watch their little joys and sorrows. I was also close with Evelyn, and that's because Louise and I were so tight. And besides, Evelyn was my first. She came out of some very strong love between two people. Louise and I had the kind of thing that you don't outlive.

I couldn't very well integrate all these children into my life. They live in faraway places, leading lives of their own. They exist on the outside of my day-to-day grind. But then again, even the boys I had with B—the kids who see me the most—have grown up with an absentee father.

Naturally many of my children are now under the jurisdiction of other men. And there's nothing I can do about that. I'm not about to break down doors and pry into other families' lives just 'cause my kids are there. And I don't really want to get involved with their mothers any more than absolutely necessary.

But the women and the kids know how I feel.

How can any of my children *not* be legitimate? "Illegitimate" sounds like the kid is damn near nonexistent. That's some cold shit. The law makes the man and woman feel like they committed some mortal sin.

It's like the rape laws where a gal is asked all these jive questions to make it sound like she halfway coaxed the cat into attacking her.

It's what we were talking about before: Marriage only got started when men wanted a way to fence off their property. So we set up these rules and started marrying gals. The gals felt like they were being protected. To them, it was their sole method of survival.

Many times women weren't allowed to learn to read or write. And they were held back the way blacks had been stifled by whites. That's how men have controlled women for so long. And that's how our attitudes got so crazy and one-sided.

I'm not a reformer and I'm not a crusader. I carry the sins and the silliness of my generation. But when it comes to children, I'm not like the rest of society. There are certain raunchy, hypocritical distinctions I just don't make.

Loosening Up

Women anchor me. They're there when I need them. They're sensitive to me, and I'm sensitive to them. I'm not saying I've loved that many women. Love is a special word, and I use it only when I mean it. You say the word too much and it becomes cheap.

But sex is something else. I'm not sure that there can ever be too much sex. To me, it's another one of our daily requirements—like eating. If I go twenty-four hours without it, I get hungry. Sex needs to be open and fun, free and happy. It's whatever you make it, and I try my hardest to create situations where me and my woman can enjoy ourselves—all of ourselves—without our inhibitions getting in the way.

You got to set your mind right and the rest will come to you naturally. No restrictions, no hang-ups, no stupid rules, no formalities, no forbidden fruit—just everyone getting and giving as much as he and she can.

Being raised in the country, I didn't start out with an open attitude about sex.

You know how 'tis: When you're poor, you hear things like, "If you bad, you gonna die, go to hell, and burn forever." That's the line a lot of folk back home be reeling out and reeling in. And if you're already suffering plenty in this life on earth, the idea of eternal damnation ain't going to rest easy with you.

You couldn't even mention sex in a little country town, in the Deep South during the forties. I imagine that when many of the gals started seeing their periods for the first time, they didn't even know what they were looking at.

Education and money can make a difference in people's attitudes. And of course it can make life—even your sexual life—more convenient. When I was coming up, the women bleeding to death from abortions were the same women nearly starving to death from malnutrition.

Go to the other side of town, though, and it was a different story: "Where's Lucille?" asks one woman.

"Oh, she went to visit her aunt in Atlanta for the week," answers the other.

Yeah, that's how folk with money handled abortions. Nice and clean. Real polite.

It wasn't till Orlando in 1946 that I understood that there were other enjoyable things to do beyond the standard me-on-top-of-you position. But why should I have been thinking otherwise? In Greensville, the emphasis was on the Lord and His holy way. When you're illiterate and poor, you're looking for salvation. And if God's own representatives are telling you that sex is a sin, you'll have a hard time bucking that idea.

But I was lucky. Mama never bugged me much about sex. She was neutral on the subject. She never brought it up, never warned me, never instructed me. If she never told me it was right, she also never said it was wrong.

And then I started to develop my own stubborn ideas 'bout God. If He was supposed to be just, I couldn't see the Man letting me burn forever. Hell, I was just doing what felt good, what felt natural, and what felt good and natural to the person I was doing it with. If that was a sin, I reasoned, then sin on!

But I've always had this shy side to me. I'm a wait-and-see-type cat. Speak when you're spoken to. I got to feel my way around. Got to see whether it's cool or not. Can't just leap into anything. If it was something new, something I never tried before, I did some testing of the waters beforehand. Once I was into the situation, though, once I knew the woman, once I was sure she was free, I'd open up the floodgates and let myself come pouring out.

In the forties, many chicks thought that uninhibited sex was odd or, even worse, dirty. They'd talk about a man like he was a dog. They'd call him crude, call him filthy, call him cocksucker.

I remember once staying in Atlanta at a friend's hotel when one of the maids—a kindly elderly lady—told me this story:

"Oh, Mr. Charles," she said, "I was cleaning up this room. And, well, Mr. Charles, I saw this man, and, Mr. Charles, his head was down there buried between this lady's legs, Mr. Charles, and, Lord have mercy, Mr. Charles, I declare, I'm a clean lady, and I couldn't imagine that two people could ever stoop so low. Could you, Mr. Charles?"

"No, ma'am," I answered in my best Southern manner.

Truth is, my attitudes about sex did take a long time to change. I wasn't about to suggest anything that a gal might not like. Mama always told me, "People may think you're a fool. Open your mouth and they'll know it."

By the time I was twenty-three or twenty-four, my attitude was more open, but the culture didn't really catch up till I was thirty or thirty-five. It wasn't till the sixties—and actually only in the last ten years—that women have been freer about letting you know what pleases them.

For so long they thought men would look down on them. And naturally it was men who gave them that attitude to begin with. Many a gal wanted you as much as you wanted her the first night you met, yet she'd refuse you 'cause she was afraid you'd think she be giving it to everyone.

Other chicks might want more from you than just straight screwing. They might want to get trimmed in another way. They might want you to do something nice with your mouth or your tongue. But they'd be scared to bring it up. Maybe—just maybe—they'd whisper something like, "Gee, have you ever wanted to . . ." but that would be a rare occasion.

Once I became looser, I saw that the name of the game was being comfortable.

"Look here, Mama," I said, "it's just you and me. We're together, and anything you do, I do. And believe me, baby, I don't do nothing I don't dig."

I've heard cats say, "Oh man, I was out with this slut last night and she did this and she did that."

"Really?" I'd say. "Well, if you were right there with her, Jack, what does that make you?"

Remember my mama's old saying? If a dog will bring a bone, he'll carry one.

To me, at least half the fun of fucking is watching a woman have an orgasm. If that don't happen, the evening's not a success.

For years, gals didn't complain and wouldn't mention the matter. And that's because of the old slave mentality. They were trained—we trained them—to think they were there only for our pleasure. They didn't realize—how could they?—that many men can derive as much pleasure from giving as getting.

I've never seen the differences I hear cats talk about in white women or black women, European women or Oriental women. I'm a curious soul, and I've wanted to experience as much as possible. I like the different feels, the different textures of the hair. I've had girlfriends in Japan and love affairs with ladies in Europe. They don't last for too long 'cause of the distance, but I've had a taste of love in several different tongues.

It's all a matter of individual chemistry—you and her—and none of the clichés are worth a damn. I've fallen into some sad lovemaking with white chicks as well as black, and I've had many thrills with members of both groups.

In fact, if I'm forced to choose between a beautiful woman and a homely one—sight unseen—I suppose I'd select the gal without the looks. That's because gorgeous chicks sometimes take the attitude that they're doing you a favor by letting you make love to them. They just lay there. You have to stick a pin in them just to get them to move a little. Another cat might look at a gorgeous chick in bed and the very picture of her beautiful body stretched out before him might damn near make him come right then and there. Not me. Far as I'm concerned, the proof of the pudding is in the eating; I require convincing beyond appearances.

Being blind keeps me honest about sex. I can't congratulate myself for having landed such a luscious chick, I can't see the expressions of envy in everyone's eye when she strolls down the boulevard with me, I can't get excited peeking at her plunging neckline in some dark corner of a nightclub. My delight is in the doing.

And there are many things to do. Many ways to see yourself through. Many ways to become you. I don't consider myself oddball or bizarre, but I certainly believe in exploration, in stimulation, in variation. For instance:

I'm not above a party. I dig 'em. And some of my happiest moments with sex have happened at parties. Those are fabulous highs, glorious hours. I've seen beautiful things come off in such settings.

Before it happens, though, you got to know the participants. If I'm the coordinator—and I prefer to be—I make sure I know everyone who's invited. My parties must be small and intimate. I prefer to be the only man.

If I have a very, very close friend and he wants to bring a girl, that's all right. But that's the exception. If he's my partner, he'll understand me well enough to make sure his lady is cool. I can't deal with more than three or four people.

I'm cautious. Before I put the party together, I weigh all the circumstances. I'm like a chemist or a cook balancing the ingredients. This is ticklish business, and there's no sense in just throwing people together and hoping it works.

When I choose the folks, I think: How will they react the next morning? I select women who will remain discreet, keep quiet, and carry on as though nothing has happened. By blabbering, they usually have as much to lose as I do.

I've seen gals in situations like this get all shy and reserved, covering themselves up over in the corner. It's something like starting a savings account: Getting yourself to begin is tough, yet when you're into it, you don't want to stop.

Once the gal sees the expressions on everyone's faces, once she understands that everyone's genuine about what's happening, she won't resist for long. Her mind will stop straying and the heat will start rising inside her.

Drugs have nothing to do with this. Don't make it no better or worse. Actually heroin is supposed to make you impotent, but I never had that experience. And if I had, then I'm sure it would have ended my addiction immediately. Yeah, I damn sure would have cut it loose, real quick. To me, sex is a stimulant that can overpower anything else running through my body.

Reefer can be nice. But it don't do no more than the right kind of music. It sets the mood, maybe mellows you down a bit, relaxes you out, and lays you back.

You don't want to be doggish at a party. You don't want to rush into things and act the fool. You got to take your time. Not everyone's in action at once, and much of the joy is just watching. If you're patient, you'll get what you're looking at. Everything falls together, like an orchestra playing a symphony. But you can't rush it; you can't get greedy.

If you can clear your mind, if you can free yourself and follow the rhythms and the motions, it's a treat. Like waiting a year and then going to Disneyland for a whole day.

I love to watch what's happening. I just don't sit on the other side of the room. I'm right there. If two women are making love, I see everything they're doing to each other. I touch. I feel. I listen. And oh man, I've seen some exciting stuff.

There's nothing lewd or obscene. Everyone's sincere—that's what makes the difference. Many of those beautiful scenes are still alive inside my brain, and I wouldn't trade those evenings for a truckload of solid gold.

Wising Up

On the straighter side, I was busy trying to take care of business in the early sixties. I became more attentive to my financial situation, and I started figuring ways to run an efficient organization. I thought long range. That's why I left the ABC royalties alone and just lived off the money I was making on the road. I was looking for security.

In 1961, B had our third boy—Bobby—and I wanted to make sure that my kids—all my kids—didn't have to face the same starvation shit that I had seen. I wasn't going to blow my bread on anything stupid.

My indulgences—women and dope—cost me something, but nothing like the stories I've heard 'bout other people. At the height, I might have been spending $20 a day for smack. Or if I spent $30, that'd be only on one of my hallelujah days. But believe me, they didn't come often.

I had a decent car, but never more than one at a time. And later on I'd even wind up owning such unspectacular vehicles as Chevy station wagons or Volkswagens. I had my airplanes, but they were for my day-to-day work.

Even when I was in New York, I shied away from limousines and crap like that. To me, a limo's a hype. When you set up those little folding seats on the floor, everyone's jammed together and crowded as hell. I ain't going to pay no $40 or $50 an hour when I can take a cab and get exactly where I want to go for maybe $5 or $6.

Fuck the status. My friends were the same folk I had always known. Some were cabdrivers, barbers, and salesmen. Sure, I met all the Hollywood stars. I was appearing on many of the national TV shows. But I didn't necessarily pal around with those people.

Not that I thought I wasn't good enough, or that I was too good. I just ain't a partygoer or a table-hopper. So I made a point of avoiding the places where the famous and the near-famous hung out.

I wasn't interested in chasing anybody or feeling like I was being chased. It's not that I didn't like many of these people. Carol Burnett's a wonderful lady; I dug Dinah Shore, Johnny Carson, and Dick Cavett; I once did a whole week with Mike Douglas and had a ball. But even when I worked TV—say for Bill Cosby or the Smothers Brothers—I did my deal and split. Didn't hang around to rub elbows.

I did rub elbows with one star, though. But that happened completely by accident:

I'm flying to New York from L.A. on the red-eye special. Woman sits down next to me—I'm in the window seat and she has the aisle —and starts telling me how she knows my music, which songs she likes, and how long she's been digging me. She rattles on.

About an hour and a half into the flight, I interrupt her.

"Look, you've been talkin' so much about me. What about you? I don't even know your name."

"Well, I'm Judy Garland."

"Come on, Mamma. Tell the truth and shame the devil."

"It's true, Ray. I'm Judy Garland."

So we talk for the rest of the trip and all through the night as we fly 'cross the country. She's a highly sensitive person. She pours her heart out to me and, from time to time, she breaks down and cries. At one point the stewardess hears her bawling and comes over to ask me what I've done to her!

Anyway, Judy had me over to her place in New York a couple of times. She saw me simply as a cat she could talk to. And she knew that what she told me would never leave the room. She was a delicate and high-strung lady, and when she cried, her tears were for real. She'd kept too many things inside for too long.

I can do the same thing. I'll go a long ways in many situations, not say a word and just absorb the blows. But if I see it's fucking me up bad, I cut it loose. You got to.

After my second country album in 1962, I continued recording the standards I've always loved, tunes like "Ol' Man River" or "Lucky Old Sun." I used the same kind of big-band settings, string arrangements, and choral backgrounds. Those were the situations which made me happiest.

I didn't stop accompanying myself on piano. That's something I'll always do. I know myself best, my piano can actually inspire my voice, and I love the feeling of the two streams flowing together.

I began my own record company in the early sixties, but I continued to use ABC for promotion and distribution. I actually recorded other artists—Percy Mayfield and Louis Jordan—before I recorded myself.

When I originally signed with ABC in 1959 for three years, I told them if everything was still cool at the end of the period, I'd sign for another three. So I wanted to keep my word. At the end of the second three years, though—in 1965—I became an exclusive artist for my own label, Tangerine.

But back in 1962, most of my business dealings were still in New York. That was a drag. It was difficult living in California and having all my main people on the other coast, so I decided to build a small office building in L.A. and centralize the operation in one spot.

I bought the property and helped design the place. I was more interested in low costs than high prestige, so I put up the building in a normal, black, working-class neighborhood of L.A. It ain't Beverly Hills.

There are two stories—I wanted to rent the bottom half because I assumed the tenants wouldn't want to walk up and down stairs, but the second floor is all mine. That's where the offices are—the publishing company and later the record company and booking agency, as well as my recording studio.

Strange thing happened while the building was going up: Joe Adams drove me over there one night to see the place. It was still under construction. We walked around the second floor just so I could see how things were shaping up.

Went back to Joe's car and there were the cops waiting for us. Wanted to know what we were doing. I told 'em it was my building. I didn't have any identification, though, and they said they didn't recognize me. They wanted to know how a cat like me had enough bread to own a building.

"I work for a living, every day of the week," I said quietly.

I guess they considered that a wise-ass remark, 'cause they hauled me down to jail and kept me there for an hour or two.

When I walked in the station, all the police who were milling around screamed out, "Hey, that's Ray! Ray Charles! That's Ray Charles!" But it took the little desk sergeant an hour or so to be convinced. In fact, he even asked me for my driver's license. Feature that.

My first love was the recording studio, my own studio. I loved it the way I loved the first car I bought back when I was with Lowell. It allowed me to be independent, to come and go as I pleased and not be tied to everyone else's whims.

Same thing here: If I wanted to sing a song at 3:00 A.M., do some mixing, or redo an instrumental track, I wasn't going to be told that the studio's reserved. That had often been the case. When you use other people's property, they call the shots. But when you own the joint, you rock when you want to rock, roll when you want to roll.

My friend Tommy Dowd—who had been my engineer at Atlantic —came over, helped me put in the recording gear together with a guy named Bob Bushnell. Tommy was my teacher, showing me what to look for and what to listen for. In a year or so, I became a reasonably competent recording engineer, and they haven't been able to get me out of the studio since.

We began in 1963 with a three-track machine, and today we have twenty-four tracks. But the principles I learned fourteen or fifteen years ago are still the same, and I'm not nearly as impressed with the advances in recording techniques as most people. I still just try to make a recording sound like me.

I'm a perfectionist—at least I strive toward perfection, knowing I'll never achieve it—and being in control of the recording equipment lets me come closer to getting everything I want.

Once I had the studio I started "tracking"—having the other instruments record first and then doing my vocal separately. This enabled me to go over something as many times as I wanted to, until I had it in place. It was a far cry from the days when all my music was done at once, in just one or two takes.

So everything moved to California—my accounting, my publishing, my recording. We started out with just three of us: Joe Adams, a bookkeeper, and myself. Joe also helped me engineer and did everything else around the place.

Today, some fifteen years later, we're in the same spot. And we ain't about to move. We have a few more people around the office—maybe nine or ten—but things haven't changed much. I don't believe in big staffs. Everyone who works in our building has a purpose. No one's there for show. I don't even have a private secretary. I don't believe in excess fat, especially when I'm footing the bills.

While I was getting my business house in order, I also decided to foot another bill: I bought property in the View Park section of L.A. —a nice upper-class black neighborhood—and put up a split-level house for my family. B did most of the planning; I only helped design my home office.

All this might sound extravagant, but it wasn't. The office building cost under $100,000 and the house less than $200,000. I tried to be practical about the location too. My house was just fourteen or fifteen minutes from where I worked, sixteen minutes from the airport, and right in the middle of the two.

Now everything surrounding me was mine: my office building with my own recording studio, my home, my investments. I bought some apartment buildings and even a small ranch, borrowing against the royalties which were piling up at ABC. All the while, though, I continued to live far under my means.

I was careful to put my bread aside for taxes. (In the beginning of my career, Uncle Sam didn't pay me much attention. I think that was true of many of the so-called race stars. But later, when I started selling big, I noticed that the IRS developed a real interest in my career.)

I had the same problems as any small businessman. I was even taken to the cleaners once for a lot of money. But that didn't make me furious or bitter. Just taught me to keep my nose closer to the books.

I trust people. Not that I'm a little lamb in the woods. If you leave a mink coat on the front seat of your car without locking the door, I know someone's going to take it—an honest man as well as a dishonest man. But if you lock the door, the honest man ain't going to try to break in.

I believe in progress—personal progress and financial progress. I never work for less this year than I got last year. When the public is ready to say to me, "Ray, you've been a good horse, but we're going to have to put your ass out to pasture," I'll go quietly and gratefully, knowing I've had many lucrative years.

The Bad Bust

Nineteen sixty-four started out normally enough. I was doing TV, recording, touring, and fooling around my new building and studio. In April or May, we went to England and Ireland where I was in a movie, *Ballad in Blue*. It was a cute story about a blind boy whose mother is overprotective. I played myself and convinced her to let the child learn to fend for himself, the way my mama had taught me.

I liked working on the film and even wrote the title tune. The movie turned out okay, but it could have been much hipper if the folk making it hadn't run out of money. It played here and there and then fizzled out.

We also did a highly successful concert in the Shrine Auditorium in L.A. which was turned into an album. By then, Lillian Fort had replaced Margie Hendrix as the head Raelett.

Toward the end of the year, we went to Canada to play a gig. We flew back to Boston on our plane and landed at Logan Field. It was a cold and wintry day. We piled out of the plane and headed for the hotel.

Got to my room and realized that I had forgotten my fix. It was still on the plane. So I had my assistant drive me back to the airport. I walked on the plane, put the shit inside my overcoat, and headed for my car. That was when I was stopped. By the Feds.

"We've been watching the plane. Would you mind stepping over here?"

"Okay."

"Did you just come back from Canada?"

"Yes."

"We got a tip that you might have some drugs on the plane."

"Oh?"

"So if you don't mind, we'd like to see that overcoat."

If I didn't mind? Oh well. I handed them the coat I was carrying. There was smack and grass inside. I was caught. I knew this could happen. I'd been busted before. But still, I had never done anything to protect myself. Obviously I had enough bread to pay someone to keep my dope and give it to me whenever I called for it. That way I'd never be in possession. But I didn't believe in that. I never sent anyone to cop for me unless the person was also copping for himself. I couldn't live with the thought of someone getting busted on my account.

They hauled me down to the courthouse. And the charges were stiff. These guys weren't airport cops. They were full-fledged narcos.

I couldn't figure out what had happened—whether someone saw me leave the hotel and called the fuzz or whether the fuzz got to the airport late, after we landed, and bumped into me. Made no difference. I stood accused. And I couldn't plead anything but guilty. I'd possessed exactly what they claimed. I wouldn't still have been fooling with drugs if I hadn't been ready to pay the price.

I was pissed off something fierce that I'd been caught. I sure as hell didn't want to go to jail. But I saw the bust as my own doing. After all, I was the cat who went back to the plane. I was the addict.

This was the end of 1964. It would be a year before I would be sentenced. So I finished touring and then headed back to California. I decided not to tour in 1965. This was the first time in twenty years that I wouldn't be performing in public. I had lots on my mind, and I couldn't see myself running around. I needed to stop and think.

Along 'bout May of 1965, I was asked to sing the title song for *The Cincinnati Kid,* a movie being made with Steve McQueen. I listened to the music and it fit me. I agreed to do it. (That's how I always work with movie songs or commercials. Just like regular tunes: I got to like the melodies before I'll sing 'em.)

We were set to record on a Thursday night over at RCA. Then my son, Ray, Jr., who was about ten then, told me there was a banquet for his Little League team on the same night. He was getting a trophy and he wanted me to be there. So I called back the movie people and explained the conflict. They said fine, they'd be happy to put it off a week—to the following Thursday. At the last minute, though, the baseball banquet was postponed a week and rescheduled for the night of my recording date, and I just couldn't change it again.

The evening arrived, and since I had promised Ray, Jr., I'd go to the banquet, I went. There was my son Ray, there was B, there were the other parents and kids. Seven o'clock came. Seven-thirty. Eight o'clock came. Ray still hadn't gotten his trophy. I kept fidgeting. I was nervous and confused. Finally I told him and his mother:

"Look, I'm sorry. I feel terrible about it. But I got to split. It's way past eight and I'm nowhere near RCA."

"But all the other daddies are here," Ray said. "You got to be here when I get my award."

He started crying. I realized I had made it worse by coming at all. Now I was leaving before the presentation. Everyone had seen me. And everyone saw that I was splitting before my boy was recognized.

Still, I left. I left B and I left Ray crying his heart out. I heard the crying while I was recording that evening. I heard it all that night. I thought about it. I lived with it. I dealt with it inside my brain. I reasoned: This kid really loves me, really wants me to be part of him.

And I thought about something else: What if I actually had to serve time? And what if my boy went to school one day and a pal of his said, "Hey, Ray, your old man's nothing but a jailbird." That'd be a drag. Ray might knock the boy in the head and fuck him up.

So that's when I made up my mind. No more heroin for me.

The next morning I walked into Joe Adams' office.

"I want you to know something, Joe."

"What?"

"I intend to check myself into a hospital. I ain't ever gonna mess with heroin again."

"You don't have to tell me that, Ray."

"I'm not talking to be talking, Joe. I'm telling you what's gonna happen."

And it did.

Kicking

I saw that if I gave up heroin it was going to have to be a deal I made with myself. No one else could be involved. No promises, no outs, no fancy footwork. I might bullshit others, but I couldn't bullshit Ray.

I decided to find a hospital, go there, and kick the shit.

That's how I hooked up with Frederick J. Hacker, a famous Viennese psychiatrist with a clinic in Austria and one in Beverly Hills. I was told he was a big cat, and if I followed a program under his care, the court might be impressed.

I went to see Hacker. He was a sweet guy, and we sat there for a while. Him checking me out, me feeling him out. Like two dogs sniffing at each other.

"Doctor, I've decided to check in a hospital and kick drugs."

"Fine, Ray, but you don't have to do it all at once. I can give you something to wean you off so you don't have to be sick."

"I understand, Doc, but you got to understand: That ain't my style. I don't want to be weaned. I'll just stop."

Sometime around August I checked into St. Francis Hospital in Lynwood, right outside of L.A. This was the place Hacker recommended—a hospital where they treated psychiatric disorders.

I arrived one evening and immediately started following my own program. From that day on, I have never fucked with heroin. I wasn't weaned. I didn't take pills. I refused to fool with their sedatives and their tranquilizers.

The first day wasn't bad. I ate a little. I slept. I waited. But by the twentieth hour of that day, the shit started coming up. I vomited and vomited and vomited till there was nothing left to vomit. And then I vomited some more. I was heaving up poison. The poison which was heroin, the poison my body was now naturally rejecting. And it was bitter—bitter as gall. You can't imagine how bitter bitter can be. I was nauseated for hours. My body stunk. My sweat stunk. Everything about me stunk.

Then the poison began to churn inside me again until my bowels were loosened. For hour upon hour, I sat there, shitting and vomiting my brains out.

This lasted a whole day and part of another. But by the time the fourth day came around, so did I. And I got to say: In spite of all the stories I've heard about cats chewing up the sheets and climbing the walls, my experience wasn't that bad.

I was uncomfortable, and for those few days I was sick. But I also knew I was getting well, and that's different from when you're normally in a hospital. Usually you don't know what's coming down. You could have a tumor eating your lungs away. But at least with dope, you know that in a couple of days you'll be straight.

I can stand almost anything for three days. Especially if I see the purpose right there before me. All I got to do is continue to breathe and I'll make it over.

The physical addiction is something you can put behind you in ninety-six hours. But the psychological addiction is the real crusher; that's the bitch.

I had already dealt with that, though. I had promised myself I would kick. And, in fact, my mind actually worked with my body through those first days. I kept my brain focused on the future, when this bad spell would be over, when I'd be able to move past the pain and sickness.

That was it. By the third day I slowly started eating again. I sipped some tomato soup and nibbled a few crackers. I drank a little milk, which had been my favorite drink since I left Greensville. (Back home we had tasteless, clean well water. Since then, I've never been able to drink city water with its weird tastes and strange chemicals. To this day, water makes me sick to my stomach.)

I slept during the day and I was up at night. I was used to nightlife. I stayed in my room, ate all my meals alone. I stuck to myself.

You'd think that'd be the end of it. But it wasn't. The hospital wasn't convinced by my cold-turkey number. They thought someone was slipping me something, so naturally they stopped all visitors. Tests seemed to show I still wasn't clean.

One morning they woke me while I was asleep. I was buck naked. They put me in a hospital gown and then searched my room from top to bottom. They went through my things, they looked under the bed and inside the toilet, they searched everywhere. They found nothing.

I sat there after they left and thought about it. At first I didn't believe what I had seen. They had already stopped my visitors; now they were rifling through my room like I was a criminal. The more I thought about it, the more goddamn mad it made me. Finally I picked up the phone and told them I was checking out. They called Joe Adams, who had just arrived in New York to take care of some business for me, and he turned around and flew back to L.A. on the next plane.

"Joe," I said to him when he walked in my room, "what did I tell you I was gonna do?"

"Give it up."

"That's right, and that's exactly what I've done. But these goddamn people don't believe me. Just 'cause I won't take their fucking pills and follow their weaning program, they're convinced I'm slipping. They've cut off my visitors and treat me like I'm a fucking convict. Man, I've had it."

Joe was confused. After all, he'd been told by the hospital that my tests showed I was getting something. He didn't know what to think. How could hospital tests lie?

On the other hand, Joe knew me. He knew that I'd promised myself that I wouldn't bullshit Ray, and I didn't. Screw the tests; I knew I was clean.

They decided to give me another test, and I welcomed the idea. This time it showed that I was straight. The first test had been incorrect. Joe, Hacker, and damn near everybody else at the hospital apologized.

Joe and Hacker calmed me down and convinced me to stay put. So I did. Actually, I never blamed Hacker. I liked him. He never did any heavy psychoanalysis, but we did meet once or twice a week so he could have a case history of me. Most of our talk, though, was about politics or current affairs or music. I'd psyched myself out before I ever saw the hospital, so I didn't require a lot of headwork.

Besides, I had done this same sort of cold turkey with women. If I decide a gal is wrong for me—for whatever reasons—I stop seeing her. I don't go back in for a treat now and then; I don't gradually lessen the number of times we meet. I stop and never turn up the flames again. I got good control over my mind, even in areas which involve my body.

Hacker proved to be even cooler than I would have guessed. He trusted me, even to the point of giving me passes so I could go out every now and then and find myself a little pussy. He knew I'd come back clean.

Sitting around doing nothing was very hard on my nerves, and so my stay in St. Francis wasn't easy. B came to visit me to help me pass the time. I learned to play chess while I was there, and at night I passed the time drinking tea and playing cards with the nurses.

My lawyers visited me once or twice to discuss the upcoming hearing in Boston when I'd be sentenced. At one point they indicated that if I "cooperated" with the judge, I might have an easier time.

I knew what they meant. They thought I should name a pusher or two. We'd tell the court that these pushers were preying on the minds of the young, getting kids hooked on heroin. We'd look good by exposing these cats.

Bullshit. I refused to do anything of the kind. I've always had to seek out the pushers; they never came looking for me. No one ever made me spend my money on dope. I dug it, and I did it.

If the judge wanted to snatch fifteen or twenty years out of my life 'cause I wouldn't tell him who was supplying me—well, that would be blackmail. I wasn't going to insult no judge that way, and no judge was going to insult me. So I told the lawyers to forget the idea. We'd take our chances. I'd already done everything I could to help myself.

Looking back, I can't say that kicking was a nightmare or the low point in my life. For a few days, I was sick—that's as far as I can go. I'm not saying other people don't have fits with the problem. I'm sure they do.

I was a junkie for seventeen years, but maybe my habit wasn't as severe as other people's. Can't tell you. I can only speak for myself and describe my own condition.

Personally, it was harder for me to give up cigarettes. I know that sounds crazy, but I mean it. At least once I was through with drugs they weren't always in my face. With cigarettes, someone is blowing smoke at you every minute of the day. You never escape the lure of tobacco.

After three or four days off heroin—if you can control your mind and get it to work with you, not against you—you should be straight.

Cigarettes and smack are the only two truly addictive habits I've known. (You might add women.) I can't put booze or reefer in that category, even though I like to do both.

Drinking's nothing new for me. I did that while I was still on drugs. I like gin. But if they passed a law against buying booze, I wouldn't be upset.

I dig pot. I like a good smoke, just like I enjoy the taste of gin, but if my day passes and I can't have either, I ain't going nuts. It's not like missing a fix.

Gin lubricates me. Reefer mellows me. And between the two of them and some strong, black coffee, I perk along just fine.

But in 1965, the big item was still smack. And when I left the hospital in early winter to fly to Boston, there was still the distinct possibility that I was going to be thrown in jail.

Sentencing

Boston ain't the best place for a bust. So I expected the worst. There were some hard-ass judges in that town.

I never testified. I just sat and listened. I really had nothing to say. I had already pleaded guilty.

Hacker testified that I was straight. He told the judge I had kicked, showed him the reports and presented all the correct documents. When he spoke, the authorities listened.

I'd had plenty of time to anticipate what might happen, so I was ready. I wasn't preoccupied with the idea of prison. I didn't want to go, and yet I was prepared to—without a whimper or a sob—on this very day. So I waited. I had done everything I could, short of pointing the finger at people I couldn't blame for my predicament.

The judge had the power to send me to Lexington for a year or two. Or he could confine me to a hospital, or, even worse, some filthy jail. But I was lucky. Jesus, I was lucky. God's little angels were looking over me and singing sweet spirituals into the judge's ear. He postponed my sentencing for another year. That meant I'd have to return to court in twelve months, but that was okay with me. Meanwhile, I was a free man. That also meant I'd have a probation officer. And the court could put me in the hospital anytime they wanted to, just to see if I was clean. But that was all right. I could walk out of the courthouse and play any gig I wanted, go wherever I pleased.

I didn't go back on the road for the rest of the year. When I finally started touring—many months later—someone approached me after a concert in Las Vegas one night. He said he was a Fed with instructions for me to appear before my probation officer in Boston. He said I had a day to get there.

But that wasn't unfair. They had scheduled my hospital check at a time when I was free, and I didn't have to cancel any gigs. They wanted me in Boston on short notice, of course, so I wouldn't have time to clean up. I was being tested.

I flew East, met my probation officer, took some psychological tests, answered a few questions. I didn't mind; I'm always up for games. That night I checked into McLean Hospital. McLean was like a giant version of St. Francis. Mainly mental patients—folk kicking drugs or drying out from booze.

I went to sleep at about eight. At midnight I woke up to go to the toilet and I was freezing to death. Goddamn, it's cold in here. Can't understand it. Don't these people care about heat? I wondered. So I put on my robe and tiptoed out to the hall. Man, it was warm as toast out there—comfortable and cozy as it could be.

I knew what they were up to. When you're withdrawing from drugs, coldness quickens your sickness. You'll probably have chills when the temperature is normal, but when it's really cold, you suffer something awful. They wanted to see how bad I'd start shaking.

I called for the head nurse.

"Look, Mama," I said, "I'm not blaming you. I know you don't make the rules. But, sweetheart, if I catch pneumonia I'm gonna sue this place so bad that everyone here is gonna be working for me. I'm gonna own this joint. Dig?"

Five minutes later warm air was flowing through the ducts and I was snuggled back in bed.

For another four days I was checked up one side and down the other. While they were poking at me, I kept myself amused with my tapes. I even found a piano and another piano player—a classical cat—who could really wail.

So it wasn't all bad. The nicest part was meeting one of the nurses who I got next to a little later on. We became close friends. And when I checked out at the end of the week, they told me I was as clean as a baby after a bath.

After all this, I wish I could tell you that my body felt different and that I had a new lease on life. In truth, I felt pretty much the same. The only difference was that I didn't need a fix every morning. Can't boast or brag beyond that. My body adjusted to the absence, just as it had adjusted to the presence of drugs. God gave me an unusually adaptable body.

Kicking was something I felt I had to do. I didn't quit because the heroin was killing me—maybe it was, maybe it wasn't—but because it was going to bring down my family and maybe even cause me to rot away in some jail cell.

I was blessed. I'd had the bread to buy decent junk, and then I had the bread to buy bail and a high grade of justice. My thing was cool. But that doesn't make me like the system. That doesn't mean I believe that justice in this country really works for the accused who are poor any more than medicine works for the sick who are poor.

Jail's the last place you want to stick an addict. Fortunately, my judge understood that. There's no rehabilitation in prison as far as junkies go. Put an addict in jail just for being an addict and he feels like he's automatically shit upon. And he's right. Throw him back out on the streets after a year or two or three, and he's hitting himself as soon as he can cop a fix.

You know I don't give advice, and I wouldn't want to speculate too much about how others might go about kicking. But if I was pressed, I'd have to say that love has a lot to do with it. Not punishment.

While I was in the hospital, it helped to know that my family, my friends hadn't given up on me. They didn't seem to love me any the less. Even B never made me feel like I was scum, although she hated drugs.

Junkies can get down on themselves so hard they never get up. They start seeing themselves as dogs, and then they're through. They can't talk to nobody. The cops want to throw 'em in jail, their parents think they stink, their friends don't give a fuck about 'em. They're alone and abandoned. To help an addict, you have tell his family or friends not to shower down on the poor cat. The people around the junkie need to learn how to respond to the problem.

Naturally the law says, "Let me take this baby"—that's the junkie —"and smash his head against the wall. I ain't going to fuck with you —you syndicates and you big-time criminals—'cause you're too big; you're a seven-foot giant." Then the jails do all they can to destroy and humiliate. It's a wonder that addicts can survive the laws and the prisons. They're just victims—victims of a system too stupid to understand how stupid it is. It's a system that mutilates decent minds and destroys beautiful hearts.

At the end of the first year of probation, I went back to Boston to face further sentencing. Just a couple of weeks before my hearing, the original judge died. And the cat who took his place was supposed to be a real hard-ass. Again, I didn't know what to expect.

Again, Hacker testified. Again, I sat and I waited. Minutes before the hearing began, someone handed the judge a sealed envelope. Turned out to be a note from the first judge, the cat who had been lenient. On his deathbed he had dictated a letter on my behalf and it said something like:

"I know this case is no longer in my jurisdiction. But I have to tell you—just as a fellow human being—that society would be better off with Ray Charles free, serving as a good example of a guy who kicked drugs, rather than being put away in prison."

The new judge was moved by this. He gave me a five-year probated sentence. Once again that meant I was free to travel and gig as I wished. I walked out of the courtroom just as I had walked in—my own man.

Coming Back

Folk can really talk some shit:

"Oh man, you've been off, Ray."

"No telling how you'll go over now, baby."

"Yeah, you been away, Brother Ray."

That's the sort of thing I was hearing. But it didn't really bother me none. When I started going out again in 1966 after a year off the road, I treated it like every other tour I had ever made—with seriousness and concern for the music.

In the year I was off, I hadn't stopped recording; I just didn't play gigs. And when I returned, my first jobs were successful. The crowds were as large as I had ever seen them.

Just about now, I had another slice of good fortune. One of the tunes I did during my rest year—"Crying Time"—took off and became very big. And around this time I also sang with some of the best Raeletts I've ever had—Merry Clayton, Clydie King, Alexandra Brown, and Gwen Berry.

In many ways, my little company anchored me and made it easier for me to return. It wasn't large, but it was mine, and it permitted me to do whatever I pleased. I didn't want floods of people around me, so I kept the firm small. When I get past ten or twelve folks, that's too much for me. I always want to know everyone who works for me, and I also want to involve myself in the different aspects of the business. In other words, keep control and run the show myself.

I remember what folk said back in the country: " 'Tain't nothing wrong with being a big fish in a little pond." And I can swim anywhere round that pond that suits me.

When we built the place in 1962 I had RPM put on the front. That's for Recording, Publishing, and Management. (Didn't see any need to advertise my name; thought that might attract unwelcome visitors.)

In past years we've recorded some talent other than my own. A lot of people have passed through—the Ohio Players, a group called the Vocals who later became the Fifth Dimension, Ike and Tina Turner, and dozens of others that I've forgotten. I never had any real hits with these people, and when they went on to become stars, they did it elsewhere. But that's okay with me. While they were over at my place, they did what I asked. I have no regrets about losing them. They just moved on.

But of the people we actually did manage, I guess Billy Preston was the most memorable. I first heard about him through some friends. They told me how he loved to imitate me and how he had all my gestures down cold. Finally I met him on the *Shindig* TV show. I liked his music and asked him to join me. He did. He played organ with my big band and also had a feature slot at the start of the show. That lasted for three years—till '67 or so—and I treasured the relationship.

There was a lot of black music in the last half of the sixties that I could relate to. More blacks sang the way they really were, instead of doing the kind of material associated with Nat Cole and later Johnny Mathis. I liked many of the so-called soul singers—David Ruffin with the Temptations, Otis Redding, Little Milton, and Sam and Dave. Some people told me that I'd invented the sounds they called soul—

but I can't take any credit. Soul is just the way black folk sing when they leave themselves alone.

One musician towered above the rest. That was Aretha. She's terrible, man. I'd been following her ever since she was fourteen or fifteen, singing in her daddy's church. And she always sang from her inners. She's my one and only sister. In many ways, she's got her father's feeling and passion. When C. L. Franklin—one of the last great preachers—delivers a sermon, he builds his case so beautifully you can't help but see the light. Same when Aretha sings. She's all a-fire.

I loved her gospel singing, I loved her when she was on Columbia, and I loved her when she started singing for Atlantic and my old friends Ahmet, Jerry, and Tommy. Some of my favorite things are the Coke commercials Aretha and I sang together. They won some awards and even made the Top 10 charts on a couple of radio stations.

If I took all the girl singers that are around and listened to them night and day, I still wouldn't be happy unless I snuck in a little Aretha. By the time the others caught up with her, she was already a mile or two ahead of 'em.

Gladys Knight has a wonderful feeling. Barbra Streisand is tremendous. I've heard her sing things—funky, nasty, swinging things—behind stage that she's never put on record. I wish she would. Younger chicks like Chaka Khan are nothing to sneeze at. But take Brother Ray's word for it: Aretha's still boss.

I ran into the Beatles much earlier in the sixties. I think it was in Hamburg, Germany, where they played intermission at one of our concerts. I've never been in love with their music, but I have liked some of their tunes, and years later I recorded four or five of them. "Yesterday" became a good record for me, and I found that I could do items like "Eleanor Rigby" or "Something" in my own special way.

Even though I'd never really appreciated what's called rock, I also haven't had eyes for what the cats call free jazz—which was also happening in the sixties. I was brought up to play through the changes when I ad-lib, and I don't like leaving that approach.

Music needs to make sense, needs to have order. From what some people consider the lowest stuff—a cat in the middle of a cotton field shouting the blues—to what's considered the highest—a symphony or an opera—it has to be structured.

Blowing out notes in whichever way, whenever you please, paying no mind to the chord changes—well, that doesn't hold me, doesn't make me want to listen. Far as I'm concerned, music should be beautiful, and the most beautiful aspect of music is its simplicity.

Same goes for all the new electronic instruments. They're okay. Hell, I've been playing some of 'em for twenty-five years. But no fad's ever going to replace the basics: the beauty of a tenor saxophone, the sound of a plain piano, the naturalness of the human voice.

I continued to listen to the things which have always sounded good to me: country music by George Jones; jazz by Stan Getz, Lockjaw Davis, or Johnny Griffin; spirituals by the Swan Silvertones or Clara Ward.

I probably should have spent more time with my family in Los Angeles in the late sixties. But I just didn't feel like I could afford it.

Maybe that was an excuse. Maybe I just couldn't stop playing, recording, and doing concerts. Maybe I just couldn't resist whatever the road was offering me.

Meanwhile, I saw the country going a little nuts. And I got to say that when everyone started yelling and screaming about the Vietnam War in 1967 and 1968, I was as confused as the next cat. I never did understand that war. Didn't understand what they meant by us having to "contain the war." Didn't understand why all these people were dying—mother's sons, brothers, fathers, husbands, and cats who might have nobody, cats without any family. I figured: If we weren't going to make a parking lot of Vietnam and take over the place, why were we fooling around letting all these young kids get their heads blown off?

But there was a lot I didn't understand in the sixties. Everyone kept talking 'bout "progress" between the races, but I took another position. I'd been thinking long and hard about the black and white questions. And at the very beginning of the decade—maybe even a little before —I threw my lot in with one cat in particular.

Following
a Leader

In the sixties I was more aware of race than any other time in my life. But how could it have been otherwise? I was living in America.

By the time I was thirty or thirty-two, I had acquired the habit of listening to the news every morning on the radio and watching it every night on TV. I kept up. But I didn't need no radio or television to tell me what was happening down South. I was right there, baby. That was still fertile territory for my music, and I got to feel those crazy vibrations firsthand, in the flesh.

I told you before how I refused segregated gigs after the incident in Augusta. I lost that case, but I felt like I won the war—at least *my* war. When I could control the situation—like my own concert—I sure as hell wasn't going to allow a promoter to insult me.

But there was little I could do about the world outside my music. I just watched and wept along with everyone else. I took notice of all the different civil rights groups forming in those days—like SNCC or CORE. I understood what they were saying, and I could see a few rays of reason in the various outlooks. But early on, I decided that if I was going to shoot craps on anyone's philosophy, I was putting my money on Martin Luther King, Jr.

I met Martin in the early sixties when I went down to Alabama to play a benefit for his cause, and it turned out to be a particularly strange night. We got nasty threats from people who said they were going to put water and sugar in the gas tank of my plane. So there were all kinds of FBI men at the airport to protect us. And then, just after we played our set and left the stage, the bandstand collapsed from too much weight. Oh Jesus, it was a nervous night.

From the start I had respect for Martin. He reminded me of Jackie Robinson. Same kind of situation. These were the first cats to break down barriers made of iron and steel. Both guys took punishment and abuse for a whole race of people.

I liked Martin Luther King's theory. I saw it this way:

Let's say I meet six brothers on the street and they're walking along with their sister. If I decide to slap that sister upside her head, I'd be stupid to think that the brothers ain't gonna waste me.

You got to know who you're dealing with. You got to be practical. You got to figure out the plan. You got to make sure your approach will get you what you want.

Martin worked with the law. Sometimes he broke it intentionally; other times he didn't; but he always had the law in mind. His aim was to get the law on *our* side.

We had been hearing this bullshit about a Constitution and a Bill of Rights. Now it was time to test the waters to see if the words applied to us as well as the folk with the power and the money.

King hated violence. He'd prefer never to see it. But in order to be a true participant in America, he believed that you needed a dramatic entrance. And the man was right. For people to notice you, for people to hear your cries and pleas, usually something bloody has to happen. Blood's red; it makes you look.

In King's case, the people protesting were not being violent. But because they were pointing to changes in the way of life in the South, they provoked violence.

Martin knew exactly what he was doing. And he told his people: Look, if you come with me, you might get hurt. You might get beat up. You might get put in jail, or even worse, you might get murdered. But if someone hits you, he said, you just got to take it. If someone beats on you, you look the other way. That's how we resist. That's how we make our point. That's how we cross over.

And then Martin said something which closed the deal for me: I'll be on the front line, right there next to you.

I've always believed that the cats who make wars should be the ones who fight 'em. Let the presidents and the prime ministers put their asses out there. Let them duck the bullets and rub their noses in the trenches instead of staying home, reading casualty lists and eating steak every night.

What Martin was telling you to do, he was doing himself. That made me sit up and take notice. He saw the black struggle in America in worldwide terms, and I liked that thought. He exposed our hypocrisy and our injustices for everyone to see. If we were judging the rest of the world, let the rest of the world judge us.

I figured that if I was going to pick up my cross and follow someone, it could only be a cat like King. Yet I couldn't see me doing any marching. And I told that to Martin personally.

A reporter once asked me why my name didn't appear in ads protesting one cause or another. Was I soft on the issues? he wanted to know. No, I said, I just don't believe that my name—as a musician or an entertainer—can do very much. Besides, that ain't my way.

I didn't march for a couple of reasons: First, I wouldn't have known when to duck when they started throwing broken beer bottles at my head. And secondly, I'd defeat Martin's purpose. My temperament just wouldn't stand certain treatment.

I can take abuse. You can call me stupid, ugly son of a bitch or motherfucker. You can put me in the dozens and cuss me out all night long. Ain't gonna make no difference. I'll just sit there. But if you touch me, if you hit me, if you start messing with my body, man, that's another story. I hit back. I don't like violence; I don't believe in violence. I am violent only if violence comes upon me.

And if a cop hits me, then he'll have to kill me. I say that 'cause I'll never do anything to make the fuzz hit me. If I'm struck, it's for doing nothing. That means I strike back. And that gives the cop his little excuse to knock my brains out.

Martin trained his people differently. If they were going to be slapped, he told 'em to duck. If they couldn't duck, he told 'em to flinch. I admired that. It made sense for the cause. But it didn't make no sense for me. I knew when I could control myself and when I couldn't.

In an organization, like in a business, not everyone does the same thing. Not everyone's a secretary; not everyone's a PBX operator. With Martin's group, not everyone had to be a marcher.

When he intentionally broke the law, he was hauled off to jail. And when you go to jail, you need money for lawyers, for legal research, for court fees, for food for the marchers. I saw that as my function; I helped raise money.

Funny thing happened to me and my band during these stormy days down South. My big band was all black then, except for the guitarist, Don Peek. We were down in Alabama playing a gig and, like I say, these were nervous times. The South was in an uproar; the danger zone was everywhere.

We were on the street, doing nothing in particular, when a cop— a son of a bitch at least six-three and 280 pounds—approached Don.

"Boy!" cop said.

"Yes?" Don answered.

"Boy, are you with these, these . . . people?"

"Yes."

"Well, boy, what does that make you?"

"I'm Mexican, señor."

That broke us up, and later I asked Don—who could easily pass for Latin—why he fibbed.

"You don't think I'm crazy enough to tell the bastard that I'm Jewish, do you?"

Later on, I saw racial turmoil that made no sense. The riots in the big cities in the sixties might have pointed out the lousy living conditions, but I couldn't understand folk burning down their own neighborhoods. That just meant they were going to have to walk twenty more blocks to get to a supermarket.

I ain't going to tear down my house unless I have another one to sleep in. I ain't going to put myself out on the street. I ain't going to do nothing to hurt *me*.

That's what I liked about Martin's program: It was positive. Practical. Geared toward achievement. And yet even with all the laws passed and the old chains smashed, I couldn't get myself to call any of the gains real progress. All we got was what was legitimately ours to begin with. Many white people felt that their lives were being invaded, and when they finally agreed to the new terms, it was as though they were giving us something which was theirs.

Bullshit. I didn't want no gifts. I didn't want no favors. These were rights that had been written down from the beginning, except that only whites had been enjoying them.

Some whites were saying, "Well, we have to *give* these people a break." They didn't have to give us shit. All we wanted them to do was play it straight.

When World War II broke out, I didn't hear any whites saying, "No, let's not send those goddamn niggers over there. This is *our* war. They have nothing to do with it." When it comes to risking our necks, everyone's mighty liberal.

In Korea or in Vietnam, the blacks were usually the first cats over there, the cats who made up the ground troops, the first motherfuckers to get blasted. And if you were black and refused to serve, you'd hear, "Don't you understand your civic duty? How can you let your country down?"

In 1941 or 1951 or 1968, no one needed to pass an ordinance giving us the right to risk our black asses on the battlefield. Yet it ain't till 1965 that we get the practical right to vote. Now ain't *that* a bitch?

I better not dwell. No use in getting bitter. Besides, I really don't dig the more militant approach. I can understand the anger. I've even shared it from time to time. And if an organization like SNCC was really dumped on back then and had one of their members messed up, I've been known to play a benefit or two. I don't have to believe in everything a group stands for to help them.

On the other hand, if I deeply disagree with some organization's ideology, I can't do nothing for 'em. I'd look like a goddamn fool supporting somethin' I don't dig. You'd have to kill me 'fore I'd play a benefit for a cause I don't believe in. But if I do believe in it, man, you got my soul.

To my mind, militancy doesn't get you far. It points to the problem, but that's all. It can even be counterproductive. And even worse, it doesn't effectively deal with reality. I see America as a house. If there are ten people living in the house, only two are black. Say I'm one of those two. I deserve as much respect as anyone. I have as many rights as anyone. But there's no way that me and my brother are going to take over and rule the roost. If we start pissing on the floor and breaking the windows, we'll be busted in a flat minute. We've got to learn to live with the other eight.

As much black support as Martin had, he also got a lot of white support. He never forgot—and neither did I—that the favorable decisions were written by white judges. When the laws were changed, for the most part they were changed by white legislators, white politicians.

I could never tell anyone not to be angry. Stokely Carmichael, Rap Brown, the Panthers—these were all cats who spoke for many people too afraid to speak for themselves. The militants of the sixties had their limitations, but they also had their purpose. And I ain't going to put 'em down.

But when the smoke settled and the fires burned themselves out, I could see that of all the people running around, one cat had the clearest and the furthest vision. That was the good Doctor King. They could gun him down and kill him, but they couldn't make us forget his lessons. He taught us, we listened, and now we know.

The Scene Abroad

I've been traveling extensively outside the United States since the early sixties. For the past seventeen or eighteen years, I've gone all over the world to play my music.

I'm not much of a tourist. There's never been enough time. I'm always running from one city or country to another. But even during my first trip abroad, I sensed there was something about my music that transcended other cultures and languages. Europe, South America, Asia, North Africa, New Zealand, Japan—the places didn't matter. The people heard who I was; they responded to me like brothers and sisters, and I responded to them. I soaked up their music.

Before I started making these trips, I'd never listened to singers like Edith Piaf, for example. But when a friend of mine in Paris played Piaf's music for me, I loved her. She struck me as a French Billie Holiday. Not her music, but her way of living, the way she hurt, the way she reached people. She didn't hold back. She exposed herself in public. Much later, I recorded a tune she had done—"The Three Bells"—though at the time I didn't know that she had sung it.

One night in Montreal I met the French singer Nicoletta. We became very tight and managed to leap over the language barrier. She was with another lady from Paris, a songwriter named Ann Gregory, who also became a good friend of mine.

The three of us still see each other in France from time to time, and we've even collaborated on some writing together. "The Sun Died" was a tune Nicoletta did in French. Later I recorded it on the *Portrait of Ray* album. "Takes So Little Time" is another of Ann's songs that I wound up singing.

In the seventies I was also in France when I heard this guy playing a haunting Charles Aznavour song called "For Mama." I couldn't help but make a record of it myself.

I dig Latin-American music. When those Spanish singers start moaning low in minor keys, I'm there with 'em. I also love Mexican three-part harmony groups with male singers. They make all sorts of interesting twists and turns, the rhythm is hot and the sound fascinates me.

Traveling round the world opened up my ears. Between the promoters, my friends, and the women I got next to, I discovered music that I never even knew existed.

I went to Paris before I ever saw London, and the first trip was strange. The Algerian War was in full blast; bombs were exploding all over town. But the Algerians sent a note to my promoter saying that there'd be no bombings on my route from the hotel to the concert hall.

"Tell Brother Ray not to worry," they said. And I didn't.

I had grave reservations at first about going to England. Other entertainers told me that British audiences were cold as ice, and I worried they wouldn't take to my hot brand of music. So I didn't go to England that first year abroad. I waited. Then one night at the Copacabana in New York, Cary Grant came backstage after my show. "Whatever you do, Ray," he said, "go to England. They love you over there. I don't know anyone who doesn't own at least something of yours."

That seemed like good authority to me. So I took his advice and made the trip. He was right. London was a gas. The British dug me. They're reserved—like the Japanese—you can't expect them to be screeching and hollering. Yet, in their own way, they let you feel their love.

I can't say whether I'm more appreciated in one country than another. Europeans and Japanese seem to have a high regard for artists —if they're really artists. That's especially true for jazz musicians. When we've played jazz festivals, I've heard ovations for cats—great jazz players—who are barely known in America, but heroes in Europe.

Europeans are more serious about black music than we are. They study it and they know it. Most Americans—even most black Americans—just take it for granted, like the grass they walk on.

I've had experiences that have knocked me out in all kinds of wild places. I played Kingston, Jamaica, in the pouring rain and had three or four people carry me through the mud, put me on the stage, and then sit themselves down with the thousands of others, refusing to budge, getting drenched while I sang my songs. I ain't sure I'd walk through the mud and sit in the rain if Jesus Himself came back to preach a sermon. He'd have to do some real sweet talking to get me to hang around.

Men and women have approached me on the streets of Hungary, Bulgaria and Yugoslavia as though they were long-lost relatives. They treated me like a king; they reacted to my concerts as though I was playing their native folk music. But the people who knocked me out the most were the Israelis.

I had always heard that I was popular in Israel, but I didn't get over there till the early seventies. Some people asked me to do a documentary. They wanted to film my concerts in Israel and have me go around doing interviews with politicians, religious leaders, and plain, ordinary people.

I liked the idea. I'd never done anything like that before. The film people knew I wasn't a scholar or a theologian, but they had heard that I had a decent working knowledge of the Bible. They had also heard that the Israelis liked me, and they hoped the two things would blend.

Like my earlier film, *Ballad in Blue,* this movie was also underfinanced and never distributed. But I still had a ball making it, and it gave me twelve days to tour the country, to look around, and learn. It was all so old—so incredibly old—that I couldn't help but shake my head with wonder. I could smell history on the streets.

The concert I mentioned before was in Jerusalem, and in thirty years on the road, I had never experienced anything like this. We were supposed to do two shows, but the first one had the crowd so crazy and happy that they wouldn't leave. The second crowd was due any minute, but the first crowd wasn't about to move. The promoter was scared, and he came to me, wanting to know what to do. Man, what did I know? *He* was the Israeli; it was *his* country.

Should he call the cops? No, I said. Anything but that. I suggested that he tell the people they could stay for the second show, as long as they gave up their seats. He made the announcement and everyone cheered. So for the second show there were Israelis everywhere— people sitting between people's legs, people in the aisles, people standing up, people on people's shoulders. I was sure glad the place didn't catch fire, 'cause we all would have burned up together. But fortunately the only fire was the one in them and in me. I can't remember ever feeling more loved.

I also met David Ben-Gurion. I traveled to his kibbutz where I was scheduled to interview him for the film for forty minutes, but I wound up being there all day.

I loved him. He was straight-ahead and honest. We talked like old friends. And he told me exactly what was on his mind—the personal problems he was having with one of his children, the disagreements he was having with his religion, and the squabbles he was trying to settle among Israeli politicians.

He said he was a vegetarian, but that if he was to eat meat, he'd also eat pork. He asked me about my life, and after our get-acquainted conversation, we walked together to a place where children were playing. We sat ourselves down at a piano—David Ben-Gurion, the children, and me—and sang songs that I taught them and songs that they taught me. Then we all ate dinner together at a big, long table.

He asked me into the small rooms where he slept and worked. He allowed the cameras and equipment to follow us in. The guards whispered to me, "We've never seen him do this. He's never done this before." He showed me his books and told me that he was still writing his memoirs. He promised me an autographed copy.

He showed me what they had done with the land. He carefully explained to me how a kibbutz is run. He introduced me to all the people—the old ones and the young ones—who lived around him. And we passed hour after hour, gossiping and chattering about everything under the sun.

Normally I have avoided such situations. Most times I hate this sort of social thing. But on this particular day in this particular place, I have never been happier or more myself.

Ben-Gurion was an open book—loose and free with himself. He died a few months after I met him, but even now I can still feel his closeness.

After a couple of weeks in Israel, I felt a lot of respect for its people —for their iron will to survive, even with the odds stacked against them and the smart money on the other cats.

Even though I'm not Jewish and even though I'm stingy with my bread, Israel is one of the few causes I feel good about supporting.

Blacks and Jews are hooked up and bound together by a common history of persecution, and that's probably why I've always been interested in Judaism. I've always seen Jews as the earliest defenders of black causes in this country, particularly at a time—in the forties—when no one else was breathing a word.

If someone besides a black ever sings the real gutbucket blues, it'll be a Jew. We both know what it's like to be someone else's footstool.

I have enormous respect for what the Jews have made of themselves, especially in America. They had their program together before anybody else, and they've kept it together, understanding how to take care of their own, understanding how to keep on going.

I've heard about anti-Semitism among blacks in America, but I've never paid that much mind. Some of the only white people that blacks have contact with are Jewish businessmen—least that's the way it used to be in the big city ghetto. That can cause resentment. But that prejudice is stupid and narrow and, fortunately, short-lived. For the most part, we're two peoples who work well together. And in many instances, there's real love between us.

I've met many of my early goals: I've played Carnegie Hall. I've got a big band. I've won some Grammys, though I forget when and for what. But I never dreamed when I started out that I'd become known in two-thirds of the world. If you had told me in 1952 that one day I'd be flying to Singapore and Sydney for gigs, I'd have said, "Baby, I may be blind, but I ain't dumb; I'll be lucky to keep working the chitlin circuit."

B and Me

B and I had some good years together. We had three boys, and we shared a home together in Dallas and later in Los Angeles. I lived in those homes. I loved my wife and my children. But I put B through a lot. First of all, I was gone. That was bad enough. I was gone nine or ten months a year, every single year. That was something she was forced to swallow. And she did. Then there were the drugs. And that —to B's mind—made things even worse. But she also swallowed that.

I think it was really those paternity suits, though, which got to her. The papers were full of the news, and it was tough for B to face her relatives and her friends. Throughout it all, even during the lawsuits, she was on my side, expressing anger at those women for being greedy. But I know that the situation ate at her and ate at her, until it nearly made her sick with anger and grief.

B's strange, though. She's someone who doesn't scream and doesn't yell. She keeps it all inside. She's not like a kettle which will explode without a valve. She's more like a pot which is half-filled with coffee and left on the stove all night. Finally, the coffee will burn itself out. So for years she just burned. And finally it became too much. By the early seventies, the tension between us was real. You could cut it with a knife. The climate was so hostile that it hurt us both.

We went through the motions—me bringing home the bread, her cooking and looking after the young 'uns. We went to the kids' graduations together—stuff like that—but that was all. Just the motions.

There came a day some three years ago when B decided that she had gone as far as she could go. She filed for a legal separation. That meant I was going to have to move out. But if I was leaving, I figured we might as well do it right. Why mess around? You don't gain any points by bullshitting yourself.

So I filed for divorce. Long as I wasn't going to be at the house, there was no reason to be married. When we went to court, the judge recommended that we try to save the marriage and go to a counselor. That seemed stupid to both of us. We weren't kids. By the time you've been married twenty years, you'd better have it together. If you don't, it just ain't going to work.

We tried doing what the judge said. We went to a marriage counselor together, then we saw a psychiatrist. All this took about six months, but it didn't change anything. By then, B and I were already set in different directions. There was no turning round.

Maybe if I had taken off in 1967 or 1968 and put in a year or two with the family, I would have had a shot at setting things right. But I was still too preoccupied with making music and making money. The chance was there, but I wasn't.

Maybe if B had gone on the road with me and shared my life— maybe that would have made the difference. Maybe.

Far as my family went, music proved to be a blessing and a downfall. It created the financial security I had sought, but it also kept me away from anything close to a normal home life.

Finally, though, I have to blame myself for 80 or 85 percent of the damage to our marriage. I was the one who fell into the dope and into the paternity suits. I knew just what I was doing. I saw the risks. I was selfish. All these babies, all these drugs, all these months and years away on the road—they took their toll.

Today my relationship with B ain't ideal, but there are times when she will call me for help and advice. There is still love between us. And when her mother died recently, I rode in the family car with B, holding her hand and doing my best to see her through her pain.

The collapse of a marriage—especially one which began so many years ago—is a sad and hurtful thing. And all I can do—all I want to do—is recall those happy, good years, when we were both singers kicking around Texas, very young and starry-eyed in love.

I can't see myself marrying again. Oh, maybe if I was seventy or eighty and shacked up just for the companionship; maybe if my old lady stayed on my case long enough I'd marry her for the sake of society.

But basically I'm through with marriage.

It's not that I live alone. No, I'll never live alone long as I can help it. It's just that my style with women—my need for women—doesn't match up with the demands and dilemmas that marriage puts in my way. And besides, to me marriage seems to mean possession and ownership of human beings as though they are television sets. And I really don't want to be owned.

Working
on the Building

My politics are a little strange. I've never figured out whether I'm a liberal or a conservative. I think I'm both. I have trouble understanding the simple shit. Why we give billions of foreign aid and then can't make sure that everyone in trouble has a decent lawyer. Why we subsidize the tobacco companies and then can't make sure that everyone who's sick has a decent doctor.

I don't dig welfare. But I can feature folk needing help to help themselves. I think it corrodes a man's or woman's integrity to get something for nothing. But I believe in incentives. The government could pay 70 percent of a poor kid's education, let's say. The government could start giving the poor some bargains—not handouts or freebies. A dollar means a hell of a lot more when you got to sweat a little blood for it.

I think simply. I see Uncle Sam popping for billions and billions—for some new giant bomber or for some country no one's heard of—

and I wonder: Where's the sense? If we can clean up their yard, why can't we clean up our own?

Politicians are even stranger than musicians. I ignore most of them, but I've supported a few. Given 'em money or hosted fund-raising parties—though I'm never there during the parties themselves.

Politicians are necessary, and it'd be foolish to blame them for our troubles. They're just doing what they've always done—looking to survive, looking to climb, trying to please everyone at once and grinning and lying while they're doing it.

I've even enjoyed some of these cats: Take Truman. I dug his style. I liked his way. He was a fiery little man. He'd just say whatever he wanted. Ike seemed like he was above the common people. I thought of Kennedy as a freshness coming out of the White House. LBJ struck me as a hard-nosed dude. He did good things we've already forgotten about. He had his program together, and I'd guess he had something on every son of a bitch in Washington.

Of all the cats, though, my man was Hubert Humphrey. I had faith in him. Humphrey was on the right side—the black side—from the beginning. He was sincere and straight-ahead and decent. And that's saying a lot for someone in his line of work. When he passed, we lost a friend.

America's made bigger promises than almost any other country in history. We're told that everyone's entitled to this and to that. We've got this hip Constitution and this precious Bill of Rights. We make the promises, we talk the talk, but often we don't do the deed. And even though I might be a little cynical—I call it realistic—about the way America's run, I still feel like it's *my* country.

I'm curious about Africa. I'd like to see what's happening there for myself. Maybe one day I will. But I don't have a burning desire to find out everything about my past. So much sickening crap has gone down that I know I'd be heartbroken learning 'bout it.

I don't see Africa as my homeland. My homeland is Florida—

Greensville, Florida—Georgia, Mississippi, Seattle, California, Dallas and Houston and New Orleans, Baltimore and the Carolinas. My homeland's right here.

I ain't gonna lie to you and tell you I don't love America. I do. But I'm also gonna tell you what gripes my ass about this country: the hypocrisy.

I dug the hippies, for example, 'cause they pointed to society's two-faced standards and fucked-up demands. I heard that some of those folk were dirty, and I'm no lover of filth—a man should always wash his ass—but sometimes you need drama to drive home your message.

Up until three or four years ago, I did very few message songs. There are some scattered examples—Percy Mayfield's "You're in for a Big Surprise" and "Danger Zone" come to mind—but the album *A Message From the People* in 1973 was really my first collection of songs about politics and society.

"Look What They've Done to My Song, Ma" was written by a French lady, but it served my purposes. I stepped right into the tune, and it fit me like a banana skin.

The words went something like, "Look what they've done to my song, Ma. The only thing I could do half right, and now it's turning out all wrong, Ma . . . look what they've done to my brain . . . they picked it like a chicken bone and I'm about to go insane . . . look what they've done to my song . . . put it in a plastic bag and then they turned the bag upside down . . . maybe it's all right, maybe it's okay, I don't know . . . if my tears were money, I'd be a millionaire today . . . I'm going crazy, Mama . . . they stole everything I had and made a million with it, and you know that hurts . . . but I'm gonna keep on working on the building just like you taught me . . . oh yes I will."

I was saying—in my own way—that the whites had taken a lot from me and from the soul community. I wasn't bitter or angry; I was just telling the truth.

For thirty years, I had seen my records—and the records of other black musicians—taken over or imitated by whites. They mutilated the songs, and they still wound up selling more by accident than the black versions sold on purpose. I remember that when I went to England to do the Tom Jones TV show I didn't even have to take my arrangements out of my suitcase. The band already had them.

I've heard a lot of praise for my work in the last ten or fifteen years. Big words have been used to describe what I've done. And yet, in spite of all the roses and the prizes, I know I'll never see the bread that a Dean Martin or a Frank Sinatra makes. We just ain't ready for that yet. We're not moving that fast.

In the fifties, many characters could do what Elvis was doing. Where do you think he learned it from? But these dudes were black, and there's no way Middle America was going to permit some dark cat to shake his ass on TV with millions of white chicks screeching and hollering for more.

Growing up in the Deep South you learn one fact real early: You cool with white folk long as you don't fuck with their women. And that attitude spills over into music.

But like I said in the song, I ain't mad, Ma. I can't afford to be. That ain't productive, and that ain't going to get me nowhere. As the old Negro spiritual says, "I keep working on the building 'cause it's a true foundation."

I tried to describe the things which were out of tune in America on *A Message from the People*. I sang "I Gotta Do Wrong" and "Hey, Mister" and "Heaven Help Us All." But I also did "America, the Beautiful." I was saying, "Listen, you need to clean up some of this shit, America, but I still love you."

A black magazine wrote that I was selling out by singing "America." Well, if I was, I had sold out a long, long time ago. Ever since I started traveling round the world and seeing other places, I've been convinced that what we got—as rotten as part of it might be—is hipper than anything else I've noticed out there.

On almost every level, America has a tighter system than other countries. Try having a phone put into your apartment in Europe. See how long it takes. Or try messing around with the courts in Latin America. See how much justice you gonna get.

So my attitude on *Message* was like a mama chastising a baby: "You may be a pain in the ass, you may be bad, but, child, you belong to me."

I believe that hard work and good luck can still do the trick in America. If taxes don't eat you up or the unions don't drive you mad, a musician can make a decent living by keeping his nose to the grindstone and playing what he thinks is right.

In my whole career—some thirty years of performing—I haven't missed more than five or six gigs. And that's only because a snowstorm closed down an airport in New Mexico or a car broke down in the middle of the highway. When my plane hasn't worked, I've chartered planes for my band rather than miss a job.

I've worked my ass off for everything I've gotten, and that's why I intend to keep my most precious reward: my independence. No one will tell me what to play. To me, that's the spirit of America.

As small and half-assed as my company might be, it's mine. That's why I love it. And I don't owe no motherfucker a single dime.

I've even turned down a president of the United States when his people asked me to play in Washington. They called the day before the gig and I just didn't think that gave me enough time. Why should I drop everything and run to Washington? I thought I deserved a little more respect than that.

In 1973 there was a confrontation between me and the president of ABC. They were still doing my distribution and promotion then, and this cat figured I should be selling more records. He thought I was a bit too free over there. He wanted to set up a producer for me. He said he'd advance my record company big bread for the production costs. He was anxious for me to have a hit.

Well, I said no. I didn't need no advance. That was just a loan. And I wasn't interested in borrowing money that I had to pay back. Besides, I didn't want a producer.

Things got chilly. He let it be known that he wasn't interested in renewing my contract. He might have thought that would make me nervous, since my money from all my past sales had been accumulating over there since 1959. Maybe he figured I'd panic at the thought of having to pay the taxes.

But I didn't budge. If y'all want to break the contract, I said, that's cool. Give me my bread, send me back my masters, and I'll pay my taxes.

That's just what happened. It stung—oh baby, you know it hurt—but I paid every dime's worth of tax.

I felt an obligation to myself and particularly to my public which had been keeping me alive all those years. If I'm going to stick my name on a record, I want to make sure I'm sincere about it. If it's a hit, fine, wonderful, great. If it ain't, that's cool too. When an entertainer lasts thirty years, he owes the public something decent.

People tell me about songs I've done which were never hits. They love them—I can hear it in their voices—so I know that sales don't mean everything. I remember one straightlaced fan—a stockbroker—telling me about some obscure songs of mine that even I had forgotten. He knew 'em all, and he really dug 'em. He couldn't have cared less which tunes had sold and which hadn't.

I've had real smashes, tunes that made me some smart money. When it happened, it was very sweet. But I never ran after it, I never got desperate, I never said, "Find me some son of a bitch who understands how to make a hit and let him shine his light on me." So by 1973, it made no sense to turn around and start chasing rainbows. By then I was a child who had got his own. Thank you, Jesus.

Even recently, when I saw that I needed help promoting and distributing my own company's records, I talked with my old friend Ahmet Ertegun of Atlantic, and I took the same approach.

I told him that I wasn't happy using independent distributors. I told him that we were just a little company and it was tough for us to compete. But I also said that if I went back to Atlantic, I had to retain control of my own product. If not, I still loved him, but there could be no deal.

Ahmet might have said, "Well, Ray, that was in the old days." But he didn't say that. He agreed. And that's how I happened to return to my old label in 1977.

It's not that I won't listen to other ideas. I will. I try to stay open to new tunes, new arrangements, new instruments. And I'll sing something—I'll sing anything—long as it suits me.

I don't know how many times I've been asked to sing "The Star-Spangled Banner." I've refused. Never sang that song once. I just don't hear myself doing it. If the shoe don't fit, I don't wear it. When I do a song, I must be able to make it stink in my own way; I want to foul it up so it reeks of my manure and no one else's.

I'm not even sure I'm a real singer. But I know goddamn well that I can interpret anything—country, blues, jazz—except opera. And I'm not so sure I couldn't do that if I set my mind to it.

I've sung everything from "My Bonnie" to "Two Ton Tessie" to "Moon Over Miami" to "Indian Love Call." I ain't real narrow in my tastes. In fact, I'm crazy about "Indian Love Call." I heard Jeanette MacDonald do it with Nelson Eddy when I was a kid, and I thought it was beautiful. I dug her kind of singing; she had real control and true feeling. I recorded the song in the late sixties and then sang it as a duet with Susaye Greene, one of the Raeletts, all over Europe and Japan. People flipped.

I've been lucky that way. I've been able to rummage through the attic of my mind and pick out all the old tunes that I like. In recent years, I've done "Gloomy Sunday," just 'cause I was struck with the way Billie Holiday once did it.

I think "Wichita Lineman" is a beautiful song. And when I recorded it, Glenn Campbell and Jerry Reed came over to my studio—free of charge. Glenn played mandolin and Jerry played guitar.

Throughout the past ten years, I've been able to go back over my life and reinterpret music—Charles Brown's version of "Drifting Blues" or Nat Cole's rendition of "Gee Baby, Ain't I Good to You?" —which I had loved as a kid.

It's crazy, I know, me singing "Oh, What a Beautiful Mornin' " or "Zip-a-Dee-Do-Dah," but those are numbers which I can honestly feel. I can be cynical about other things, but never my music.

I love ballads, for example—real corny ballads. Songs like "Cry," "Tears," and "If You Go Away" are among my favorite records. They haven't been smashes, but they came from inside me.

I dig George Gershwin. The cat was a stone writer. Norman Granz once suggested that I do *Porgy and Bess,* and I liked the idea of doing a whole book. I saw the challenge. I decided to record it 'cause I felt like I could crawl inside and get under the skin of the score.

Frank DeVol did the charts and Cleo Laine sung the Bess part. The record's okay, but it would have turned out much better if Frank and I had had time to get together before he wrote the arrangements. He did a fine job, but because we didn't collaborate beforehand, I think something's missing.

I also try to be current. I don't believe in using iceboxes when you got refrigerators around. I try to find material which isn't antiquated —like "I Can See Clearly Now"—and adapt it to my own low purposes. I never stand still, and I ain't running after no one.

Case in point: A woman can be in her forties or fifties and still dress in style without looking the fool. She doesn't have to go crazy, doesn't have to turn herself into a teenager. But she can still wear clothes like she knows what's happening. That's how I feel about myself and my music.

My own personal style is uncomplicated. My hair is short, just the way it's been my whole life except that now it's a little gray. I keep it short 'cause it's coarse and thick, and it's much too hard to comb when it's long. I don't care much about being stylish. I don't wear jewelry 'cause it's expensive and it don't do nothing.

My business style is also simple. A friend of mine says I never get excited about anything. He claims he can tell me 'bout a big deal, something which will earn me lots of bread, and I'll just sit there— nodding and thinking. He'll get nervous and want to know if I really understand how fabulous this deal is.

What's wrong with me? Don't I understand good news?

Sure, I like juicy contracts as much as anyone else—maybe even more. Sure, I like the taste of new money and, sure, I'm crazy 'bout those guarantees, that up front cash, and those fat royalties. But I also know that I got to pay for it, because obviously the man ain't going to give it to me. Just as sure as you're reading this, I know that the other side is coming. I know costs will be involved. So if I'm cool, it's 'cause I'm busy reflecting on those costs.

You can run into wild happiness now and then, but some suffering is also going to arrive, and there ain't no way to stop it. You can duck, but you can't hide. So I try to strike a balance. I count my ability to stay calm as a blessing.

Then I'm blessed another way. I've always been able to find many great musicians for my band—Fathead Newman, James Clay, Leroy Cooper, Donald Wilkerson, Hank Crawford, Marcus Belgrave, Wilbur Hogan, Phil Guilbeau, John Coles, Cliff Solomon, Billy Preston, Edgar Willis, Ernie Vantrese, Cliff Hugo, Mr. Chambers, Henry Coker—to name just a few.

And I've been rewarded. I got a wall full of awards—from governments and cities and magazines and schools. I dig 'em all, but the one that moved me the most was being B'nai Brith's Man of the Year in 1976 in Los Angeles. They had a banquet, and people like Sammy Cahn wrote special songs for me. That touched my heart.

Being honored while you're still alive is a gas. 'Cause when all is said and done, when the party's over and the building comes tumbling down, you ain't sure what's coming next.

Living
and Dying

I release feelings inside me through my songs. I take some of the sadness, some of the heartache, and turn it out. I'm able to stave off the severity. By expressing myself in music, I can soften the blow. But those melodies and rhythms can only do so much. An aspirin can cure a headache for an hour or two, but if the pain's really deep, nothing short of brain surgery is going to make it go away.

Music has made me a good living and helped keep me whole. But it's not my religion or my salvation; it's only something I do because it's a part of me and I love to do it.

I'm not sure what my religion is. I'm not sure why man is born and why man dies. I have trouble understanding why a young, beautiful child must contract leukemia. I have a problem rationalizing that.

I don't have the answers, but I do have faith in a Supreme Being. It may just be a way for me to rid myself of my fears—I'm not certain —but I do believe in God. I believe in God because I believe in life —and, man, that's my only reason.

How else did all this begin? Who started it, who created it in the first place? The world is so ordered, so perfectly balanced, that I can't see it happening by accident or chance. No, the measurements in the universe are exact. A scientist knows when the sun will eclipse fifty years from now to the very second. We can shoot rockets to Mars and make them land exactly where we want. The elements are dependable.

We live inside this unbelievable cosmos, inside our unbelievable bodies—everything so perfect, everything so in tune. I got to think that God had a hand in it. This marvel didn't just fall into place. There's got to be something greater than us. You and I will never reach our potential. We'll never gain full control of our destinies. Man can't handle everything.

And when you can't handle it, that's when you start praying. Don't matter what you're praying to—the sun, the moon, or the stars. The act of praying will do you good. If you believe in the doctor—even if the cat's only giving you sugar pills—that belief can contribute to your cure. Folk need hope, purpose, a feeling that they matter. And I'm no different.

I don't mean prayer will get you what you want. May get you nothing. But even if I was a skeptic, I'd pray anyway—just in case God might be listening. I mean, why take a chance?

I told you how I say the Lord's Prayer every night before I go to bed. And from time to time I've been known to pray for other reasons. But that's only after I've done all I could on my own. Far as I'm concerned, it's stupid to go to God every time you prick your finger or stub your toe. You don't want to use up your favors or exhaust God's patience.

I say: As long as I can stand it, God, I'll keep on keeping on. I say: When I can do a little bit more on my own, Lord, I'll do it. I say: If I have strength left in me, then I'll use it.

Mama said, and I still believe her, that God helps those who help themselves. Now that's the truth.

Everything must start with me. I can dig that. But when the well is dry, when there's nothing left to pump and no more digging to be done, I say: Lord, I understand that Moses never got to see the promised land, and I ain't asking for no bed of roses, but please help me understand. I can't go no further without You.

Looking back at the sad and bad times in my life, I can't say God got me through. I just kept hearing Mama say, "Boy, you got to learn to take care of yourself." That's the faith I've tried to keep.

But there were moments when I couldn't do it alone. After Mama died, and my head was in a mess, it was only with the help of Ma Beck —who might well have been the instrument of the Lord—that I was able to shake out the cobwebs and make sense of the world.

I'm not sure why we're put here, but because I can see God's handiwork, I also got to believe in His presence. And if He's around, there's no reason not to pray to Him.

I'm like Job and the Jews: I pray directly to God, without a middle-man.

I'm neutral on the question of Jesus. Maybe He was the son of God, maybe not. I can go either way without any trouble. I can understand that Jesus was born of Mary without coming from Joseph's sperm. And I can understand that Joseph married her to save her from the town's scorn. I have a harder time, though, believing that Joseph never touched Mary till after Jesus' birth. To me, that's not human.

I can see a guy trying to save a woman's character. He might say, "That's fine, Mama. If you're carrying a special something in your womb, I can dig it. But listen here: That's no reason why we can't get together."

That's not the only thing in the good book that I question:

I also wonder why Jesus couldn't convince the Jews that He was the Messiah. After all, He was a Jew. They were His people. And the Jews —the folks who were there at the beginning of the Bible—didn't turn away from the truth. It worries me that Jesus wasn't able to persuade the very people He came from.

My relationship is really with the Supreme Being, not with Jesus. I suppose I consider myself religious since I believe in God. But I never thought about joining any particular faith just 'cause then I'd have to face someone else's set of rules, and I don't see much sense in that.

I like the singing in the Baptist church and the preaching in the Methodist church. But I could go sit in any church. I ain't particular.

If I think about the wonders of God, I also wind up wondering 'bout the mystery of death. I'm as scared of dying as anyone else, even though I know there's nothing I can do about it. It's one of those constants —a flat-out certainty—that you can't escape.

Friend of mine tells a story about a farmer who looks up one day and sees Death coming across the field. So the farmer runs and hides. Next day the farmer's out there plowing his field when he spots Death again. He starts to run, but Death stops him:

"Hey, man, hold it. Where you running to? I just came to tell you something."

"Oh, that's all?" the farmer asks.

"Yeah, baby, that's all," Death says.

"Well, what you wanna tell me?"

"Remember yesterday when you saw me and you started to run?"

"Yeah."

"Well, look here," Death says, putting his arm around the farmer, "I was just gonna tell you that I'd be back for you 'bout this time today."

I've lived through scary business without being afraid. The big earthquake in L.A. didn't even wake me. It was my kids crying and my wife praying that got me up. I thought there was a burglar loose in the house with a shotgun, and I screamed my head off for everyone to keep quiet so I could sniff out the son of a bitch.

Turbulence on planes doesn't worry me none. I'm usually fast asleep, dreaming that I'm flying. I don't worry 'bout the bomb and I ain't ever scared anyone's going to shoot me.

But the word cancer puts chills through my bones.

It's not how long I live, but how well I live—that's something I've been saying for a long time.

If God made us perfect, then down through the ages our genes somehow started messing up. That's the only explanation I can come up with for some of the dread diseases that knock us off early.

Cancer's a bitch. It eats and eats and eats at you; it's the most destructive process I can feature in my brain, and like everyone else, I'm frightened of what it might do to my body.

We had a maid once. Her name was Myrtle—we called her Myrt —and everyone loved her: the kids, B, and me. She was a beautiful person, always full of good spirit and warmth. She got cancer, and we watched her die. That hurt me so bad. It tore us all up something awful.

I'm sure a heart attack would shake me and leave me nervous about every twinge of pain that passed over me. But there's something about cancer—the idea of lingering away, withering away—which is more frightening. And in those last days, I'd be the kind of cat who wouldn't be able to sleep alone.

Sometimes I imagine death to be like sleep. When death comes to you, you just pass out, just the way you passed out last night. It's easy.

We don't know where we were before we got here, so why worry about what's going to happen after we split? I can't see God taking eight hundred or nine hundred million people and saying to them, "Okay, y'all, you didn't believe in me so I'm gonna burn your asses in the fires of hell and torture you for all eternity." Now that just don't make no sense. The idea of heaven and hell is a little far out for me.

What does happen, though? At times I can dig the idea of our bodies becoming dust and fertilizer, being ground up with the rest of the earth. And at times I also think that the soul—apart from the body— might have a shot. If God created us, maybe He can keep our souls going after our bodies collapse. Maybe.

I can see where the soul might be reawakened from the sleep of death and sent out on another trip, much different from the one which just ended. I can see where the soul could keep pushing on, to places we've never seen or felt before.

But I can see a lot of stuff. Meanwhile, I'm content to keep on living. It may not be the best thing we have, but it'll do for right now.

Besides, we know about sleep. We've been asleep before. But there ain't no one who's come back to tell us what death is like. When we die, it's sure enough for the first time. I'll be interested to see how it comes out, but I'm in no hurry.

Since I have no control over when I die, I hope I can live reasonably well in the meantime, getting my small pleasures as often as possible.

I could see myself paralyzed from the waist down, for example, and still be able to go on. It'd be painful and difficult, but I'd make it.

There's something else, though, which frightens me more:

One time I had a serious problem in my left ear. It was paining me something awful. For a week or so, it got worse and worse till I couldn't take it anymore. At the point where the hurt reached its height, I was out in Arizona. I went to a doctor's office. I could hear him talking on the phone.

"The doctor will be with you in a minute," the nurse said to me.

"No, ma'am. The doctor will see me right now."

And I walked right in—that's how bad I was hurting. He looked in my ear and said, "Wait a minute. I see what the trouble is."

He lanced a boil inside my ear and pus shot out like ink squirting from a pen. There was so much pus that it filled a little pan which he was holding under my ear.

"Another day or two," he told me later, "and you'd be dead."

The pus was poison and it was about to spread all over my body. That's why my arm had also been hurting. And naturally that's why I couldn't hear out of my left ear.

This little episode didn't really get to me until a few years later. That's when I began thinking about what would have happened to me if I had lost my hearing.

If I had lost my hearing, I wouldn't be able to hear music, I'd eventually lose the ability to speak or sing right, I'd no longer be able to get around by myself.

With me, so much depends on my hearing. When I walk, I listen to where I'm going. I know people—I feel people—by their voices. I see the world with my ears.

I know all about Helen Keller. But Helen Keller was a miracle. There's been only one Helen Keller as far as I know. She was an amazing and inspirational person. I sure don't put myself in her category.

Now you already know that I'm not one to take individual handicaps all *that* seriously. I can do damn near what any sighted cat can do, and some things he can't. Even though I stopped viewing my blindness as a handicap a long time ago, I've never forgotten my limitations.

A pilot once told me that the hippest thing to know about a plane is what it can't do. Same goes for me.

I remember one time when my blindness actually helped me. A mechanic was trying to put in a gasket on one of my planes and couldn't see up inside the engine. He fooled with it for hours. Finally, I asked if I could help. I wasn't about to wait there while the cat disassembled the whole fucking engine just to replace a simple part. I reached in and did it in five minutes. My eyes didn't get in the way.

Folk underestimate the blind. Big insurance companies, for example, don't understand that blindness doesn't have to be a dangerous handicap. The blind don't have to live in fear and the blind don't have to tremble in the dark.

Blindness can be overcome. That's fact. But blindness *and* deafness . . . well, that's another matter. I shudder at the thought. And the worst part would be depending on others. Now I'm able to do what I want, when I want. I've been that way since Mama died. But being deaf and being sightless, I wouldn't know what was going on. I'd probably have to lock up with one woman, and then I'd be telling myself that the only reason she hung around was 'cause she felt sorry for me.

I wouldn't know who or what was around me. I'd lose my music and I think I'd eventually lose my mind. I could see myself saying, "Well, your life has been all right up till now. But this dependency business is too much."

Adjusting to a handicap is rough. But adjusting in middle age—at forty-seven or forty-eight—is plain murder. For me, losing my ears could be the final fuck-up; I'm not sure I'd have the strength to get past it. Might just take some high-powered sleeping pills and check out early.

I ain't telling the Lord what to do. God knows His own mind. But just in case He's looking over my shoulder or reading this book, let me repeat myself:

I know I ain't getting out of death. When the cat comes a-knocking, I got no choice but to let the motherfucker in. But in between time, if there's any way to avoid getting cancer or going deaf, I'd be mighty grateful.

Nothing New

Looking back over what I've heard and seen, I can't say I've witnessed much progress in the world. If you tie up my hands and then release one finger, I don't call that progress. And that's the only sort of advances I've seen man make in the past forty or fifty years.

Actually, I don't think man's made much progress—other than scientific progress—since Biblical days. The Bible's my main book, the only thing I've read twice. And when I tell you I've been over it twice, I mean slowly and carefully—from the first word in Genesis to the last word in Revelations.

I don't believe everything in there—far from it. I don't analyze or interpret the Bible. I never think, "Well, it says this, but it *means* that." I just nod my head yes or shake my head no.

But I think the Bible's basic. It describes men and women the way they are. It shows people acting according to their true nature. It tells the truth 'bout the way we behave. And it proves to me that we haven't changed much.

Bring me today's *L.A. Times*, give me a few minutes, and for every major news story I'll find a comparable tale in the Bible. I rest my case.

The Bible say, "Ye shall hear of wars and rumors of wars." And that's the truth.

We've learned very little, and if we've learned at all, we've learned very slowly.

If someone has something we want, we just go ahead and grab it. If someone does something we don't dig, we just go ahead and stop it. That's if we're stronger. We pry and push, dictate and declare our superiority. And it don't matter none if it's a person or a country.

I believe in leaving people and countries alone. Impositions and interferences, zealots and evangelists, cats coming down on you for this, chicks trying to convert you to that—man, it's all wasted energy as far as I can see.

Let people be who they are.

Things were bad down South in the old days. Racial hatred was open. You saw it and you felt it. It was harsh. But at least you knew it. Least you knew what to expect.

Now it's subtle and quiet. And in a way, I'm fearful. I think that's even more dangerous. You keep a motherfucker talking and you know where he's at. Once he shuts up, though, you don't know what's happening.

Still waters run deep.

It'll take another twenty-five, thirty, or forty years for people of different races to respect each other in this country—if ever. Many folk have to die out before we're going to see any real change.

And if you want to see proof, just look at the busing question. Parents say they don't want their kids riding on a bus, that they want the kids going to neighborhood schools, that they're worried about the kids being so far from home.

Bullshit. They just don't want their kids going to school with little niggers. That's what they really mean.

Too many white kids are bused way crosstown to private schools—

schools that charge an arm and a leg—for me to buy those arguments. And naturally it ain't the kids who mind—they love riding on buses—it's Mommy and Daddy.

To me, the hippest solution would be to bus the teachers. Ship them to different parts of town every day and rotate them each year so the schools would have an equal distribution of the good teachers. But naturally that ain't ever going to work; the teachers' unions would scream bloody murder.

You can change the lyrics, but it's still the same song.

Folk can chatter away all day about how they believe in racial equality, but when it comes home—like this busing business—oh man, it's a different story.

Just like the gay question now. Everyone pretends to be so tolerant and liberal until someone starts talking about gay people's right to teach in school. "Shit no!" all the parents scream. "It's wrong, it's immoral, it's sinful, it's criminal." When it comes down to their kids, they show you how tolerant and liberal they really are.

It's that same tired old story: I love to watch those darkies a-singing and a-dancing in the streets, long as they don't come crosstown and start messing with my women. Long as they know their place.

I'm not sure there's been much progress in music either—even with all the new instruments and university courses. Least I don't hear it.

From the forties on back, singers and even individual instrumentalists weren't that important. If you became a star back then, you had to knock off so many great musicians that you just had to be good.

The band played the first 32 bars before the singer even came in. Today the band hits one chord and the cat's singing—right off the bat. Today money's gotten cheap. Fame's gotten cheap. And musicianship has suffered.

When I was coming up, the competition was about knowing your instrument. If cats like Lucky Thompson or Don Byas, Dexter Gordon or Gene Ammons were blowing on the bandstand and the drummer messed up, they'd turn around and stare at that motherfucker till he be ready to crawl inside his tom-tom.

Drummers—like Sonny Payne or Buddy Rich—knew how to keep time.

Singers—like Ella or Lady Day—knew how to sing in tune.

I remember hearing an album that Jo Stafford made with Paul Weston. She sang slightly out of tune, but you can bet your ass it was on purpose, and it sounded beautiful. But before you can go off, you got to be on.

If you look at the really good musicians around today—Joe Pass or Oscar Peterson, Milt Jackson or Clark Terry, Leroy Cooper or John Coles—you'll hear that they can burn past a chorus or two. These cats play. And they ain't young men anymore.

I see a lot of kids who can play loud. They can play their little rock 'n' roll beats. They can scream and find themselves a hip manager. They can read three chords and figure out how to get to the recording studio.

But I want to know: Can they keep time? Can they sing in tune?

I was coming in when the old school was going out. I saw cats get smothered in sessions. But I also saw how they'd come back and play even harder the next time. They learned that they weren't such hot shit. And, man, that's a valuable lesson.

I appreciate cats who are studying. I have guys in my band who went to college, and they play good. I think the universities who teach music are cool. Nothing wrong with that. But believe me, the real shit ain't in the books. It's just not there. You got to go out and get your ass kicked. You got to get wiped out two or three times. And then you'll start learning what music is about.

This sounds tough-nosed and hard. Well, it was. That was the forties. I caught it on its last go-round, and I count that as a blessing. And I don't mean the starving part. I don't think you got to go hungry. But I do believe that instruments—and naturally I'm including the human voice—are there to be mastered, not to be toyed with.

Little Bit
of Soul

I've seen good and bad. And I suspect that the rest of my life will be
the same. I'm prepared. I don't understand what retirement is, and I
don't intend to find out. Music is nothing separate from me. It is me.
I can't retire from music any more than I can retire from my liver.
You'd have to remove the music from me surgically—like you were
taking out my appendix.

I believe the Lord will retire me when He's ready. And then I'll have
plenty of time for a long vacation.

I'm still on the road nine months a year, traveling the globe with my
big band and five Raeletts, working for very decent bread. The other
three months I spend recording, doing some TV, making commercials,
playing a benefit here and there. I still run very hard, and I'm busy—
maybe busier—than I've ever been.

I've got enough bread to keep playing the music I want to play. And
unless they drop a bomb on this place, I should be straight for the rest
of my life—with food, shelter, clothing, a phonograph, a TV, some

kind of transportation to get me around. And if I can continue getting a little pussy to set off my day, I suspect I'll be a reasonably happy man.

I've heard other cats my age talk about not being able to raise a hard. That hasn't happened to me yet, thank the Lord, and I don't go around worrying 'bout it. I've recently been tested by some serious lovemaking. Actually I trust that as much as a cardiogram. When I can come from under that and still be breathing normally—well, I know I'm in real good shape.

I think that aside from some sure-enough nasty disease, most of your health is in your head anyway. I've had all kinds of strange shit running through my body and the doctor says I still have the heart of an eighteen-year-old.

I dream.

Before the bust in Philadelphia, I dreamt the whole thing was going to happen—not in Philly, but in Pittsburgh. That's happened to me two or three times, and I don't like it. It scares me. These dreams are clear and realistic. They bug me. I have no interest in knowing the future. I don't want to see ahead of my time. I just want to keep up with myself.

But on other days I dream of other things. I dream of dead folk.

I dream of Miss Georgia. I see her boarding house and her café back there in Greensville. She's talking to me like I'm a little boy. But in the dream I'm a man.

I dream of my grandma, Muh. She's telling me stories 'bout how the Old South used to be. She talks for a long time, and I listen hard.

I dream of Ma Beck. She reaches in and shakes me loose. She's a saintly woman, and everyone knows that if there's a heaven, she's sure to be among the blessed.

I dream of Mary Jane. She hasn't changed. She offers me candies and clothes. She looks after me. She loves me.

I dream of Mama. She's sweet and soft. She's telling me things I need to know. I see her hair—such beautiful black hair—falling down her back till it reaches the top of her buttocks. Her hair is like a fine cat's fur.

I hear Mama's voice comforting me, telling me that the world ain't all that bad. There's pain, there's joy, and there's a way to deal with them both.

Sometimes my dreams are so deep that I dream that I'm dreaming. I wake up inside myself. I watch myself sleeping and I look like a baby or a boy—tired from playing all the day long, a small soul hungry for peace and rest.

Afterword

by David Ritz

I am twelve. The walls of my bedroom are plastered with pictures of
Billie Holiday, Charlie Parker, Miles Davis, Bud Powell, Thelonius
Monk, Clifford Brown, Sonny Rollins. My religion is jazz. It's my High
Art, the thing which separates me from the other kids in high school
who are listening to Elvis and Pat Boone. Today I'm cataloging my
record collection.

In the middle of my work, my sister Esther—a year older than me
—comes in with her friend from down the street, Marilyn Lipman.
They have a new record that Marilyn is raving about.

"Show David," Esther urges. "He likes that kind of music."

"What is it?" I ask.

"Oh, it's really wild," Marilyn says.

She shows me the album. It's by Ray Charles.

"Come on," I mutter, "that's pop crap."

The girls pay no attention to me and put the record on my father's
phonograph.

I listen to "Hallelujah, I Love Her So."

I'm shaken. I recognize the song from the radio. It's a hit, but I can't help myself; I'm drawn to it; I love it.

The next day I buy "Drown in My Own Tears" and "A Fool for You" by the same man. I do not want to like the songs as much as I do. They are *commercial*—an unpardonable sin in the mind and the heart of a twelve-year-old who knows that True Art cannot also be popular. My distinctions and categories are starting to blur. My understanding of music is being threatened. I am hooked on Ray Charles.

I am sixteen, and my friend Richard Freed and I have driven from Dallas to Fort Worth.

We are in an immense arena usually reserved for livestock shows and rodeos. The eight-piece band plays for an hour. They play rhythm and blues and they play what is then called hard-bop jazz.

There is an intermission. I look around and see only twenty or thirty other white faces in an ocean of black. The dark screaming fans seem to me a crazed army—there are five or ten thousand of them—dressed in shocking pink, Popsicle orange, Wizard of Oz green.

We are a mile from the stage, high in the rafters.

From the back door I see them leading him out. He is shaking. From afar, his sunglasses look like a bandage hiding some mysterious pain. When he comes closer, the glasses appear to be sewn into his face. He is twitching and laughing. It is difficult to tell his age—he looks neither young nor old—but I have read that he is thirty.

I am surprised to find myself afraid. He is a freak, and I am apprehensive about what will happen. He is in possession of magic. Inside him wild spirits run amok.

He opens his mouth and the spirits come charging out, like convicts escaping prison.

He sings his new song—"Them That Got"—two times, to remind us to buy it.

I witness the ritual: They call him High Priest. His singing is coarse and romantic; he phrases like the great jazz masters of old. "What I

Say," the hottest song in the country, brings the crowd to the very edge
of its ecstasy.

He throws back his head and smiles, flashing his teeth like a horse.
He is grotesque and beautiful. He cannot stop moving. He screams, and
the scream lasts for ten, twenty, thirty seconds. The scream is the
breaking point, and the show is over.

He is led from the livestock arena. It will be sixteen years before I
will be in the same room with him again.

In 1976 I decide to meet Ray Charles and convince him to let me
write the story of his life. I am thirty-two; he is forty-six.

Here is how Ray and I work:

I call his office each day at noon and learn whether he wants to talk
that night. We rarely interview during the day—that is time reserved
for music. If I'm in the building in the afternoon, I'll ask him at four
or five o'clock whether he is in a talking mood.

He hates planning ahead more than a half-day. He lives and works
according to his moods, and he knows better than anyone that those
moods cannot be anticipated.

He has set up his life in this small building—and in thousands of
motel and hotel rooms throughout the world—to accommodate himself and his mercurial nature. He is a tremendously vigorous worker, but
the work moves only in time with his peculiar rhythms; he cannot be
completely satisfied by any drummer except himself.

Out of seven days, we spend at least three or four evenings together,
and the interviews last anywhere from three to seven hours. We do this
for a year.

Several times he calls me in the middle of the night—at 2:00 or 3:00
A.M. He says he cannot sleep. He has just completed a mix and wonders
if I'm in a mood to talk.

Our conversations take place in his building, either in his office or
in the control room overlooking the studio. He likes to leave the
machines in the control room running as we talk. He likes the sounds
of the soft buzz of electrical power, likes to move his fingers over the

buttons and levers. For a man to whom control is everything, this is the right environment.

He is compulsive. If our meeting is at six and he is still recording, he may not stop till nine or ten o'clock. In the same way, he will talk to me three or four hours longer than we have planned.

In the interviews themselves, he lets me drive—and that is unusual for Ray. On some nights, I bring tapes and we listen to music together —boogie-woogie or swing or bop or early Ray Charles—and then discuss it for the rest of the evening. Once in a while I will play him someone he has not heard, like Phoebe Snow, just to watch his reaction. (He takes to Phoebe immediately.)

On a typical night, though, I throw him questions, he answers them, and if they lead us into an argument or a deeper discussion, he never backs off. In fact, he revels in debate. He loves to catch me in contradiction or factual error. He is a chess player, a dominoes player, a crapshooter, and one of the most combative, competitive people I have met.

His vocabulary is full of fight metaphors. He speaks favorably of musicians or politicians or athletes when they can whip ass, kick ass, stomp ass, when they can destroy, fracture, or wipe out. He is a rabid sports fan.

He turns men into sparring partners and women into daughters or mothers.

There are two moods which he exhibits: extreme highs and extreme lows. He knows this, and before he plans a move of considerable consequence, he waits until he is operating in the middle ground.

When he is excited, he is an obsessive and poetic talker; he will chew your ear off until you are exhausted and beat. When he is down, he becomes nonverbal. His responses are monosyllabic—"I don't know," "I can't remember," "How can I tell?"

At the end of a lousy interview he will say, "Oh, well, we'll go at it again tomorrow," understanding that I have not gotten what I need.

When he is exhilarated, his face shines from within; he radiates warmth and twinkles like a star. When he is glum, he hangs his head, his face goes blank, and he slips into a dark, silent funk. Both moods are strong, and his sullen look will grip him as suddenly as his smile.

Talking to a blind man—especially if he is Ray Charles—takes some adjustment.

We are dependent on eye contact; we seek approval in visual expression.

With Ray, there are only his sunglasses. And they tell you nothing. If you are uncertain to begin with, his mere physical presence will make you doubly nervous.

"When I want to talk to him," one of his employees tells me, "I always write down what I'm going to say or else I'm speechless. When he looks at me, I freeze. It's like he can see through me."

One day I hear him ask everyone he meets about the configuration of the moon after it is full.

"Does it go back to being a sliver, or does it get small gradually?" he wants to know.

No one can answer the question.

"With all that twenty-twenty, y'all don't even look at the moon," he giggles.

"Timing is everything," Ray likes to say. "Hit me at the right time and you got a shot," he explains to his agent who needs a decision, "but right now I can't fuck with nothing." And with that, he turns his head towards the tape machines.

His reactions to the day's events are always genuine: He is genuinely angry, genuinely upset, genuinely moved by a piece of music, genuinely grateful for a call from an old friend.

He is incapable of faking a feeling.

"I like it myself," he says when he's pleased with his own singing. He smiles and nods and does his dance as he listens to how he has fouled up—in his own sweet way—Gershwin's "How Long Has This Been Going On?"

His vocal belches and farts break him up. After hearing a particularly nasty lick, he will say, "That's me" or "That's stupid" or ask me rhetorically, "Does that stink enough for you?" Then, realizing he may be enjoying this too much, he will add, "I better go back inside and record. No use in getting hung up on myself." On the other hand, if he doesn't like what he has done, he'll curse himself.

He knows his strengths and weaknesses, and while he is recording he seeks no opinions other than his own.

He is a confident and self-centered man, all right, but listening to him listening to himself, his reaction reminds me of my own: He is simply a fan in love with the voice of Ray Charles.

Respect for Ray is so widespread and exuberant among the people I interview that my conversations with colleagues and friends soon become repetitive and dull. Musicians and entertainers see him as a master in their own particular fields—jazz or pop, country or soul—and take hours describing his contributions. Ex-sidemen praise his music but often complain about his being cheap or strict. Hundreds of magazine articles over the past twenty years treat him with boring reverence.

I meet people from Tampa, Orlando, Jacksonville, Seattle, Baltimore, Houston, New Orleans, Atlanta, and Dallas who will swear before witnesses and under oath that Ray Charles is a native of their cities. They can hear it in his music.

Everyone claims him. He belongs everywhere and nowhere.

It takes four or five months before Ray and I become friends and start sharing intimacies. Toward the sixth month, he becomes emotionally involved in the book and begins understanding it as a work of passion. I write a hundred pages which are transcribed to Braille. Ray takes six weeks to read them.

One day I catch a glimpse of him reading. It is as though he is playing piano. Running his fingers over the page, he responds viscerally to what is written. He will grunt in approval or disapproval, muttering, "Oh yeah" or "Hmmmm, don't think so." He talks back to the page. When he is through, he is not entirely pleased. He calls me into his office to explain. He is gentle with me, almost apologetic about letting me know that he has problems with the text. The facts are there, he says, but the tone is wrong. He makes a suggestion: He will read these hundred pages out loud to me and stop every time he thinks I have used an inappropriate word or phrase. Then I can take notes and later make repairs.

For nearly two months we stop our interviews as Ray reads to me —slowly, cautiously—every word that I have written. He is patient— far more patient than I am—and determined to be properly represented.

He is not concerned that I have included large sections on sex or drugs, but only that the words I have chosen for him are sometimes too harsh, sometimes too demure. He understands that writing is no different than music: Every note must be the right one. When the interviewing is over and a first draft—over five hundred pages—is written, we go through the process again. He carefully reads each page in Braille, indicating what he likes and what he does not like.

For months, I have been listening for Ray's music in his speech. But one night I suddenly realize I have the process reversed: His speech is in his music. Talking comes first.

We talk before we sing, and now I see that the Ray I hear—the Ray speaking to me night after night—is the essential Ray. His style of singing is born out of his style of talking. He talks crazily. He talks quickly. He slurs and he stutters and he cannot find the right words. Or, like a machine gun, he sprays you with all the right words for hours on end. He screams at will. He will moan a phrase rather than utter one. He will whisper to make a point. He will shout the news in your ear.

His speech is full of surprises. His accent is essentially Southern, but he is able to bend away from that when he wants to. He does precise imitations of white people, for example, whom he has spoken to during the day. The parodies are not scornful or angry—just funny. He will speak the language too properly, pronouncing all the Rs and making a joke of the correctness and rigidity of it all.

"This cat say to me, 'Yes, sir, Mister Charles. Your ee-quip-ment will be ready x-act-lee by five o'clock. On the dot, sir.' Yeah, that's what the cat say."

He does a respectable Lyndon Johnson imitation ("Friends and feller Americuns") and a decent Rex Harrison ("She's got it, by God, I think she's got it").

His voice is flexible, the instrument of his moods. If he is excited, he howls in falsetto. If he is mellow or melancholy, he broods in the bass clef and transforms himself into a baritone. As a conversationalist, his vocal charms are overwhelming. If he wants to, he will sell you in a minute. His enthusiasm is electric, his giggle infectious. His speech is magical. He is magical. There is no telling what sound will come out of his mouth. His favorite expression in telling me that I have understood him is, "I like that; that's me."

The Last Days of
Brother Ray
by David Ritz

The sheer strength of his life force made me less afraid of death, but now that he is dead, now that our endless discussions about the nature of death are over, now that his own struggle with death is resolved, the question of death is more on my mind than ever. "Death," he said to me when he first learned that cancer was devouring his body, "is the one motherfucker that ain't ever going away."

I met Ray Charles in 1975, at a time in my life when I was haunted by the fear of death. This had been the case since I was a little boy. In college I had read the line by seventeenth-century poet Andrew Marvell, "At my back I always hear Time's winged chariot hurrying near." I took Time to mean Death. To defy death meant to hurry into life. If I could convince Ray to let me write his life story in his own words, my own life would change. I could go from being an advertising copywriter to an author. The obstacles, though, were daunting. Ray was unrelentingly private. When not performing, his whereabouts were well-guarded secrets. His underlings were instructed to stop people like me from approaching him. What's more, I lacked the qualifications. I'd never written a book before.

But frantic determination was my ally. My future was in the balance. I had to find a way to get past his handlers. Salvation came in the form of Western Union. By sending him long telegrams in Braille, I reasoned rightly that no one but Ray could read them. The telegrams set out my impassioned argument: that I could capture his voice and translate the pulse of his music into musical prose. Ray bought the argument. We met, bonded and went to work.

The work of a ghostwriter is strange. Your job is to disappear and then reappear in the guise of another spirit. You lose yourself before finding yourself in someone else's skin. To do that you listen. You listen to the cadences, the stories, the beating heart beneath the stories. In listening, you pray for a mystical marriage between your soul and the soul of your collaborator. In listening to Ray, I was transported. I didn't merely like the way he spoke; I loved it. Early on I heard how the thrill of his music was even more thrilling in his speech. He was vulgar, refined, funny, sexy, spontaneous, outlandish, brave, brutal, tender, blue, ecstatic. He was wholly unpredictable. He wrapped his arms around his torso, hugging himself in a grand gesture of self-affirmation. To make a point, he beat his fist against his chest. His gesticulations, like his articulations, were wildly unrestrained. In normal conversation, he preached and howled and fell to the floor laughing. He had no trace of self-consciousness, no pretensions. He was, in his own words, "raw-ass country."

Because my job was to take the raw material of our dialogues and weave them into a first-person narrative, I had to make sure the dialogues were deep. I had to ask tough questions.

I began tentatively by saying, "Now if this question is too tough . . . "

"How the fuck can a question be too tough? The truth is the truth."

The truth—at least Ray's truth—came pouring out. That his life had been rough. That his life had been blessed. That he had followed his musical muse wherever it led. That he had been gutsy in traveling the long dark road, blind and alone. That he had been a junkie. That being a junkie never stopped him from working day and night, touring, recording, succeeding. That he had given up junk only when faced with prison. That every day he still drank lots of gin and smoked lots of pot and worked just as tirelessly. That he had a huge appetite for women. That he never curbed that appetite. That he wasn't even certain of how many children he had fathered. That he was unrepentant about it all. That he was more than confident; he was cocky; he knew his own powers—as a man, a musician, a lover, an entrepreneur who had outsmarted a ruthless industry, maintained ownership of his product and stashed away millions.

I'd never met anyone braver. He had no fears. He walked through the world like a lion. If anything, his handicap gave him an edge. His sightlessness intimidated adversaries. Rather than look *at* you, he looked *through* you. His mind was quicker than yours, his memory better, his instincts keener. Keeping up with him required resilience.

"We're flying out tomorrow," he said, a week into our interviewing.

My heart sank. I was deathly afraid of planes, especially small private planes like the one Ray was taking. But I said nothing. He was the star, I was the ghost. It was his book, not mine. My job was to catch him when I could.

Next day we ascended into an overcast sky. For the first hour, the little jet danced around the thunderstorms. Then darkness descended, lightning flashed, thunder boomed. We rocked from side to side; we dropped precipitously. Ray remained impervious. He was discussing his childhood. I was taping him and taking notes. The pilot opened the door to the cabin to tell us it would get even rougher. Ray didn't react. He couldn't have cared less. And suddenly I realized that, for all my years of fear, for all my paranoia about planes, I too was fearless.

As long as I'm with this man, I silently said, *God will dare not touch me. God will dare not touch me because God will dare not touch Ray.*

Ray doesn't fear God. If anything, God fears Ray.

The senselessness of my thoughts made perfect sense to me. The plane landed safely in Chicago, and that night, after the gig, Ray and I were deep into a discussion about fear and faith, the Grim Reaper and the Almighty.

"When my mother died, I didn't understand death," he said. "Couldn't feature it. What do you mean she's gone forever? I was 15, living at a school for the blind 160 miles away from home. She was all I had in the world. No, she couldn't be dead. She'd be back tomorrow. Or the day after. Don't tell me about no death. Death can't take this woman. I need her. Can't make it without her.

"That's when I saw what everyone sees—you can't make a deal with death. No, sir. And you can't make a deal with God. Death is cold-blooded, and maybe God is too. So I'm alone, and I'm going crazy, until Ma Beck, a righteous Christian lady from the little country town where I grew up, wakes me and shakes me and says, 'Boy, stop feeling sorry for yourself. You gotta carry on.' "

I wondered if the experience made him more religious.

"Made me realize I had to depend on *me*," he shot back. "No one was going to do shit for me. You hear me? *No one.* I could praise Jesus till I'm blue in the face. I could fall on my knees and plead. Pray till the cows come home. But Mama ain't coming back. So if Mama gave me religion, the religion said, 'Believe in yourself.'"

"And not Jesus?" I ask.

"Jesus was Jewish, and if he couldn't convince his own people he was the messiah, why should I be convinced? I could believe in God. I was scared not to. And I sure as shit could believe in the devil. But I had problems with Jesus."

Early the next morning we flew on to New York. I was eager to continue the conversation.

"Ray, I just want to ask you another question about death . . . "

"Look, man," he said, irritated and tired, "I wouldn't talk to my mama now if she came out the grave." And with that, he fell asleep.

Most of our discussions took place in the recording studio in the back of the modest office building at 2107 West Washington Boulevard he had built in 1964. The place was in the shadow of downtown Los Angeles, and he owned it outright. Because he had memorized the floor plan years before, he knew every inch. The moment he stepped inside, he was no longer blind. He ran up and down the halls like a kid. The studio was his playpen, the place where his fascination with machines and music forged into a permanent obsession. The studio was also where he exercised absolute control.

He routinely called me after he had been recording for several hours and was ready to wind down. That was usually the middle of the night. When I arrived, the first thing I noticed was the enormous key ring he carried with him. Keys to his house, cars, studio, cabinets, safe.

"Every key unlocks something I own," he explained. "Don't owe nobody nothing. Ain't afraid of nobody."

I wondered if his hard-earned wealth was one of the reasons he didn't seem to fear even God.

"Wrong," he said bluntly. "The thing about me, man, is that I never change. *Never*. Back in the fifties, when I was taking little gospel songs and turning them into rhythm-and-blues, I caught hell. Preachers calling me a dirty dog. Saying I'd rot in hell. Well, I didn't have no money then. I was broke as a motherfucker, but I was the same Ray then as now. I was going to do what I had to do. I wanted to change up the music. Wanted to make some bread. And if God was going to strike me down dead for perverting his spirit, so be it."

We talked about the church—the country church of his childhood—projecting the same spirit of his blues-based music. "I loved the church," said Ray. "Loved the jump-up-and-down feeling in there. Loved the ladies hooting and hollering. Loved the tambourines. Loved the shuffles and the back beats. Loved every goddamn thing about it. The church is my base. Without church, there's no me. But that don't mean I believe everything the church says. Years later I had an experience that made me think about the church. You'll appreciate it because you're Jewish. A friend took me to a synagogue, and guess what? No shouting. No tambourines. No amen corner. No red-hot music."

"I know," I said. "It's boring."

"Not to me. To me it was chilled out. Calm. I dug it."

Brother Ray: Ray Charles' Own Story came out in 1978. Ray liked the book because, as he said, "it's me—and I like me." Our friendship continued. He'd occasionally invite me to recording sessions and concerts. I'd hand him the books I'd written with people he knew—Marvin Gaye, Aretha Franklin, BB King, Jerry Wexler, Etta James, Little Jimmy Scott—and he'd listen to them on a machine given to him by Stevie Wonder. I'd watch a half-dozen different producers try to produce his music. Finally, though, no one could produce Ray but Ray. Just as no one could manage Ray but Ray. That he fell out of fashion with the record business meant little to him. He still toured the world, still made millions. He knew that his seminal influence on American culture was permanent, his place in history secure. His bravado never waned.

"I can still sing my ass off," he said. "Besides, even if I never earn another penny, I got enough money to survive World War III."

His bravado was momentarily undermined in the eighties when an inner-ear infection had him afraid of going deaf.

"Being blind is one thing," he told me. "But being blind *and* deaf is some Hellen Keller shit I can't fathom. No ears, no music, no Ray."

But the infection healed and, after donating money to organizations aiding the deaf, life went on.

"I'm a man of routine," he explained. "Don't like changes. Don't like surprises. Just let me keep doing what I'm doing. If I can play a concert, if I can cut a record, and if at the end of the day I can top it off with a nice piece of pussy, well, what else can a man want?"

When he turned sixty in 1990, I asked him if he had regrets.

"About what?"

"Paternity suits from women who claimed they had your babies, law suits from musicians who claim you owe them money . . . "

"Mother-fuck it," he spat. "I paid what was due. Fact is, no one's paid dues like me. If someone can prove I owe him, I'll pay. If they can't, I won't."

When he turned seventy in 2000, I asked him if he wanted to collaborate on a sequel to his autobiography.

"All the facts are in *Brother Ray*. What would we talk about?"

"We'd reflect."

"About what?"

"The changes you've been through since 1978."

"I don't see no changes, baby. I'm still me. Still kicking plenty ass."

He beat his chest with his fist, leaned back in his big chair and grinned like a Cheshire cat.

Then in the summer of 2003 everything changed.

I read an article in the paper saying he was having hip problems and was canceling his world tour. Ray never cancels tours. I knew something was deeply wrong.

When I called Ray to express concern, he didn't sound right. Usually focused, always ebullient, he was distracted and subdued.

"My liver's not right," he said. "I'm not putting out no press release, but I heard them use the word cancer."

I was stunned. Other people got cancer, not Ray. Meanwhile, his office kept telling the press it was his hip. He'd have surgery. He'd be back in no time.

A month later my phone rang shortly after midnight. Ray wasn't talking about cancer but rather the fact that we used the same doctor, Alan Weinberger, who had diagnosed the disease.

"Alan's a beautiful guy," said Ray. "He always has hope in his voice. He says chemotherapy can do a lot of good."

Ray's voice was different, softer, almost vulnerable.

"I'm thinking," he went on, "that we need to add some stuff to the book. But right now I'm tired. I'll call you when I can."

Another five or six weeks passed before he called.

"Chemo kicked my ass," he said. "Nearly did me in. I was at death's door. It wasn't pretty."

"I'm sorry. The pain must be . . . "

"It ain't just physical, man. It's mental. It has you thinking."

"About?"

"Everything."

I waited for an explanation but none came. I let the silence linger. I didn't know what to say. I knew what I wanted to ask— *How are you dealing with the prospect of death? How are you feeling about God?*—but I couldn't initiate that subject. Only he could, and he chose not to. I could only tell him that I loved him and would keep him in my thoughts.

My thoughts were confused. His office gave out reports that he'd soon be touring. He was to give a concert in New York. He was going to Europe. He was giving the impression that all was well. But every time we spoke, he sounded weaker. I knew he couldn't tour, yet understood that he, the most determined of men, wanted the word out that nothing or no one would stop him.

"Someone said," he told me a little later, "that if you picture yourself well, you get well. If you can conceive it, you achieve it. I'm focusing on the future. But I got to say, man, that the past keeps coming up."

"What part of the past?" I ask.

"Some of it is funny shit. Like this one time from the early days. I was fucking someone's old lady when Mr. Someone came home. I didn't even know there *was* a Mr. Someone. But there we were, screwing like rabbits, when we hear the door opening and she's whispering, 'Oh, my God, it's my husband.'

"'What husband?' I want to know.

"'The one who's crazy jealous and carries a razor.'

"So she hides my naked ass in the closet where I'm praying to God for the guy to leave in a hurry. Man, I'm shivering. If I cough, I'm dead. If he opens the closet to look for his hat, I'm dead. No *What I'd Say*, no *Georgia on My Mind*, no *I Can't Stop Loving You*, no Grammys, no career, no nothing. But God hears me. God delivers me. The man splits. I'm saved. Now am I supposed to believe that the Good Lord spared me so I could have me some hit records, make me some money and get me some more pussy? Well, that don't make sense because God sure didn't save Sam Cooke. Sam was fucking the wrong girl in the wrong place at the wrong time and he got shot dead. Why Sam and not me? Church folks said 'cause Sam traded in gospel for the devil's music. Well, I did the same. No, man, you got to believe that God works in mysterious ways. And you got to believe that I've been blessed. My life has been beautiful. I've gotten to go everywhere I've wanted to go. Got to do it all. So I shouldn't have any attitude. None at all. Just accept my blessings and say, 'Thank you.'"

I found the courage to say, "Sounds like you're trying to convince yourself."

"You mean I should be angry about getting sick?" Ray retorts.

"You're entitled to whatever feelings you're feeling."

"I'm feeling like I want more time. Something wrong with that?"

"Nothing."

"But there's no appealing. There's no making deals. God doesn't work that way."

"How does He work?" I asked.

"He worked through Ma Beck—that's for sure. After Mama died, she kept me from going crazy. She set me straight. I know that woman sure-enough saved me. Or maybe it was God who saved me. God working through Ma Beck."

"Ma Beck would say it was Jesus working through her."

"What do you know about Jesus? Jews have a thing about Jesus."

"Mable John has been talking to me about Jesus," I said. "Mable has church in her home."

Mable John, the great rhythm-and-blues artist for Motown and Stax/Volt, is a former lead Raelette and one of Ray's closest confidants. Now she is a minister.

"I need to call Mable," said Ray. "Need to see her."

"I saw Ray," Mable told me a few days later. "Went over there and sat with him."

"Was he receptive?" I asked.

"He listened. He let me pray. He loved that I prayed. He said, 'John, never stop praying for me.' We read the 23rd Psalm together. He knew it. He had it memorized. It's taken him awhile to get there, but he knows his own strength isn't enough."

"I'm getting stronger," he said the next time he called. "I can feel it."

"Great. Heard you talked to Mable."

"Man, I been talking to Mable for 40 years. For 40 years she's been trying to save my sorry ass."

"Any progress?"

"How about you?" he asked.

"I've been reading the bible."

"I got my Braille copy. Always keep it with me."

"What's it telling you?"

"When we were writing my book I remember telling you that I'm not really looking at Jesus, I'm looking at God. Well, I'm looking at it differently now."

"How so?"

"I think about stories. Songs are stories. And if you're going to write a good song, you're going to have praise a woman. That's the key. And if you're writing a book about God, you're going to have praise God. That's what Jesus did. Praised the Father. Taught us about praise."

"Wasn't the church of your childhood all about praise?"

"Hello!"

"So you're wanting to praise?"

"I used to think all that church praise, all that hooting and hollering, was overdone. Stop shouting. Be cool. Besides, if God is God, why does He need all this praise? Now I'm thinking it ain't God who needs the praise; it's *us* who need to do the praising. The praise makes us stronger. That's why I'm getting stronger."

"What's the source of the strength?"

"Used to think it was me."

"You always preached self-sufficiency. Wasn't that your mother's lesson?"

"'Once I'm gone,' she said, 'you're alone. Nobody can help you but you.' If she had said, 'Once I'm gone, Ray, pray to God and you'll be delivered,' that wouldn't have worked. I'd be back in Georgia with a dog and a cane. She knew me. She knew the world. She knew I'd have to fight the fucking world and bend it my way. So I bent it my way. That made me feel strong as Samson. But now I see my strength has limits. I see my strength starting to sap away."

"That's a scary thought."

"I ain't afraid to admit it. Folks say, 'Ray, you got balls. When you were just a little scrawny-ass kid you caught the bus from Tampa to Seattle and somehow got over. You rode a bike. You drove a car. You put together a band when everyone said you'd go broke. You ain't scared of nothing.' Well, maybe I got caught up in hearing that. Maybe that made me proud. Maybe that got me thinking, 'I'm in control of this whole motherfucking operation—my music, my band, my life, my ladies.' But soon as you start thinking that way, brother, run for cover. 'Cause someone's about to kick your ass."

"Is God kicking your ass?"

"God's teaching me to depend on something I can't see. I've always seen ahead of myself—how to buy a car or buy a building, how to start a publishing company or a record label, how to make more bread this year than last. They call that foresight, don't they? Well, I've been blessed with foresight. Thank you, Jesus. But now it ain't serving me. Now I need another kind of sight."

A part of me wanted to see him; a part of me didn't. I'd heard that he was frighteningly changed. "You'll be horrified," said one of his close associates. "You won't want to look."

But when Ray called and said I could come by the studio, I dropped everything and ran. For nearly 30 years, that had been our way. When he was ready to talk, nothing got in my way. I cherished every minute I spent with him.

He was seated where he loved to sit most—behind the control board, his fingers running up and down the switches of the elaborate recording console that anchored his musical life. He looked smaller, thinner, certainly diminished but far from defeated. I thought of the hundreds of hours I had spent in this room eliciting the thoughts of his secret heart. I thought of the hundreds of thousands of hours he had spent here— singing, writing, playing keyboards, rehearsing singers, musicians, mixing his songs, recording his voice. That voice, once an instrument of unprecedented power, was reduced to a whisper. I had to lean in to hear. The great sensuality that once emanated from deep inside his soul was missing. His robust frame had melted into the frail body of a sick old man. I felt alarmed by the transformation, but also intrigued, excited, grateful to be by his side.

He was thinking about other musicians, now gone.

"Did I mention Erroll Garner in my book?" he asked, referring to the great jazz pianist.

"Can't remember. I think so."

"I think I talked too much about my own playing. Too much about myself."

"That's the nature of autobiography."

"I never came up with that 'genius' tag. Someone else did. I don't like the genius business. It's not me. Erroll Garner was a genius. Art Tatum. Oscar Peterson. Charlie Parker. Artie Shaw. Dizzy was a genius—the way he wrote, the way he played. I'm a utility man. I can do a lot of little things well. But I learned it all from others. Piano from Nat Cole. Singing from Nat and Charles Brown. I copied."

"And then innovated."

"The innovation was copying. Good copying. Great copying. But I wouldn't put me up there with Bird and Diz."

"And when they say you invented soul music, you're going to argue?"

"Maybe I put together two things that hadn't been put together before, but, hell, give credit to the church singers—Archie Brownlee, Claude Jeter—and the bluesmen—Big Boy Crudup, Tampa Red—where I got it from. I got enough credit. Let people know that it didn't come from me. It came from before me. Way before me."

"And way before Big Boy and Tampa Red. Didn't they get it from someone else?"

"But they didn't no get money for it, and I did."

"And you regret that?"

"I love that, man," he said, his voice growing a bit more animated. "Be lying if I said I didn't. Got bread to leave behind. Bread for charities. Bread for my kids. But for every musician out there who's made a name, there's a dozen cats back in Jacksonville or Dallas twice as bad as them. They just never got known. Think of my own band. Everyone knows Fathead Newman and Hank Crawford. And rightly so. Fathead and Hank are beautiful. But no one remembers Donald Wilkerson or James Clay or Leroy Cooper or Marcus Belgrave or Johnny Coles or Clifford Solomon. These are cats up there with with Coltrane and Miles. Mention them, man. Don't let them be forgotten. They got me where I needed to go."

"What else do you want to mention?"

"That I hurt some musicians."

"How?"

"Being too much in a hurry. Too impatient. Looking for everything to be perfect. Lost my head. Said some nasty shit to guys who didn't deserve it. You know me, man. I'm always fucking with the drummers. If they don't get my time, I pitch a bitch. Treat them bad. I feel like I hurt people. I know I hurt people. Well, tell them I'm not an asshole. Tell them I have feelings too. I can feel their feelings, man. Tell them I appreciate them. Tell them . . . just tell them Brother Ray loves them."

He started crying. I'd never seen him cry before. Not like this. I fought to keep my composure, but couldn't. He turned away and signaled me to leave.

"I'm getting stronger," he said when we spoke again. "Having a good day and feeling *a lot* stronger."

"I'm glad."

It wasn't the hallelujah Ray Charles voice we know and love, but I could feel him trying.

"So I'm reading the Bible and seeing how Jesus cured all these blind people. What do you take that to mean?"

"He could change things."

"You don't take it literally?"

"I love metaphors," I said. "Jesus used them all the time."

"So if I pray for healing, can a metaphor heal me?"

"Why not?"

"When I was a kid and went blind, never dawned on me to pray for sight. When I got to the school for the blind, lots of kids did just that. I'd hear them at night. 'Sweet Jesus, let me see.' I laughed at them. 'Waste of time,' I said. 'You fools better play the hand you were dealt.' So what's I did. But now I'm going to tell you something that'll surprise you. I'm changing. I'm praying for healing. I don't want to see. I just want to live. See anything wrong with that?"

"How can I argue with you? I'm praying with you."

"And expecting the miracle?"

"Your whole life's been a miracle."

"Hello! So it's gonna happen. It *is* happening. Mable was talking about it the other day. She came over here, walked right in, kissed me on the forehead and squeezed my hand. 'Ray,' she said, 'I've seen folks a lot weaker than you get healed. You're a man with a strong will. God likes that. God can work with that. Now you got to work with Him.' 'Mable,' I said, 'I'm working hard as I can.'"

"You've always worked hard."

"Strange part is that this work ain't hard. It's easy. It's about letting go of a whole of dumb shit. Not feeling afraid. Feeling calm. I tell you, man, I'm feeling like I felt when I was a little boy in church when all the ladies would come round and hug me and make me feel safe. Those ladies had no fear. What does the bible say? 'A perfect love casts out all fear.' You believe it?"

"I believe the part that says God is love. If God is alive and well inside us, we'll never die."

"Is that the Right Reverend Mable John talking, or is that you?"

I laughed and said, "I thought *you* were the Right Reverend."

"I'm getting there, baby. I truly am."

The last time I saw him we didn't speak. He could hardly speak at all. It was at the end of April, 2004, less than a year since he had been diagnosed. By then much had changed. His deterioration was dramatic. Although the mainstream press left him alone, one tabloid ran a ghastly picture of him on page one under the screaming headline, "Ray Charles Dying!" I hadn't been able to reach him for six or seven weeks. His people told me he was talking to no one. Minister Mable John said otherwise.

"I was there the other day," she told me. "He's still going to his building every day. He's still goes into his studio. He's maintaining his routine. Routine is Ray's life. He'll never give up his routine. So they set up a bed for him where he used to work. He has all the nurses he needs. He says he has all he needs to get through. And I believe him."

"Is he peaceful?" I asked.

"He's determined. He can't be any other way. He's determined to come outside today for the ceremony."

The outdoor ceremony was to commemorate Ray's beloved professional home, 2107 West Washington Boulevard, as an historical monument. Mable and I arrived early and sat on the front row. The afternoon sun was hot. The festivities began without Ray. Where was he? Politicians and movie stars—councilmen, the mayor, Clint Eastwood, Cicely Tyson—testified on Ray's behalf. The media came out in force. I was relieved to know that the utilitarian complex Ray designed would not be torn down for a strip mall. He had spent more hours here than anywhere. This was his refuge from the world, his work space, his musical lab, the hub of his entrepreneurial soul. The speeches droned on. We waited. We wondered. And then the door to his building opened.

Seated in a wheelchair, Ray appeared in a crisply-pressed pinstriped suit. We stood to applaud. He was in obvious pain. Slowly, carefully, he was lifted from the chair and brought to the podium where his long-time manager Joe Adams placed Ray's hand over the plaque. Then Joe brought the microphone to Ray's mouth. The sound of the singer's voice was slight, distorted, slurred. His words were barely audible. He thanked the city for the honor and then paused. It was clear that he more to say. The pause was excruciating. I felt him struggling for energy, for a single stream of breath. Finally the breath came:

"I'm weak," he said, "but I'm getting stronger."

The news came six weeks later on June 10. Ray was gone. My reaction was immediate: I had to hear him sing. I put on his live versions of "Drown In My Tears" and "Tell the Truth." Those were the songs that bonded his heart to mine when I was still a boy. After a good long cry, I called Mable.

"I know he's all right," she said. "I know he's found his strength."

—David Ritz
Los Angeles, June 2004

Discography
and Notes
by David Ritz

What follows is a listing of all the records that Ray Charles has made. The recordings have been divided into four periods, each preceded by a few thoughts I have about the music.

No personnel are given. Much of that data is lost and, I suspect, of no great interest to the general reader. The musicians who have played in Ray's key groups—the trio, the septet, the octet, and the big band —have already been mentioned in the body of the book.

PART I
Pre-Atlantic

When Ray was seventeen, he inadvertently recorded his voice for the first time, fooling with a primitive wire recorder at a friend's house. We still have the four amazing songs—his first recordings—that he sang on that day down in Tampa. "St. Pete's Blues," "Walkin' and Talkin'," "Wonderin' and Wonderin'," "Why Did You Go?"

Ray sounds more like a fifty-year-old man than a boy. There is not the slightest hint of youth or frivolity. Instead, there are these classic blues, songs which stand with Robert Johnson's "Love in Vain," Bessie Smith's "Empty Bed Blues," Lightnin' Hopkins's "Wonder Why," Billie Holiday's "Fine and Mellow."

He uses the Nat Cole/Charles Brown instrumentation—trio without drums—and his voice echoes Brown's, though this time it is more than flat-out imitation. The suffering belongs to Ray. He is moaning for his mother; the pain is still fresh, the wounds still open.

Ray's piano is neither ornamental nor ostentatious. These are the simple, stark blues. Ray is a teenage professional devoid of a teenage sensibility. There is no adolescent groping. He is already alone, already full grown, twenty or thirty years ahead of himself, singing as though he has been on the road for a decade, giving the 1948 postwar public the cool, shaded, romantic music they are seeking—the California blues-and-cocktail sound of Cole and Brown.

There are dozens of samples of the work of McSon Trio—"Ain't That Fine?," "Honey, Honey," "She's on the Ball"—but sadly, there are no recordings with Ray and the Lowell Fulson band. We do have the four tunes recorded in L.A., however, with members of Lowell's band—Earl Brown, Billy Brooks, Fleming Askew, Stanley Turrentine—in which Ray tests the new waters. For the first time, he stops imitating and sings in the raw. On "Hey Now," "Kissa Me, Baby," "The Snow Is Falling" and "Misery in My Heart," we hear his real voice: a coarse and harsh voice which is the very antithesis of Cole's, a terribly lonely, ecstatically happy sensual voice which seems to contain the whole of black suffering and celebration.

This is the most difficult period to catalog. The masters of these songs have been sold and resold many times, and you are likely to find them on dozens of different albums. The reissues are everywhere, on labels like Premier, Design, Hurrah, Coronet, Spectrum, Grand Prix.

The most recent reissue is *Best of Ray Charles* on MCP (8029), a superb collection of the early material, including "Baby, Let Me Hold Your Hand," "Walkin' and Talkin' " and "Hey Now." The bulk of Ray's Nat Cole material is on two Everest LPs (FS-244, FS-292). And there are also two excellent, if somewhat misleading, LPs on Upfront: UPF-170 contains three of Ray's original recordings; in fact, on UPF-170 there is "I Found My Baby There" and on UPF-192 the same song is listed as "St. Pete's Blues." Also on UPF-192, a tune called "Ray's Blues" is actually the guitar and piano solos lifted from "Baby, Let Me Hold Your Hand." The fourth original recording—before Ray signed with Swingtime—is "Why Did You Go?" on Mainstream (MRL-310).

In 1970, Specialty reissued Guitar Slim's "The Things That I Used to Do" on an LP (SPS 2120) which also has Ray on "Well, I Done Got Over It." The entire album—even the parts without Ray—is sensational.

You are likely to find early Ray coupled on LPs with Harry Belafonte, Solomon Burke, Jimmy Witherspoon, and madman tenor honker George Brown. (Ray does not sing with these people; their old songs are just put on the same album as his.)

Searching for Ray's first material is tough. You will find songs listed by the wrong name and, even worse, material said to be sung by Ray but actually sung by someone else. The only compensation is usually the price: Most of these albums sell in the $2 to $4 range.

The title confusion, by the way, is as much due to Ray's casualness as the labels' sloppiness. He often wrote songs and never gave them a name.

Naturally, all these early songs were released as singles. Beginning around the first months of 1949 and concluding somewhere in 1951, the titles were:

St. Pete's Blues (*also called* I Found My Baby There *and* Done Found
 Out)
Walkin' and Talkin' (*also called* Talkin' 'Bout You)
Wonderin' and Wonderin'
Why Did You Go?

I Love You, I Love You (*also called* I Won't Let You Go)

Confession Blues

Baby, Let Me Hold Your Hand (*also called* Oh Baby)

Going Down Slow *(also called* I've Had My Fun; *there are two versions —the one Ray did originally and another some nameless entrepreneur engineered, putting choral and organ tracks over Ray's vocal)*

Blues Before Sunrise *(two versions—the original and then Ray with organ overdub)*

If I Give You My Love *(two versions, as above)*

Alone in This City *(two versions, as above)*

Baby, Won't You Please Come Home? *(two versions, as above)*

C.C. Rider (*two versions, like* Going Down Slow)

Can Anyone Ask for More?

Let's Have a Ball (*also called* Here Am I, By Myself, *and* All Alone Again)

Rocking Chair Blues

How Long

A Sentimental Blues

You'll Always Miss Your Water

Sittin' on Top of the World

Ain't That Fine?

Don't Put All Your Dreams in One Basket

What Have I Done? (*also called* Ray Charles' Blues *and* Tell Me, Baby)

Honey, Honey

She's on the Ball

Ego Song (*also called* All the Girls in Town)

Late in the Evening

I'll Do Anything But Work

I Wonder Who's Kissing Her Now?

I'm Just a Lonely Boy

I'm Glad for Your Sake

All to Myself Alone *(on which Ray plays celeste)*

Kissa Me, Baby (*also called* All Night Long)

Hey Now

The Snow Is Falling (*also called* Snowfall)

Misery in My Heart (*also called* Going Down to the River, Givin' It Up, *and* I'm Going to Drown Myself)

Blues Is My Middle Name (*also called* Someday)
Guitar Blues
Easy Riding Gal
This Love of Mine
Can't You See, Darling?
Going Away Blues

PART II
Atlantic

In 1954 Ray was sick of third-rate pickup musicians. He wanted to form his own band, and the success of his Atlantic singles—"It Should Have Been Me" and "Don't You Know, Baby?"—gave him the confidence to start shaping music entirely in his own image.

To convey the radical originality of Ray's first band, I have to go back to 1925, 1926, and 1927 and Louis Armstrong's Hot Five and Hot Seven. Like Louis, Ray was a man in his mid-twenties when he formed his sextet. And like Louis's, Ray's invention is historical: he finds a new musical context for the blues.

In the twenties, Louis's group was immediately successful, as though the world had been waiting for Armstrong's stop choruses and scat singing. Popular vocalizing was suddenly handed a thousand new possibilities. It would take another decade or two for the white musical community to catch on, but Louis's lesson was clear: Daring improvisation need not be limited to instruments; the human voice can be sung like a horn.

In the fifties, Ray Charles found a new musical context for the blues. Like Louis's band, Ray's was immediately popular and permanently influential. It became the model of all the great rhythm-and-blues bands to follow—James Brown, the Muscle Shoals groups, the Memphis horns, Tower of Power. Its basic function was to kick the singer in the ass, and it did so with a kind of energy and precision which would help Ray create dozens of major hits. (If there is a precedent for the instrumentation of Ray's septet, it is Basie's original nonet from the thirties. Ray uses piano, bass, drums, two trumpets, two reeds—or three when Ray plays alto—whereas Basie had piano, bass, drums, two trumpets, three reeds, and trombone. The Basie influence is extremely strong, especially on the jazz charts which Ray himself wrote.)

So the band is there, a pistol in Ray's pocket, a weapon to attack the music he finally understands he must play. Now he has his idea. It is plain, and it is cautious. He will take gospel songs—the rhythmic, hot-blooded spirituals he loves best—and change the words. Man will replace God. Sweet baby will stand in for the blessed Madonna. He will not alter the songs' structure, he will not change the chords, he will simply replace the lyrics. If he is going back, he figures, he might as well go back all the way—back home to the church, the country blues, to the very beginning in Greensville where his deepest and most passionate relationship to music was forged.

It is suddenly apparent that the great church singers of his day—Archie Brownlee and Claude Jeter—have as profound an influence on his music as T-Bone Walker and Louis Jordan.

There is a coupling of two bodies—the blues and the church—which have been sleeping and teasing each other in the same bed for over a hundred years. No one before Ray has had the courage to shove one spirit into the other. But once the intercourse starts, it never stops. Today, twenty-five years later, it continues with as much drive as that afternoon in 1954 when Ray Charles first sang "I Got a Woman" with his brand-new band.

The mid-fifties were also the time of hard bop, and one of the more astounding aspects of Ray's R & B band was its ability to play jazz as though that were its bread and butter. When the group stormed into the Newport Jazz Festival in 1958, it caused a sensation. (Atlantic recorded the concert.)

As Ray was turning out R & B hits, there was also a series of relaxed jazz sessions which revealed the quality of his piano work. And when, on the Milt Jackson dates, he takes off on alto, he sounds not like Charlie Parker, but like Buster Smith, who was Parker's actual teacher and Ray's jamming partner during his Dallas days.

Nineteen fifty-nine was *the* year for Ray. He did the concert in Atlanta (which Atlantic has reissued) with the long, masterful version of "Drown in My Own Tears." And on "To Tell the Truth," after Margie Hendrix rasps and claws her way through a chorus and Fathead plays one of his emerald-cut solos, Ray pulls the hair from his head and the lightning from the sky, screaming as though he has just discovered a gold mine or a murder.

Four months before, he had recorded "What I Say," his first across-the-board hit, his first song to bring the mass market to his doorstep. Here Ray achieved what Nat Cole had been doing for years—selling whites—but he did so through the excitement of his black and holy blues.

And between these two dates in 1959—"What I Say" and the Atlanta concert—he did something even more portentous. On May 6, Ray sings a half-dozen popular ballads with string arrangements by Ralph Burns. All the songs he selects are from his past—"Am I Blue?" "Just for a Thrill," "Tell Me You'll Wait for Me." And in my own mind, the date is linked to one of Billie Holiday's last albums, *Lady in Satin*, made a year or so before Ray's. Both efforts are small miracles, records of almost incalculable human pain squeezed into the delicate format of pop ballads. They are wrenching experiences, and I know of no other recordings like them.

In June there was another session, this time with a big band, and later in the same month—this is still 1959—Ray cut his last three songs for Atlantic. One of them, "I Believe to My Soul," is the finest in his down-and-out, blow-my-brains-out genre. To make matters even more hypnotic, he throws out the Raeletts and does the three-part harmony himself. The session also includes a baptized version of Hank Snow's "I'm Movin' On." Hardly anyone thought twice that Ray Charles had cut his first country song.

His early Atlantic years were now over. And even though Ray had sung ballads with strings and big-band jazz, he was not ready to leave his already established base as a rhythm-and-blues singer. For the next two years, he would do all three things—jazz, ballads, and R & B— hoping that one would click. As it turned out, they all did.

Nineteen years after Ray first left the label to go to ABC, Atlantic still has seven of his albums in their current catalog, and, of all Ray's past records, these are the easiest to locate. They are also among his best:

The Great Ray Charles (1259)—The Ray/My Melancholy Baby/Black Coffee/There's No You/Doodlin'/Sweet Sixteen Bars/I Surrender, Dear/Undecided

Soul Brothers, with Milt Jackson (1279)—Soul Brothers/How Long Blues/Cosmic Blue/Blue Funk/'Deed I Do (instrumental version)

The Genius of Ray Charles (SD 1312)—Let the Good Times Roll/It Had to Be You/Alexander's Ragtime Band/Two Years of Torture/When Your Lover Has Gone/'Deed I Do (vocal version)/Just for a Thrill/You Won't Let Me Go/Tell Me You'll Wait for Me/Don't let the Sun Catch You Cryin'/Am I Blue?/Come Rain or Come Shine

Soul Meeting, with Milt Jackson (SD 1360)—Hallelujah, I Love Her So/Blue Genius/X-Ray Blues/Soul Meeting/Love on My Mind/ Bag of Blues

The Best of Ray Charles (SD 1543)—an anthology of cuts from various albums—Hard Times (from the Fathead album, see below)/Rockhouse/Sweet Sixteen Bars/Doodlin'/How Long Blues/Blues Waltz

The Greatest Ray Charles (SD 8054)—another anthology—Tell Me How Do You Feel?/I Got a Woman/Heartbreaker/Tell the Truth/What I Say/Talkin' 'Bout You/You Be My Baby/Leave My Woman Alone/I'm Movin' On

Ray Charles, Live (SD2-503)—two LPs, the 1958 Newport concert and the 1959 Atlanta concert—Newport: The Right Time/In a Little Spanish Town/I Got a Woman/Blues Waltz/Talkin' 'Bout You/ Sherry/Hot Rod/A Fool for You. Atlanta: The Right Time/ What I Say/Yes Indeed/Hot Rod (even though the liner notes list this as Spirit-Feel)/Frenesi/Drown in My Own Tears/Tell the Truth—also, Fathead plays an alto intro to The Right Time, not tenor as the notes indicate

Ray also appears on one song—"Spirit in the Dark"—with Aretha Franklin on her 1971 Atlantic album (SD 7205), *Live at the Fillmore West.* (She calls him "the Right Reverend Ray . . . the Righteous Reverend Ray.")

The Hank Crawford reissue from 1973 has several examples of Ray's early band (without Ray): *The Art of Hank Crawford,* The Atlantic Years (SD 2-315), two LPs.

Here are Ray's singles—with the approximate dates of their release —on Atlantic:

The Midnight Hour/Roll With Me, Baby—'53
The Sun's Gonna Shine Again/Jumpin' in the Mornin'—'53
Mess Around/Funny, But I Still Love You—'53
Feelin' Sad/Heartbreaker—'54
It Should Have Been Me/Sinner's Prayer—'54
Losing Hand/Don't You Know, Baby?—'54
I Got a Woman/Come Back, Baby—'55
A Fool for You/This Little Girl of Mine—'55
Blackjack/Greenbacks—'55
Mary Ann/Drown in My Own Tears—'56
Hallelujah, I Love Her So/What Would I Do Without You?—'56
Lonely Avenue/Leave My Woman Alone—'56
I Want to Know/Ain't That Love?—'57
It's All Right/Get on the Right Track, Baby—'57
Swanee River Rock/I Want a Little Girl—'57
Talkin' 'Bout You/What Kind of Man Are You?—'58
Yes Indeed/I Had a Dream—'58
You Be My Baby/My Bonnie—'58
Rockhouse (part 1)/Rockhouse (part 2)—'58
Tell All the World About You/The Right Time—'59
That's Enough/Tell Me How Do You Feel?—'59
What I Say (part 1)/What I Say (part 2)—'59
I'm Movin' On/I Believe to My Soul—'59
Let the Good Times Roll/Don't Let the Sun Catch You Crying—'60
Just for a Thrill/Heartbreaker—'60

Sweet Sixteen Bars/Tell the Truth—'60
Tell Me You'll Wait for Me/Come Rain or Come Shine—'60
A Bit of Soul/Early in the Morning—'60
Am I Blue?/It Should Have Been Me—'60
Ray's Blues/Hard Times—'60
Talkin' 'Bout You/In a Little Spanish Town—'60
Doodlin' (part 1)/Doodlin' (part 2)—'60

And here are Ray's Atlantic Albums:

Hallelujah, I Love Her So (also called *Ray Charles*) (8006)—'57—Ain't
That Love/Drown in My Own Tears/Come Back, Baby/Sinner's
Prayer/Funny, But I Still Love You/Losing Hand/A Fool for
You/Hallelujah, I Love Her So/Mess Around/This Little Girl of
Mine/Mary Ann/Greenbacks/Don't You Know, Baby?/I Got a
Woman
The Great Ray Charles—'57—listed with current reissues above
Soul Brothers, with Milt Jackson—'58—listed with current reissues
above
Ray Charles at Newport—'58—listed with current reissues above (live)
Yes Indeed (8025)—'58—What Would I Do Without You?/It's All
Right/I Want to Know/Yes Indeed/Get on the Right Track,
Baby/Talkin' 'Bout You/Swanee River Rock/Lonely Avenue/
Blackjack/The Sun's Gonna Shine Again/I Had a Dream/I Want
a Little Girl/Heartbreaker/Leave My Woman Alone
What I Say—spelled "What'd" I Say on the album, but Ray prefers the
simpler form (8029)—'59—What I Say, parts 1 and 2/Jumpin' in
the Mornin'/You Be My Baby/Tell Me How Do You Feel?/
What Kind of Man Are You?/Rockhouse, parts 1 and 2/Roll With
Me Baby/Tell All the World About You/My Bonnie/That's
Enough
The Genius of Ray Charles—'59—listed with current reissues above
Ray Charles in Person—'60—listed with current reissues above (live)
The Genius After Hours (1369)—'61—The Genius After Hours/Ain't
Misbehavin'/Dawn Ray/Joy Ride/Hornful Soul/The Man I
Love/Charlesville/Music! Music! Music!
The Genius Sings the Blues (8052)—'61—Early in the Mornin'/Hard

Times/The Midnight Hour/The Right Time/Ray's Blues/Feelin'
Sad/I'm Movin' On/I Believe to My Soul/Nobody Cares/Mr.
Charles' Blues/Someday, Baby/I Wonder Who

The Greatest Ray Charles (also called *Do the Twist with Ray Charles*)
—'61—listed with current reissues above

The Ray Charles Story (ATC 2–900)—'62—a two LP anthology—The
Sun's Gonna Shine Again/Losing Hand/Mess Around/It Should
Have Been Me/Don't You Know, Baby?/Come Back, Baby/I
Got a Woman/A Fool for You/This Little Girl of Mine/Mary
Ann/Hallelujah, I Love Her So/Lonely Avenue/Doodlin'/Sweet
Sixteen Bars/Ain't That Love?/Rockhouse/Swanee River Rock/
Talkin' 'Bout You/What Kind of Man Are You?/Yes Indeed/My
Bonnie/Tell All the World About You/The Right Time/What I
Say/Just for a Thrill/Come Rain or Come Shine/Drown in My
Own Tears/Let the Good Times Roll/I'm Movin' On

The Ray Charles Story, Vol. 1 anthology (8063)—'62—The Sun's
Gonna Shine Again/Losing Hand/Mess Around/It Should Have
Been Me/Don't You Know, Baby?/Come Back, Baby/I Got a
Woman/A Fool for You/This Little Girl of Mine/Mary Ann/Hal-
lelujah, I Love Her So/Lonely Avenue/Doodlin'/Sweet Sixteen
Bars/Ain't That Love?

The Ray Charles Story, Vol. 2 anthology (8064)—'62—Rockhouse/
Swanee River Rock/Talkin' 'Bout You/What Kind of Man Are
You?/Yes Indeed/My Bonnie/Tell All the World About You/The
Right Time/What I Say/Just for a Thrill/Come Rain or Come
Shine/Drown in My Own Tears/Let the Good Times Roll/I'm
Movin' On

Soul Meeting, with Milt Jackson—'62—listed with current reissues
above

The Ray Charles Story, Vol. 3 anthology (8083)—'63—Sinner's
Prayer/Funny, But I Still Love You/Feelin' Sad/Hard Times/
What Would I Do Without You?/I Want to Know/Leave My
Woman Alone/It's All Right/Get on the Right Track, Baby/
That's Enough/I Want a Little Girl/You Be My Baby/I Had a
Dream/Tell the Truth

The Ray Charles Story, Vol. 4 anthology (8094)—'64—Blackjack/Alex-
ander's Ragtime Band/I Believe to My Soul/A Bit of Soul/Green-

backs/Undecided/When Your Lover Has Gone/It Had to
Be You/Early in the Mornin'/Heartbreaker/Music! Music! Mu-
sic!/Tell Me How Do You Feel?/In a Little Spanish Town/You
Won't Let Me Go

The Great Hits of Ray Charles Recorded on 8-track Stereo (SD 7101)
anthology—'64—Tell Me/ How Do You Feel?/I Had a Dream/
Carrying That Load/Tell All the World About You/I Believe to
My Soul/What I Say/I'm Movin' On/You Be My Baby/The
Right Time/Yes Indeed/Tell the Truth/My Bonnie/Early in the
Mornin'

There is also *Fathead/Ray Charles Presents David Newman* with
Ray on piano (1304)—'59—Hard Times/Weird Beard/Willow
Weep for Me/Bill for Bennie/Sweet Eyes/Fathead/Mean to
Me/Tin Tin Deo

PART III
ABC

Contrary to what a slew of critics and serious fans believe, Ray's finest
small-band work was not done on Atlantic—at least not in my view.
It was when the septet became an octet that the group finally matured,
and the new, fuller sound was due to Hank Crawford switching from
baritone to alto and the presence of the remarkable Leroy Cooper on
baritone. It was Cooper who gave the group a new undercoating, a fat
bottom it lacked before. And Cooper came after Ray had switched
labels.

With the octet, Ray recorded "I Wonder," "Sticks and Stones,"
"Unchain My Heart," "Hit the Road, Jack," "Danger Zone," and
"But on the Other Hand, Baby" (with Phil Guilbeau's especially nasty
trumpet behind him). These were the last tunes Ray did as singles.
From now on, he would think in terms of albums.

From the first such album, *Genius Hits the Road*, "Georgia" emerged as his biggest record to date. From the second album, also in 1960, came "Ruby," another hit, in addition to lovely renditions of "Candy," "Nancy," and "Stella by Starlight."

And in the same year, Ray recorded his brilliant jazz album, using the Count Basie band (minus Count and plus Guilbeau) for six songs and another band of New York free-lancers on four other tunes. Quincy Jones and Ralph Burns wrote the charts. The hit was "One Mint Julep," but the most devastating cuts are two blues—"I've Got News for You" and "I'm Gonna Move to the Outskirts of Town"—which will live for as long as there is enough fuel to power our turntables and tape recorders.

In the following year there was the seductive duet album with Betty Carter who sounds like a female vocal version of Miles Davis. Ray is sandpaper, Betty, silk; the contrast is sharp and, like Louis Armstrong's duets with Ella Fitzgerald, strangely satisfying.

In 1962, he recorded his first country album, with phenomenally successful results in the marketplace. The arrangements—and the style of Ray's singing—are no different from what he had done on *Genius Hits the Road* or *Dedicated to You*. Only the tunes are different. "I Can't Stop Loving You" became the number one pop song, R & B song, and country song in the nation.

Ray's country hits—"I Can't Stop Loving You," "Born to Lose," "You Don't Know Me," "Your Cheatin' Heart," "You Are My Sunshine, "Take These Chains from My Heart," and later, "Crying Time" —delivered him America's great white market and made him an international star. In 1962 and 1963 he was the most popular singer in the country.

After those years, most of his albums would be in the same mold— a few R & B songs, a few country songs, some standards, with very little of his own material. Still, there are gems to be culled in this period: "Making Whoopee" from his 1964 concert album made in L.A.; his loving tribute to Charles Brown—the medley of "Traveling Blues and Drifting Blues" from the 1966 *Crying Time* album; *Ray Charles Invites You to Listen* (1967) in which he sings sustained and haunting falsetto choruses on "I'll Be Seeing You," "Love Walked In" and "People";

his impassioned version of the title song from *In The Heat of the Night;* his treatment of "America" and "Look What They've Done to My Song, Ma" from his *Message From the People;* his boozy rendition of "Rainy Night in Georgia" from *Through the Eyes of Love.*

The comparison again must be to Armstrong who, after having carved the new wood so early in his life, spent decades interpreting and reinterpreting the music he thought had the most universal appeal— "C'est Si Bon," "Mack the Knife," "Blueberry Hill."

Ray owns the masters for all twenty-four albums and fifty-three singles that were released on ABC from 1960 through 1973. Currently none of them is available in the ABC catalog, and so far Ray has not reissued any of the material. He says that one day he will, but until then, the music exists only as closeouts and remainders in inexpensive secondhand record stores or as rare finds in high-priced collectors' outlets.

Here are his ABC singles, with release dates:

My Baby (I Love Her Yes)/Who You Gonna Love?—'60
Sticks and Stones/Worried Life Blues—'60
Georgia on My Mind/Carry Me Back to Old Virginny—'60
Them That Got/I Wonder—'60
Ruby/Hard-Hearted Hannah—'60
One Mint Julep/Let's Go—'61 (on Impulse)
I've Got News for You/I'm Gonna Move to the Outskirts of Town—
     '61 (on Impulse)
Hit the Road, Jack/The Danger Zone—'61
Unchain My Heart/But on the Other Hand, Baby—'61
Baby, It's Cold Outside/We'll Be Together Again (both with Betty
     Carter)—'62
At the Club/Hide Nor Hair—'62
I Can't Stop Loving You/Born to Lose—'62
You Don't Know Me/Careless Love—'62
You Are My Sunshine/Your Cheating Heart—'63
Don't Set Me Free/The Brightest Smile in Town—'63
Take These Chains from My Heart/No Letter Today—'63

No One/Without Love (There Is Nothing)—'63
Busted/Making Believe—'63
That Lucky Old Sun/Ol' Man River—'63
Baby, Don't You Cry/My Heart Cries for You—'64
My Baby Don't Dig Me/Something's Wrong—'64
No One to Cry to/A Tear Fell—'64
Smack Dab in the Middle/I Wake Up Crying—'64
Makin' Whoopee (vocal)/Makin' Whoopee (piano solo)—'64 (from
    L.A. Concert)
Cry/Teardrops from My Eyes—'65
I Got a Woman, parts 1 and 2—'65 (from L.A. Concert)
Without a Song, parts 1 and 2—'65
I'm a Fool to Care/Love's Gonna Live Here—'65
The Cincinnati Kid/That's All I Am to You—'65
Crying Time/When My Dream Boat Comes Home—'65
Together Again/You Be Just About to Lose Your Clown—'66
Let's Go Get Stoned/The Train—'66
I Chose to Sing the Blues/Hopelessly—'66
Please Say You're Fooling/I Don't Need No Doctor—'66
I Want to Talk About You/Something Inside Me—'67
In the Heat of the Night/Something's Got to Change—'67
Here We Go Again/Somebody Ought to Write a Book About It—'67
Never Had Enough of Nothing Yet/Yesterday—'67
Go on Home/That's a Lie—'68
Understanding/Eleanor Rigby—'68
Sweet Young Thing Like You/Listen, They're Playing My Song—'68
If It Wasn't for Bad Luck/When I Stop Dreaming—'68
I'll Be Your Servant/I Didn't Know What Time It Was—'69
Let Me Love You/I'm Satisfied—'69
We Can Make It/I Can't Stop Loving You, Baby—'69
Claudie Mae/Someone to Watch Over Me—'69
Laughin' and Clownin'/That Thing Called Love—'70
If You Were Mine/Till I Can't Take It Anymore—'70
Don't Change on Me/Sweet Memories—'71
Feel So Bad/Your Love Is So Doggone Good—'71
What Am I Living For?/Tired of My Tears—'71
Booty Butt/Sidewinder—'71

Will I Ever Get Back Home?/I'm So in Love—'71
Bad Water/Booty Butt—'71
There'll Be No Peace Without All Men As One/Hey, Mister—'72
Every Saturday Night/Take Me Home, Country Roads—'72
I Can Make It Thru the Days (But Oh Those Lonely Nights)/Ring of
    Fire—'73

ABC Albums:

Genius Hits the Road (335)—'60—Alabamy Bound/Georgia on My
    Mind/Basin Street Blues/Mississippi Mud/Moonlight in Ver-
    mont/New York's My Home/California, Here I Come/Moon
    Over Miami/Deep in the Heart of Texas/Carry Me Back to Old
    Virginny/Blue Hawaii/Chattanooga Choo-choo
Dedicated to You (355)—'61—Hardhearted Hannah/Nancy/Margie/
    Ruby/Rosetta/Stella by Starlight/Cherry/Josephine/Candy/
    Marie/Diane/Sweet Georgia Brown
Genius Plus Soul Equals Jazz (A-2, Impulse, ABC's jazz subsidiary)—
    '61—From the Heart/I've Got News for You/Moanin'/Let's
    Go/One Mint Julep/I'm Gonna Move to the Outskirts of Town/
    Stompin' Room Only/Mister C/Strike Up the Band/Birth of the
    Blues
Ray Charles and Betty Carter (385)—'61—Ev'rytime We Say Good-
    bye/You and I/Intro: Goodbye, We'll Be Together Again/People
    Will Say We're in Love/Cocktails for Two/Side by Side/Baby,
    It's Cold Outside/Together/For All We Know/Takes Two to
    Tango/Alone Together/Just You, Just Me
Modern Sounds in Country and Western Music (410)—'62—Bye Bye
    Love/You Don't Know Me/Half As Much/I Love You So Much
    It Hurts/Just a Little Lovin'/Born to Lose/Worried Mind/It
    Makes No Difference Now/You Win Again/Careless Love/I
    Can't Stop Loving You/Hey, Good Lookin'
Greatest Hits (415) anthology—'62—Them That Got/Georgia on My
    Mind/Unchain My Heart/I'm Gonna Move to the Outskirts
    of Town/The Danger Zone/I've Got News for You/Hit the
    Road, Jack/I Wonder/Sticks and Stones/But on the Other Hand,
    Baby/One Mint Julep/Ruby

Modern Sounds in Country and Western Music, Vol. 2 (435)—'63—
You Are My Sunshine/No Letter Today/Someday/Don't Tell Me
Your Troubles/Midnight/Oh, Lonesome Me/Take These Chains
from My Heart/Your Cheating Heart/I'll Never Stand in Your
Way/Making Believe/Teardrops in My Heart/Hang Your Head
in Shame

Ingredients in a Recipe for Soul (465)—'63—Busted/Where Can I
Go?/Born to Be Blue/That Lucky Old Sun/Ol' Man River/In the
Evening (When the Sun Goes Down)/A Stranger in Town/Ol'
Man Time/Over the Rainbow/You'll Never Walk Alone

Sweet and Sour Tears (480)—'64—Cry/Guess I'll Hang My Tears Out
to Dry/A Tear Fell/No One to Cry to/You've Got Me Crying
Again/After My Laughter Came Tears/Teardrops from My
Eyes/Cry Me a River/Baby, Don't You Cry/Willow Weep for
Me/I Cried for You

Have a Smile With Me (495)—'64—Smack Dab in the Middle/Feudin'
and Fightin'/Two Ton Tessie/I Never See Maggie Alone/Move
It on Over/Ma, She's Making Eyes at Me/The Thing/The Man
with the Weird Beard/The Naughty Lady of Shady Lane/Who
Cares (For Me)

Live in Concert (500)—'65—Swing a Little Taste/I Got a Woman/
Margie/You Don't Know Me/Hide Nor Hair/Baby, Don't You
Cry/Makin' Whoopee/Hallelujah, I Love Her So/Don't Set Me
Free/What I Say

Country & Western Meets Rhythm and Blues (also called *Together
Again*) (520)—'65—Together Again/I Like to Hear It Some-
time/I've Got a Tiger by the Tail/Please Forgive and Forget/I
Don't Care/Next Door to the Blues/Blue Moon of Kentucky/
Light Out of Darkness/Maybe It's Nothing at All/All Night
Long/Don't Let Her Know/Watch It Baby

Crying Time (544)—'66—Crying Time/No Use Crying/Let's Go Get
Stoned/Going Down Slow/Peace of Mind/Tears/Traveling Blues
and Drifting Blues medley/We Don't See Eye to Eye/You're In
for a Big Surprise/You're Just About to Lose Your Clown/Don't
You Think I Ought to Know/You've Got a Problem

Ray's Moods (550)—'66—What-Cha Doing in There?/Please Say

You're Fooling/By the Light of the Silvery Moon/You Don't Understand/Maybe It's Because of Love/Chitlins with Candied Yams/Granny Wasn't Grinning That Day/She's Lonesome Again/Sentimental Journey/A Born Loser/It's a Man's World/A Girl I Used to Know

A Man and His Soul (590) anthology—'67—2 LPs—I Can't Stop Loving You/What I Say/Ol' Man River/One Mint Julep/Crying Time/Makin' Whoopee/Busted/Takes Two to Tango/Ruby/ Let's Go Get Stoned/Cry/Unchain My Heart/Georgia on My Mind/Baby, It's Cold Outside/Worried Mind/I Chose to Sing the Blues/I Don't Need No Doctor/Born to Lose/Hit the Road, Jack/You Are My Sunshine/From the Heart/Teardrops from My Heart/No Use Crying/Chitlins with Candied Yams

Ray Charles Invites You to Listen (595)—'67—She's Funny That Way/How Deep Is the Ocean?/You Made Me Love You/Yesterday/I'll Be Seeing You/Here We Go Again/All for You/Love Walked In/Gee Baby, Ain't I Good to You/People

A Portrait of Ray (625)—'68—Never Say Naw/The Sun Died/Am I Blue?/Yesterdays/When I Stop Dreamin'/I Won't Leave/A Sweet Young Thing Like You/The Bright Lights and You Girl/ Understanding/Eleanor Rigby

I'm All Yours, Baby (675)—'69—Yours/I Didn't Know What Time It Was/Love Is Here to Stay/Memories of You/Till the End of Time/I Had the Craziest Dream/Someday/Indian Love Call/I Dream of You (More Than You Dream I Do)/Gloomy Sunday

Doing His Thing (695)—'69—The Same Thing That Can Make You Laugh (Can Make You Cry)/Finders Keepers, Losers Weepers/You Ought to Change Your Ways/Baby, Please/Come and Get It/We Can Make It/I'm Ready/That Thing Called Love/If It Wasn't for Bad Luck/I Told You So

Love Country Style (707)—'70—If You Were Mine/Ring of Fire/Your Love Is So Doggone Good/Don't Change on Me/Till I Can't Take It Anymore/You've Still Got a Place in My Heart/I Keep It Hid/Sweet Memories/Good Morning, Dear/Show Me the Sunshine

Volcanic Action of My Soul (726)—'71—See You Then/What Am I

Living For/Feel So Bad/The Long and Winding Road/The Three
Bells/All I Ever Need Is You (with Ray's alto solo)/Wichita Line-
man/Something/I May Be Wrong/Down in the Valley

25th Anniversary in Show Business Salute to Ray Charles (731) anthol-
ogy—'71—3 LPs—Hit the Road, Jack/Hallelujah, I Love Her So*/
Mary Ann*/Unchain My Heart/Don't Let the Sun Catch You
Cryin'*/Georgia on My Mind/What I Say*/I Got a Woman*/
One Mint Julep/I Can't Stop Loving You/If You Were Mine/
Busted/Crying Time/Yesterday/Let's Go Get Stoned/Eleanor
Rigby/Born to Lose/Don't Change on Me/It Should Have Been
Me*/Mess Around*/Don't You Know, Baby?*/A Fool for
You*/You Are My Sunshine/Drown in My Own Tears*/Ain't
That Love?*/Lonely Avenue*/Swanee River Rock*/I Believe to
My Soul*/Ruby/Rockhouse*/Just for a Thrill*/The Right
Time*/Yes Indeed*/Understanding/Booty-Butt/Feel So Bad

A Message From the People (755)—'72—Lift Every Voice and Sing/
Seems Like I Gotta Do Wrong/Heaven Help Us All/There'll Be
No Peace Without All Men as One/Hey, Mister/Look What
They've Done to My Song, Ma/Abraham, Martin and John/Take
Me Home, Country Roads/Every Saturday Night/America, the
Beautiful

Through the Eyes of Love (765)—'72—My First Night Alone Without
You/I Can Make It Through the Days (But Oh Those Lonely
Nights)/Someone to Watch Over Me/A Perfect Love/If You
Wouldn't Be My Lady/You Leave Me Breathless/Never Ending
Song of Love/Rainy Night in Georgia

PART IV
Tangerine/Crossover and Miscellaneous

In this most recent period, the gems are still there. On *Renaissance*,
I especially like "Living for the City" in which Papa Ray gives the son,

*Indicates original Atlantic version.

little Stevie Wonder, a taste of his own medicine. It is the blind wondrously leading the blind. And there is also the autobiographical "Then We'll Be Home" and Ray's definitive version of Randy Newman's wildly sarcastic "Sail Away."

The live concert made in Japan in 1975 is a good illustration of Ray's current road show. (Unfortunately the record is only available overseas.) He tears the heart out of "Till There Was You"—if you listen closely, you'll hear him cry—and throughout the evening his band sparkles like polished silver. There is also the fine Ray/John Coles duet on "Am I Blue?" a song he has recorded twice before.

The first few bars he sings of "Summertime" on his *Porgy and Bess/Cleo Laine* record are almost enough to save the day.

And after a decade of slumping record sales, the switch to Atlantic shows signs of paying off. At the time of writing—1978—the first album that Atlantic is distributing, *True to Life*, is selling. From that album I especially like "Oh, What a Beautiful Mornin' " and "How Long Has This Been Going On?," which is as shattering as any ballad from his first string session on Atlantic, some eighteen years before. "Game Number Nine" is, ironically enough, much the same kind of novelty blues as "It Should Have Been Me," Ray's first big single for Atlantic in 1954.

From 1968 through 1973, Ray's records carried a Tangerine logo as well as ABC's. He used his own recording company, but depended on ABC for marketing and distribution in this period. In 1973, however, the association with ABC ended, and Ray released his records on his newly named label—Crossover. In 1977, he rejoined Atlantic, agreeing to a marketing/distribution arrangement similar to the one he had with ABC.

Tangerine issued two albums of Ray's big band, without assistance from ABC:

My Kind of Jazz (TRCS 1512)—'70—Golden Boy/Booty-Butt/This Here/I Remember Clifford/Sidewinder/Bluesette/Pas-Se-O-Ne Blues/Zig Zag/Angel City/Señor Blues
Jazz Number II (TRC 1516)—'73—Our Suite/A Pair of Threes/Morn-

ing of Carnival/Going Home/Kids Are Pretty People/Together-ness/Brazilian Skies

There is a third Tangerine album on which Ray appears—playing and occasionally singing background:

Ray Charles Presents the Raeletts, Yesterday . . . Today . . . Tomorrow (TRC 1515)—'72—You Must Be Doing Alright/Bad Water/Come Get It, I Got It/You Have a Way With Me/Love Train/I Want to (Do Everything for You)/Leave My Man Alone/After Loving You/Keep It to Yourself/Here I Go Again

In the late sixties Ray played on several cuts on two LPs by the great blues singer and composer, Percy Mayfield: *My Jug and I* (TRC 1505) and *Bought Blues* (TRC 1510). Both records are on Tangerine.

To date, Ray has issued four singles on Crossover:

Come Live With Me/Everybody Sing—'73
Louise/Somebody—'74
Living for the City/Then We'll Be Home—'75
America, the Beautiful/Sunshine—'76

There are also four Crossover albums:

Come Live With Me (CR9000)—'74—Till There Was You/If You Go Away/It Takes So Little Time/Come Live With Me/Somebody/Problems, Problems/Where Was He?/Louise/Everybody Sing
Renaissance (CR9005)—'75—Living for the City/Then We'll Be Home/My God and I/We're Gonna Make It/For Mamma/Sunshine/It Ain't Easy Being Green/Sail Away
My Kind of Jazz, Part 3 (CR 9007) (Ray's big band)—'75—I'm Gonna Go Fishin'/For Her/Sister Sadie/¾ of the Time/Ray Minor Ray/Samba de Elencia/Metamorphosis/Nothing Wrong/Project "S"
Live in Japan (GSW 535–6) (released on Crossover, distributed

by London overseas)—'75—2 LPs—Metamorphosis/Pair of Three's/Spain/Blowing the Blues Away/Let the Good Times Roll/Then I'll Be Home/Till There Was You/Feel So Bad/ Georgia on My Mind/Busted/Am I Blue?/Living for the City/I Can't Stop Loving You/Take Me Home, Country Roads/Don't Let Her Know/What I Say

There are several anthologies of Ray's hits compiled for special order groups—the Capitol Record Club, for example, or the Longines Symphonette Society—similar to the ABC reissue on his twenty-fifth anniversary in show business.

He sings the title songs for two major motion pictures and is featured on the sound track albums:

The Cincinnati Kid (MGM Records SE 4313)—'65—Lalo Schifrin, composer
In the Heat of the Night (United Artists 5160)—'67—Quincy Jones, composer

In 1974, he sings two songs—"Every Saturday Night" and "Just a Man"—on:

Recorded Live at Newport in New York (Buddah BDS 5616) which also features Stevie Wonder, Aretha Franklin, Donny Hathaway, and the Staple Singers

In 1976, he plays and sings:

Porgy and Bess with Cleo Laine (RCA CPL 2-1831)—2 LPs—Summertime/My Man's Gone Now/A Woman Is a Sometime Thing/ They Pass By Singing/What You Want With Bess?/I Got Plenty o' Nuttin'/Buzzard Song/Bess, You Is My Woman Now/Oh, Doctor Jesus/Crab Man/Here Come de Honey Man/Strawberry Woman/It Ain't Necessarily So/There's a Boat That's Leavin' Soon for New York/I Loves You, Porgy/Oh Bess, Oh Where's My Bess?/Oh Lord, I'm On My Way

And in 1977 Ray calls his return-to-Atlantic album:

True to Life (SD 19142)—I Can See Clearly Now/The Jealous Kind/ Oh, What A Beautiful Mornin'/How Long Has This Been Going On?/Be My Love/Anonymous Love/Heavenly Music/Game Number Nine/Let It Be

Finally, there are the commercials. In most instances Ray has produced them himself, just as he has produced his own records. Among the best are the ones done for Coca-Cola, alone and with Aretha Franklin, in 1966 through 1968; the Olympia beer commercials, 1975 through 1977; and the Scotch recording tape television spots, 1977.

PART V

1978–1991

When *Brother Ray* was originally published in 1978, Ray had recently re-signed with Atlantic. His initial album, *True to Life*, was followed by three others, the high point of which may be his poignant version of Barry Manilow's "One of These Days" on *Ain't It So*. His latter-day Atlantic albums:

Love and Peace (SD 19199)–'78–You 20th-Century Fox/Take Off That Dress/She Knows/Riding Thumb/We Had it All/No Achievement Showing/A Peace That We Never Before Could Enjoy/Is There Anyone Out There?/Give the Poor Man A Break
Ain't It So (SD 19251)–'79–Some Enchanted Evening/Blues in the Night/Just Because/What'll I Do/One of these Days/Love Me Or Set Me Free/Drift Away/(Turn Out the Light And) Love Me Tonight
Brother Ray Is At It Again! (SD 19281)–'80–Compared to What/Anyway You Want To/Don't You Love Me Anymore?/A Poor Man's Song/Now That We've Found Each Other/Ophelia/I Can't Change It/Questions

In 1983, he switched to the country division of Columbia Records, where he cut six albums. The cover photographs show a pensive, mellow Ray, and the music reflects much the same mood. Typically, Ray self-produced the first two albums, but on the third effort — the successful *Friendship* — he turned the reins over to veteran country music man Billy Sherrill who fashioned a series of duets, employing, among others, Hank Williams, Jr., George Jones, Merle Haggard, and Johnny Cash to sing along with Ray. "Seven Spanish Angels," the Ray/Willie Nelson collaboration, hit number-one on the country charts. (*Seven Spanish Angels* was also the name of Ray's Columbia greatest hits package.) Sherrill co-produced *From the Pages of My Mind*, although it was Ray and Ray alone who put together *The Spirit of Christmas* — "I'd been waiting to do a holiday album for years," he told me — and *Just Between Us*, his final album for Columbia, featuring duets with B.B. King, Gladys Knight, Jim Johnson, Kenny Carr and Lou Rawls.

The Columbia albums:

Wish You Were Here Tonight (FC 38293) — '83 — 3/4 Time/I Wish You Were Here Tonight/Ain't Your Memory Got No Pride at All/Born to Love Me/I Don't Want No Stranger Sleepin' in My Bed/Let Your Love Flow/You Feel Good All Over/String Bean/You've Got the Longest Leaving Act in Town/Shakin' Your Head

Do I Ever Cross Your Mind? (FC 38990) — '84 — I Had It All/Do I Ever Cross Your Mind?/Woman Sensuous Woman/Then I'll Be Over You/(All I Wanna Do Is) Lay Around and Love on You/Love of My Life/They Call It Love/If I Were You/Workin' Man's Woman/I Was on Georgia Time

Friendship (FC 39415) — '84 — Two Old Cats Like Us (with Hank Williams, Jr.)/This Old Heart (Is Gonna Rise Again) (with Oak Ridge Boys)/We Didn't See a Thing (with George Jones and featuring Chet Atkins)/Who Cares (with Janie Fricke)/Rock and Roll Shoes (with B.J. Thomas)/Friendship (with Ricky Skaggs)/It Ain't Gonna Worry My Mind (with Mickey Gilley)/Little Hotel Room (with Merle Haggard)/Crazy Old Soldier (with Johnny Cash)/Seven Spanish Angels (with Willie Nelson)

The Spirit of Christmas (FC 40125)—'85—What Child Is This/The Little Drummer Boy/Santa Claus is Comin' to Town/This Time of Year/ Rudolph The Red Nose Reindeer/That Spirit of Christmas/All I Want for Christmas/Christmas in My Heart/Winter Wonderland/ Christmas Time*

From the Pages of My Mind (FC 40388)—'86—The Pages of My Mind/Slip Away/Anybody with the Blues/Class Reunion/Caught a Touch of Your Love/A Little Bit of Heaven/Dixie Moon/Over and Over (Again)/Beaucoup Love/Love is Worth the Pain

Just Between Us (FC 40703)—'88—Nothing Like a Hundred Miles (with B.B. King)/I Wish I'd Never Loved You at All (with Gladys Knight)/Too Hard to Love You (with Jim Johnson)/Now I Don't Believe That Anymore/Let's Call the Whole Thing Off/Stranger In My Own Hometown (with Kenny Carr)/Over the Top/I'd Walk a Little More for You/If That's What'Cha Want/Save the Bones for Henry Jones (with Lou Rawls and Milt Jackson)

By the start of the nineties, he had left Columbia and was working with longtime associate and songwriter Jimmy Lewis who co-produced, along with Ray, Charles's debut album for Warner which contained "Ellie, My Love," a number-one hit in Japan.

Would You Believe? (263453-2)—'90—I'll Take Care of You/Your Love Keeps Me Satisfied/Ellie, My Love/I Can't Get Enough/Let's Get Back to Where We Left Off (featuring Peggy Scott)/Child Support, Alimony/Fresh Out of Tears/Living Without You/Where're the Stairs/Leave Him!

Brother Ray dueting with other artists on their albums:

Susaye Green and Sherrie Payne, *Partners*, "Love Bug" (Motown M7-920R1), 1979

---

*Ray Baradat, who, along with France's Joel Dufour, ranks as the world's most knowledgeable Ray Charles discographer, reports that in 1978 a single appeared on Atlantic entitled "Christmas Time," a different song than the one on Ray's Columbia Christmas album.

Clint Eastwood, *Any Which Way You Can*, (movie soundtrack album, Warner-Viva 23499), "Beers To You," 1980

Willie Nelson, *Angel Eyes*, "Angel Eyes" (Columbia FC 39363), 1984

Hank Williams, Jr., *Major Moves*, "Blues Medley" (Warner Brothers 9 25088-1), 1984

Billy Joel, *The Bridge*, "Baby Grand" (Columbia OC 40402), 1986

Tony Bennett, *The Art of Excellence*, "Everybody Has the Blues" (Columbia 40344), 1986

Lou Rawls, *At Last*, "That's Where It's At" (Blue Note 91937-2), 1989

Three items from France in 1989: Ray signs "Love Makes the Changes" (Philips), a Michel Legrand/Alan & Marilyn Bergman song from Legrand's film *Cinq Jours En Juin*; he duets with Dee Dee Bridgewater on "Precious Thing" (Polydor); and he appears on the charity LP *Silences On Crie* (CBS/France) for the Foundation Pour L'Enfance, singing "A Childhood."

In late 1989, Quincy Jones released *Back on the Block* (Warner 9 26020–2) which includes a spirited duet with Ray and Chaka Kahn doing the Brother Johnson's "I'll Be Good to You." The song earned Ray and Chaka a Grammy.

Ray Charles: Birth of Soul, The Complete Atlantic Rhythm and Blues Recordings, 1952–1959 (Atlantic 82310–2), a comprehensive 3-CD box set with insightful notes by Robert Palmer issued in 1991.

PART VI:
1992–2004

The Birth of a Legend (1949–1952) (Ebony 80001/80002) was released in 1992 as a two-disc retrospective of Ray's work on Down Beat/Swingtime labels. It's invaluable.

Ray continued his relationship with Warner in 1993 with *My World* (8 26735–2). Proving his old adage—"I can't be produced by anyone but me"—the relationship between Ray and producer Richard Perry was strained. "I didn't even let Perry in the studio when I sang my vocals," Ray told me. One track—Leon Russell's "A Song for You"—won a Grammy for best R&B male vocal performance and about another—Paul Simon's "Still Crazy After All These Years"—Ray said, "I really relate. I'm happy not to change, happy to be crazy in the same ways I've always been crazy."

Ray Charles Live '93 (Jazz Door 1263). Contains live versions of Percy Mayfield's poignant "Stranger In My Own Town" and the overlooked "Brightest Smile in Town" which Ray recorded thirty years earlier. Plus a breathtaking "How Long Has This Been Going On?"

Strong Love Affair (Qwest/Warner 9 46107–2). In 1995, Ray collaborated with his Parisian friend Jean-Pierre Grosz, who produced eight of the twelve tracks. Initially released in Europe and ultimately picked up by Ray's best friend Quincy Jones for Quincy's Qwest label, the album quickly disappeared.

In 1995, Ray also signed a mega-deal with Rhino Records to re-release his back catalogue. The highlight of the ambitious enterprise, supervised by James Austin, is *Genius & Soul, the 50th Anniversary Collection*, a 5-CD box issued in 1997. In addition, some twenty Ray albums from his glorious past—including his duets with Betty Carter and his immortal *Dedicated to You* (Rhino R2 75229)—were also meticulously repackaged.

A compilation of his country material—*The Complete Country & Western Recordings, 1959–1986* (Rhino R2 75328)—came out in 1998 as a 4-CD box with a comprehensive history by Daniel Cooper.

In the wake of 9/11, Rhino compiled the patriotic *Ray Charles Sings for America* (Rhino 76098) in 2002 with versions of "America the Beautiful" and "God Bless America."

Ray briefly revised his Crossover label in 2002 and, coproducing with Billy Osborne, sang 11 new songs and a redo of "What I

Say" on *Thanks for Bring Love Around Again* (Crossover/E-Nate Music 3956040002). The record languished.

Artist's Choice: Ray Charles (Rhino Special Products OPCD–1991) from 2002 includes Ray's favorite artists. He himself doesn't play or sing but rather hand-picks sixteen songs from Harry James' "Boo Woo" to Willie Nelson's "Always On My Mind." Available at Starbucks.

Ray's final record was for his first for Concord/Hear Music, *Genius Loves Company* (2248), a collection of duets posthumously released in 2004. Because Ray was sick for much of the recording, quality varies. But it's astounding — and moving — to hear how, despite his weakness, he manages to mold the material to his creative strengths. The highlight is his duet with B.B. King on "Sinner's Prayer," a riveting blues that Ray recorded for Atlantic in the fifties and first sang when he led Lowell Fulson's band. His other partners are Elton John, James Taylor, Norah Jones, Diana Krall, Johnny Mathis, Willie Nelson, Natalie Cole, Van Morrison, Michael McDonald and Gladys Knight. Given his epic career, it is not inappropriate that on this, Ray's swan song, he tries to give something to everyone.

A soundtrack of the bio-pic movie "Ray," starring Jamie Foxx, is slated for release from Rhino in October, 2004, and includes original Ray Charles vocals of his major hits.

PART
VII

Videos:

Ballad and Blue. The English movie from 1964 in which Ray acts and performs. Worth it just for the opening credits rolling over "Let the Good Times Roll."

We Are the World: The Video Event (RCA/Columbia Home Video), with Bob Dylan, Michael Jackson, Bruce Springsteen, Stevie Wonder, Paul Simon, etc. 1985.

Limit Up. A feature film from 1988 in which Ray plays God.

Ray Charles: The Genius of Soul. The documentary originally shown on PBS as part of the Masters of American Music Series, 1992.

Concert performances on video include:

That Was Rock (Music Media). A Compilation of the TAMI and TNT shows from Santa Monica, California in 1964–65.

An Evening with Ray Charles (Optical Programming Associates), Alberta, Canada, 1981.

Gladys Knight and the Pips and Ray Charles: Together, Live in Concert (Vestron/HBO), 1982. Listen to Ray and Gladys sing "Neither One of Us."

Fats Domino and Friends (HBO/Image), with Jerry Lee Lewis, Ron Wood, and Paul Shaffer, 1986.

The Legends of Rock 'n' Roll (HBO/Image) with Jerry Lee Lewis, James Brown, Bo Diddley, B. B. King, Fats Domino, and Little Richard, from Rome, 1989.

Ray Charles Live 1991: A Romantic Evening at the McCallum Theater (Atlantic/Vision).

Live at the Montreux Jazz Festival (Geneon Entertainment). Filmed in 1997, released 2002.

Ray Charles Celebrates a Gospel Christmas with the Voices of Jubilee, (Urban Works 14882–7), 2003.

In Concert (Image Entertainment), includes duets with Diane Schuur. 2004.

O-Genio, Ray Charles Studio Session. Brazil, 1963. Fabulous DVD slated to be released by Rhino in late 2004. Ray with his big band doing heart-stopping versions of "My Bonnie," "Carry Me Back to Old Virginia" and "In the Evening." Plus riveting solos by David "Fathead" Newman and the great Margie Hendrix, the Raelett who belongs in the highest category of soul divas along with Big Maybelle and Etta James.